TRANSMOVIMIENTOS

**Expanding Frontiers: Interdisciplinary Approaches
to Studies of Women, Gender, and Sexuality**

SERIES EDITORS:

Karen J. Leong
Andrea Smith

Transmovimientos

LATINX QUEER MIGRATIONS, BODIES, AND SPACES

Edited by Ellie D. Hernández, Eddy Francisco Alvarez Jr., and Magda García

University of Nebraska Press | LINCOLN

A version of chapter 6 was originally published as Katherine Steelman, "Home(Bodies): Transitory Belongings at LA's Oldest Latina/o Drag Bar," *Graphite: Transit* 10 (2019): 118–28, https://issuu.com/graphitejournal/docs/graphite _sendtoprint05.03.19__1_.

Library of Congress Cataloging-in-Publication Data
Names: Hernandez, Ellie D., editor.
Title: Transmovimientos: Latinx queer migrations, bodies, and spaces / edited by Ellie D. Hernández, Eddy Francisco Alvarez Jr., and Magda García.
Description: Lincoln: University of Nebraska Press, [2021] | Series: Expanding frontiers: interdisciplinary approaches to studies of women, gender, and sexuality | Includes bibliographical references and index.
Identifiers: LCCN 2020047083
ISBN 9781496225894 (hardback)
ISBN 9781496226754 (paperback)
ISBN 9781496227140 (epub)
ISBN 9781496227164 (pdf)
Subjects: LCSH: Transgender people—United States. | Gender-nonconforming people—United States. | Gays—United States. | Latin Americans—United States.
Classification: LCC HQ77.95.U6 T74 2021
DDC 306.76/8—dc23
LC record available at https://lccn.loc.gov/2020047083

Set in Garamond Premier Pro by Laura Buis.

Frontispiece: *Amor Eterno* by Olivia Levins Holden

We dedicate this book to Zoraida Reyes, whose memory reminds us that we must always move toward justice.

Contents

Illustrations

Acknowledgments

Ellie D. Hernández

One never journeys alone. Our book is a voyage rarely traveled. I wish to recognize the various people who have made this book project possible. I embarked on this journey not alone but with two of the most talented and respected people in academe today. Magda García, PhD candidate at the University of California, Santa Barbara, and Eddy Francisco Alvarez Jr., assistant professor of Chicana/o studies at Cal State Fullerton, have been a joy to work alongside. Their prescience and acumen grace this book. We all felt a deep commitment to organize a book about the intersectionality of LGBTQ immigrant experience, and I am truly grateful for their dedication to this book.

I wish to acknowledge the fine people at the University of Nebraska Press's Expanding Frontiers series for their dedication and commitment to our book. The coeditors and I believe we are expanding the frontiers of our own thinking and trying to create a path for others to follow. Emily Wendell, assistant editor, carried us to the finish line. A great deal of thanks goes out to the dean of social science, University of California, Santa Barbara, Charles Hale, for providing funding assistance for production costs and graduate assistance. Thank you also to the Chicana/o Research Institute for providing funding for graduate assistance in the early stages of the book project. This funding support has been helpful for completing our project. I also want to thank the contributors to this book.

They have been patient and honored all of the aspects of the revision process. This book is about these thinkers and scholars who feel the urgency to write about a major issue in Latinx studies.

I offer recognition of the many trans immigrants who travel the long, arduous road of self-fulfillment. I am inspired by the many people who inhabit the space of the trans world. The search for home is necessary and imperative and a life-changing experience.

Eddy Francisco Alvarez Jr.

First, I want to thank my parents: my father, Eddy Francisco Alvarez Sr., who I know watches me from wherever he is, and my mami, Ramona, whose undying and unconditional love heals and cradles me as it did during my time away from California. To my sisters, Gabriela and Patricia: life is unimaginable without our daily texts and doses of memes and chisme, especially during these pandemic moments and on the days when life feels too hard. On the days when academia feels like I am in a bad movie, you remind me of why life is so precious. To my nieces and nephews: your laughter, funny antics, and intelligence are healing, and they give me hope for the future! Undoubtedly, there are so many people to acknowledge and not enough space. Please know that even if you are not named explicitly here, your brilliance, bravery, camaraderie, kindness, and generosity helped usher this project into being.

Horacio Roque Ramírez, ¡presente! You believed in me from day one, fought for me even, and for that I am eternally grateful. Bamby Salcedo, you have inspired me since the day we met, and you continue to do so. Eres una guerrera siempre en movimiento. I love you very much!

To my hermanxs from the Association for Jotería Arts, Activism, and Scholarship: gracias for showing me how to think in comunidad, organize, and imagine through an ethic of friendship and love!

To my friends from graduate school at the University of California, Santa Barbara: we've been through *a lot* together. Your cariño, support, brains, and laughter sustain me.

Chela Sandoval, thank you for reminding me of the power of revolutionary love!

I must express my gratitude to my former students at SUNY Oneonta and to my former students and colleagues at Portland State University. I am a better scholar and teacher because of all of you! Kara Jinks and Leith Ghuloum, thank you for your skills and dedication as research assistants.

When this project started I was finishing graduate school and was an adjunct at California State University, Fullerton, in the Department of Chicana and Chicano Studies. Today, I am back there in a tenure-track position and among familia. I feel blessed for the nurturing and encouragement of my colleagues at Fullerton.

To my coeditors, Ellie and Magda: I have grown so much in your company through the process of assembling this transformative project. I will always be grateful for this journey.

Lastly, Jorge, Oscar, and Maggie, our nest and our rituals are sacred and a reminder of the beauty of everyday life and of the power of love.

Magda García

I want to begin by thanking my coeditors, Ellie Hernández and Eddy Francisco Alvarez Jr., for inviting me to partake in this meaningful and powerful project. I am incredibly grateful and forever indebted to jotería scholars, activists, and writers for maintaining the liberatory visions of queer 1980s Chicana feminists such as Gloria Anzaldúa alive and growing. Thank you to all the mentoras who have gifted me with community throughout my intellectual growth as a first-generation Tejana/Chicana: Norma Cantú, Sonia Saldívar-Hull, Norma Alarcón, and Chela Sandoval. Many thanks to Larissa Mercado-López, Jason Treviño, Sara Ramírez, Michael Lee Gardin, Christy Gutiérrez, and Micah Garza for their friendship, which sustains me. Always, gracias to mis queridos Roberto, Archie, and Paloma, who are my home.

Introduction

Trans vida in Extraordinary Times

EDDY FRANCISCO ALVAREZ JR., MAGDA GARCÍA, AND ELLIE D. HERNÁNDEZ

This book takes as its central concern the subject of immigration and LGBTQ identities. Within a trans-embodied framework, we identify *Transmovimientos* as the creative force or social mechanism people utilize to change their location and calibrate their consciousness. In thinking of the last four years, nothing could have prepared us for the refugee crisis or the reign of political terror on trans bodies. Nothing in the political field offers a comprehensive logic and true reasonable perspective on the impact on our lives. We arrive at the completion of this book with alarm and distress, with yearning for new ways of thinking and being, and we present a need for hope and the dissolution of distress. Living under the Trump administration has posed a direct threat to the lives of so many, and yet there is still a pushing forward, a desire for movement forward, a trans movement of everything we know. At no other moment in U.S. history has the subject of immigration been so tenuous, rendering queer, transgender, nonbinary and gender-nonconforming immigrants the targets of so much contempt.

We reflect on this time with apprehension and dismay. At the same time, we believe it is time to tell our stories and shape the narratives told about our lives. Decades of irregular immigration policy and upheaval across Central America, Mexico, and globally has led to widespread movement of populations, creating mass migrations as necessary responses to violence and economic displacement. The coeditors of *Transmovimientos* view the intersection of immigrants and LGBTQ people to be central to the larger discussion that we have identified in the specifics of each issue and story laid out across the pages of this book. As a critical anthology, this collection forms a nuanced conversation between scholarship and social activism that speaks in concrete ways about migratory LGBTQ communities that seriously suffer from immoral immigration policies and political discourses that produce an untenable living situation. In this collection we look at the effects of migratory movements; anti-immigrant sentiment; homophobia and dogma; stigma toward gay, lesbian, queer, transgender, and nonbinary immigrants and refugees; and most recently the climate of hate aroused and policies established by the Trump administration.

Transmovimientos unveils a critical perspective with the emphasis on queer immigrants, trans-identified dissidents, and gender-nonconforming folks who reflect and write about migratory movements within actual geographical spaces, as well as the trans and nonbinary body, all crucial elements of the trans movements we see taking place in this time in the United States. We reflect on the immigrant, transgender, and transmigrant experiences in United States and those currently undergoing problematic and challenging times as immigrant, migratory, and diasporic subjects. We view this challenging moment as an opportunity to look deeper at the issues and to draw from various perspectives that compose the transmovimiento experience. We view the intersection of these twenty-first-century paradigms of change, of migration, and of desire for mass movement beyond the limited world. These are deliberate consciousness-based expressions designed to realign awareness about the body in transit, the diasporic experience, of relocating and emerging into new possibilities.

We editors believe it is a timely moment to have a much-needed discussion on the place of Latinx queer communities, immigration policy, and migration(s) of various types, especially those that center trans and gender-nonconforming peoples. While the United States has witnessed a dynamic progressive social movement around same-sex marriage, we also note a difficult, problematic, and unsustainable perspective on immigration stemming from global economic disruptions, neoliberal economic policy, and emergent nationalisms, as well as the current administration, which has waged a war on LGBTQ, poor people, Muslims, and immigrants. The urgency for an anthology like this is perceptibly necessary. This book project creates a conversation between several critical essays on the subject of queer brown LGBTQ communities, immigration, migration(s), and diasporas and the affective, activist, literary, and cultural worlds that collide or the economies they navigate. Transmovimientos are rooted in the embodied experiences, struggles, theorizations, and creativity of LGBTQ im(migrants), Chicanas/os(x), Latinas/os(xs), and those identities in between.

Actual LGBTQ transmovimientos take place across geographical and psychic spaces, their impact seen and felt across the United States, Latina/o America, and beyond. Transmovimientos are about embodied movements across time, space, and memory. They are inspired by social movement activism and by the multiple daily physical and ephemeral crossings of queer and trans bodies. They are about critical dialogue, new frameworks, difficult conversations, generational gaps, creative solutions, and a futurity that takes us to the space of hope and urgency that centralizes queer lives as it creates junctures for interventions. From this, the artistic, poetic, creative, and psychic life of queer Latinx comes to life and is offered a space to develop a perspective on queer im/migrant and migratory lives.

This critical anthology fills a critical void but also creates new possibilities, poses new questions, creates visibility, and tells stories without obfuscating the issues or erasing the problem. In trans-movimientos we see trans bodies and queer bodies moving into the future, critically and unapologetically. Kai Green and Treva Ellison refer to *tranifesting*, or "transformative manifesting," which, they argue, "calls attention to epistemologies, sites of struggle, rituals, and modes of consciousness, representation, and embodiment that summon into being flexible collectivities" (2014, 222). "Flexible collectivities," they continue, "are those that are capable of operating across normative and violative configurations of race, gender, class, sex, and sexuality" (Green and Ellison 2014, 222). This book, like the authors and subjects of the essays within, seeks this type of transformative rupture toward collectivity.

To "tranifest," Green and Ellison explain, is to "mobilize across the contradictions, divisions, and containment strategies produced by the state and other such large-scale organizations of power that work to limit our capacity to align ourselves across differences in ways that are necessary for social transformations" (Green and Ellison 2014, 222). This time of change, this continuous flux in the midst of transnational migrations along with threats to build a wall on the U.S.-Mexico border, as well as sexual and gender identities, demands a collective critical response to the issues, problems, and crossroads that arise as we take seriously LGBTQ immigrant lives and stories. In this book we bring together academically oriented and creative essays that address a critical perspective on what it means to be Chicanx/a/o or Latinx/a/o and queer and immigrant, navigating the often-tenuous place and conditioning of citizenship, state formation, and many related issues. We have curated a collection of writings that highlight these intersections.

In a 2008 issue of *Women's Studies Quarterly*, Susan Stryker, Paisley Currah, and Lisa Jean Moore argue that "trans-" has the potential of being a productive prefix: "Because we believe some vital and more generally relevant critical/political questions are compacted within the theoretical articulations and lived social realities of 'transgender' embodiments, subjectivities, and communities, we felt that the time was ripe for bursting 'transgender' wide open, and linking the questions of space and movement that that term implies to other critical crossings of categorical territories" (2008, 12). What do these "critical crossings of categorical territories" mean for Latinx, Chicanx, immigrant, and diasporic people in the borderlands? How does the "bursting" of trans across Latinx modes of thinking and being expand our understanding? How does it enable transformation? How do we make sense of these intersections, and how do trans movements, or transmovimientos, provide that schema for more inclusive and just worlds?

As editors, we are building on the works of queer of color theorists, trans studies, Chicanx and Latinx studies, and jotería studies to answer the questions above, make connections, and highlight a few concepts that have shaped our thinking about transmovimientos. We follow Francisco J. Galarte, who asks that we be attentive to trans Latinx lives and how these inform how we understand the interconnections of race, gender, sexuality, and nation: "New reading practices for listening for the iterations of silences within the analytic boundaries between race and sexuality, can push us to think of gender as much more dynamic and as spatially and temporally contingent" (2014, 233). We also understand trans in the way Stryker, Currah, and Moore define it above and merge it with the concept of movimientos, which we articulate as political, social, and conceptual "crossing," to borrow from M Jacqui Alexander (2006, 21). We build on past and present activism and transformative and field-defining scholarship. An exhaustive literature review is beyond our scope; however, we briefly discuss several concepts, provided below, that speak to what scholars refer to as "transing," or the showing of how trans is and always has been a part of materiality (like queering) (Cuevas 2018; Stryker 2017; Crawford 2016; Stallings 2015). "Acts of transing," according to Lucas Crawford, "are happenings or movements not objects or presences" (2016, 14). These ideas *move* us and provide a working, *moving*, and undulating basis not only for connections among the essays in this book but also for how we conceive of transmovimientos. These terms are nodes within a framework or model for thinking about LGBTQ Latinx and queer Latinx immigrants while keeping trans bodies, lives, *and* trans as a mode of analysis. The examples we share, "transvisible," "translocas," and "post-boderlandia as a gender variant critique," are but a few within the arsenal of concepts available today to talk about these topics. However, as the scholarship compiled in this book demonstrates, we need more.

Scholarship and cultural production by Latinx, Chicanx, and queer and trans scholars, activists, and artists of color illustrate a map of how trans and queer intersect with racialized forms of existence within a neoliberal system and across militarized borders and how resistance occurs at those spaces of contact (DiPietro 2016; Cárdenas 2012; Rodriguez 2003). These works go "beyond hetero/homo normativities" (Martinez-San Miguel and Tobias 2016) and other binaries. One example is T. Jackie Cuevas's (2018) proposal of a perspective that expands Chicanx queer and gender-nonconforming beyond the dichotomous ways we have thought about Chicana lesbian identity. Cuevas provides a critical transmovimiento of ways to understand gender outside of binaries and not as a new phenomenon. Cuevas asks how genderqueerness can provide a lens to construct an alternative affective queer history of the borderlands (2018, 103). While our focus is not limited to the Chicanx experience and expands to other identities within the category of Latinx, we, too, are interested in such alternatives. This expansion is also about visibility or the "transvisible" based on the TransLatin@ Coalition, Bamby Salcedo and Karla Padrón's report about trans Latina immigrants in the United States, and a film about Salcedo, *Transvisible: Bamby Salcedo's Story*, an intimate look into the activist's life (Alencastre 2013). The usage of "transvisible" is about visibility for trans Latina immigrants. While it is true, as others have argued, that visibility and mere survival are not enough, these texts made visible the intersections of trans and Latina, which had otherwise been ignored. The release of the report and the film came at a critical time in jotería history. Another example is Lawrence La Fountain-Stokes's translocas, which he describes as performers, lovers, beauties, and exiles, among others and argues that we not see "trans" as necessarily as unstable or in between but as a key aspect of transformation, "change, the power or ability, to mold, reorganize, reconstruct, construct, and of longitude, the transcontinental, transatlantic but also transversal" (2011). The transloca, then, for La Fountain-Stokes is a contradictory, numerous, and "polysemic affair." While just a few examples, these scholars illustrate the ability of trans and gender nonconformity to make visible, expand and reshape across and within borders. A transing happens, which we further elucidate in our discussion below of the relevance of movimientos.

While we as editors continue to emphasize that transmovimientos is not only about transgender experiences, we must recognize the role of trans Latinx leadership from Sylvia Rivera to Bamby Salcedo, Alexandra Rodríguez de Ruíz, Isa Noyola, Jennicet Gutierrez, and others, all of whom have inspired action across borders. The recent caravans of LGBTQ people from Central America are an example of the trans-border movements that people embark on to find liberation and safety. As Suyapa Villeda Portillo (Latino Media Collective 2018) reminds us, the caravans are not a new phenomenon. The movement of bodies, many of them trans, required and built solidarity and community efforts on both sides of the border. Social movement activism is about creating change, sparking revolution and shifts in consciousness and language, and improving lives. The modes of doing this are multiple (Sandoval 2000). However, movement is also as simple as an energetic shift, a tilt of the body, an inspiring idea, a cumbia. Through a performance and dance studies lens, movimientos in the context of this book is about activism (past and present) and about the everyday political and social encounters that have taken place on the streets, in nightclubs and bars, and in leisure spaces where movement(s) finds new meanings in the midst of dancing and socializing (Alvarez 2019; Rivera-Servera 2012; Roque Ramirez 2007; Rodriguez 2006). However, social movement activism, whether in a march or through a performance, has been central to our authors and how we conceived this book, especially when the Trump administration has moved many of us into fear but also into action. Social justice warriors like Sylvia Rivera and Alicia Garza from Black Lives Matter, among others, have been pushing boundaries, making demands, and moving the struggle forward. As the editors of *Queer Brown Voices* remind us, queer brown people have been part of ethnic struggles but also moved forward queer rights, participating in AIDS organizing, founding organizations like LLEGO, and creating social and political spaces that intersected their various identities (Quesada, Gomez, and Vidal-Ortiz 2015). To this point, Jennicet Gutierrez from Familia: Trans Queer Liberation Movement told one of us editors recently, "The work of Familia builds on the work of others who have come before us" (Jennicet Gutierrez, phone conversation with the author, September 22, 2019). In these movements, movidas, transits, and choreographies, how do we, to borrow from Cuevas, strive to "turn away from heteronormativity and gender non-conformity" (2018, 92)? Cuevas would say the blueprints for transmovimientos are everywhere. We agree.

We also weave varied selections that speak to the need for interdisciplinary and multimethod perspectives while also articulating embodied knowledge and providing "theories in the flesh" about the experiences we highlight here. For example, the Undocuqueer Movement, composed largely of young, undocumented, queer immigrant activists, who have been unafraid to demand visibility and inclusion, building off the impetus of the marches of 2006, shed light on many facets of the queer Chicanx/a/o and Latinx/a/o immigrant experience and urged us to think about these intersections. These narratives see the DREAMers as vital to the immigrant rights movement, but they also problematize any notion of assimilation and push for intersectional decolonial approaches to "citizenship."

As coeditors, we see these struggles reflected in the social sphere, cultural production, politics and aesthetics, migration narratives, activism by undocuqueer, both a movement across historical moments, bodies, and subjectivities, a process of shifting identities, ideas, and actions, literally, movimientos—*movements*. Through the various essays, we explore what transmovimientos means in the current times of viciously renewed xenophobia and nationalism. Collaborators' essays range from the experience of queer love affairs, to lesbian street vendors in Los Angeles, to transgender Cuban migration, to a San Diego trans bar. This book is an attempt to map queer Latinx memories and moments across various geographies and temporalities. This collection is important to Chicana/o studies, Latinx studies, immigration studies, queer studies, transgender studies, and cultural studies as it brings together conversations that might otherwise be disparate, and it recognizes the valuable frameworks these various fields have provided.

Transmovimientos tracks the personal, public, and intellectual sites across which an array of queer, transgender, and feminist Latinx/Chicanx resistance occurs, from the front lines of the demand for im/migrant rights beyond DACA in Las Vegas, Nevada, to the coming into being as a queer intellectual and scholar through the experience of grief. While our volume plots a series of points across queer, transgender, and feminist Latinx movements, we do not conflate these sites or identities.

Rather, the selections that we present here are but a glimpse into the multiplicity of ways, practices, and sites in which consciously nonheteronormative, nonhomonormative, and noncisnormative Latinx movements claim ground—a claiming that becomes yet more imperative due to the violences against the environment and brown peoples, rendered even more stark each passing day. Significantly, these violences reminds us of how the brown body is marked with or without its consent—made explicitly clear in the August 3, 2019, act of terrorism in El Paso, Texas, in which brown people were targeted for death in a city similarly targeted because of the many borders it represents. This act of terrorism reminds us that the practices, readings, confrontations, and genealogical interventions made by each of the contributors to our volume take place not just as resistance but as a myriad of ways to survive—physically, emotionally, and intellectually.

Our volume begins by tracing the creation of current queer of color student movements. In our first chapter, "Triunfando con o sin papeles: Muxerista y jotx-historias of DACA-mentation and Activism in Las Vegas," Joanna Núñez, Jasmine Rubalcava-Cuara, and Anita Tijerina Revilla place Las Vegas at the forefront of queer of color activism by examining how the city has played a significant role in the im/migrant rights movement nationwide. Significantly, Núñez, Rubalcava-Cuara, and Revilla recognize and correct the dearth of research on the activists at the forefront of this movement, who are predominantly queer and feminist. Núñez, Rubalcava-Cuara, and Revilla place these queer and feminist activists' experiences at the center of their research by focusing on activists' narrations of their own encounters with DACA, including lack of access. In our second chapter, "Somos jotería: UCLA Chicanx Latinx Student Activists Fighting for Social Justice," José Manuel Santillana documents queer of color student activism in real time through La Jotería de UCLA. In the first part of his chapter, Santillana discusses students' relationship to the term "jotería" and how it relates to their activism within La Jotería de UCLA. The second part of Santillana's chapter focuses on the experiences of La Jotería de UCLA committee members with other Latina/o and Chicana/o student organizations on campus. Through these avenues, Santillana illustrates how La Jotería de UCLA was constructed on a foundation of love and acceptance, which provides the impetus for their activism on- and off-campus.

Shifting to reading and analytical practices, in our third chapter, "Working Trans in Jaime Cortez's *Sexile/Sexilio*," Carlos Ulises Decena iterates a queer of color reading practice that recognizes transgender Cuban immigrant Adela Vázquez's *Sexile/Sexilio* as an artifact of queer Latinx activism, ultimately rejecting the understandings of Vázquez's work that elide cisgender and transgender queer identities. From Cuba, our volume then returns readers to the space/ place that is the U.S.-Mexico border, specifically El Paso / Ciudad Juárez. Even before the August 3, 2019, act of domestic terrorism that claimed twenty-two lives, the Texas-Mexico border had drawn national attention as a gateway for Central American refugees and subsequent increased militarization, establishment of family separation, and expansion of detention centers. In our fourth chapter, "Wonder Woman, Pancho Villa, and the Shifting Rio Grande: Transnational jotx Identity, Desire, Pleasure, and Death on the El Paso / Juárez Border," Omar González describes their own experiences and the experiences of "border joto/as" in negotiating a transnational queer identity on the border between El Paso and Ciudad Juárez, as well as the social and physical violence that accompanies the act of inhabiting the identity and space of "joto/a." Drawing on historical accounts of revolutionary queer figures like Teresa Urrea, Carmelita Torres, and Hector Arturo "Arlene" Díaz, González demonstrates how border queers embody a specifically queer revolutionary spirit. In doing so, González constructs an explicitly queer of color border and revolutionary genealogy.

In our fifth chapter, "Vaqueros: Muy machos, Wearing the Pants, and Living la vida loca," Carlos-Manuel joins Mandujano's and González's discussions of transphobic and homophobic violences. Written from the intersection of research, interview findings, and personal hypothesis, Carlos-Manuel attempts to make sense of how secret same-sex acts between Mexican/Chicano men contribute to both existing machismo in Mexican/Chicano culture and the constant retributions lived by men who are considered "effeminate," "putitos," and "maricones."

We turn to queer of color temporalities and continue our return to Los Angeles in our sixth chapter, Katherine Steelman's "Home(bodies): Transitory Belonging at LA's Oldest Latina/o Drag Bar." In this chapter, Steelman focuses on La Plaza, the oldest operating gay bar in Los Angeles and a place where time and space are disrupted, rendering La Plaza a transitory spatial phenomenon. Through interviews with people in La Plaza, Steelman examines how drag performance, transgender identity, and migration interact within the confines of La Plaza. Steelman demonstrates how La Plaza functions as a queer "home" for those who inhabit it, despite the space being in constant flux due to realities such as deportation, AIDS, incarceration, and gentrification. Steelman, then, interrogates this concept of "home," its inclusions and exclusions, and how this influences race, transgender identity, and performativity.

We shift to the ever-significant genre of memoir and theme of memory in our subsequent section. Our seventh chapter, "Pesadilla convertida en sueño: El sueño nunca soñado / A Nightmare Turned Into a Dream," by recognized trans Latina activist Bamby Salcedo, is a nonfiction essay / poem / testimonio / dream sequence / prayer that blurs genres as it tells an individual story of trans Latina resilience and an investment in community. Through narrating her journey from Guadalajara, Mexico, to Los Angeles, Salcedo describes the personal experiences that formed the impetus for her creation of Angels of Change and the TransLatina Coalition. In her chapter, Salcedo re-members how she started working at a young age to help her mother, the abuse she suffered, her struggles with addiction, and how she navigated the gender binary. Weaving in and out of poetry and prose, Salcedo recounts the impact of HIV, prison, and the depths of addiction as she writes about those "guardian angels" that came into her life to help her move out of despair and into a space of hope.

Our eighth chapter, Nicholas Duron's "'¿Qué harás si algo me pasa?': An ofrenda," traces queer intellectual formations and reading practices shaped by, but nevertheless always beyond, the realm of the personal. Duron tells how he came to understand his identity as a queer Mexican American through his experiences as a queer scholar of color and through his relationship with his amante. Invoking an archive of Chicana writers, his experiences in academia, his family history, and the memories of his deceased lover, Duron's essay is equal parts memoir, love letter, and bucket list. His contribution to this volume is a heart-wrenching testimonial of his journey across time and space from his biracial, third-generation Mexican upbringing in Texas and the family stories that shaped him, to his academic sojourn in New York City, and finally to the lessons he learned from his amante, who died too soon and too young. Duron explores themes of language, identity, literature, love, memory, and desire as he grieves and heals.

Our last section shifts readers from the urban landscape to sites of incarceration. In our ninth chapter, "Queering el barrio: Latina Immigrant Street Vendors in Los Angeles," Lorena Muñoz focuses on space/place. The chapter challenges perceptions of street vending as a heteronormative space through the experiences of two Latina immigrant street vendors to display the queer and gender constructions of the Los Angeles street vending space. Muñoz offers that, due to the negotiation of the queer and gendered identities of Latina immigrants who operate within those spaces, they are reconstructed as "pseudo" heteronormative spaces. She situates the gendered performance of Latina street vendors within both the street vending space and how that space is perceived. The chapter further elaborates upon these experiences through discussion of the gendered and queer performances of the vendors' home life.

In our last chapter, "The Privatized Deportation Center Complex y la trans mujer," Verónica Mandujano intervenes in the political dialogue concerning immigration policy to center the experiences of asylum seekers with a focus on gender and sexuality. Situated within an understanding of privatized deportation centers as operating along the gender binary as an organizing structure, Mandujano's work engages the multiple levels of violence against transwomen, specifically, the violence that causes transwomen to flee their homelands in Latin America and ironically exposes them to similar transphobic and sexual violence from guards and prison inmates while in U.S. privatized deportation custody. Mandujano engages transnational forms of transphobic violence through analysis of government reports, literature, and released revenues of private prison corporations, as well as testimonies of and by transwomen to convey the importance of the transwoman's immigration experience within an era that aims to commodify the incarceration of human bodies regardless of their asylum-seeking process.

Transgender Latina/o activism and burgeoning scholarship in the United States and transnationally have made urgent the need for including trans bodies and narratives and thinking about trans as a framework for understanding queer immigrant, Chicana/o, Latina/o communities. We are interested in the ways different generations of LGBTQ im(migrants) have experienced the borderlands, including regional differences across the United States. We believe there is much more to consider. In light of these emerging trends and growing issues surrounding migration and problems with legitimacy, citizenship, and decoloniality, this book project draws from current insights by scholars and community activists who are researching and dealing with many facets of the struggles that confront us daily. These insights add a critical dimension to our understanding of the policies on immigration, the narratives that are told about the lives of Chicana/o and Latina/o LGBTQ communities and people, especially in light of the 2016 election, which projected a precariousness for the lives of the communities discussed here. This book project endeavors to add a critical dimension to the policies on immigration, the narratives that are told about the lives of Chicana/o and Latina/o LGBTQ communities and people, and the everyday ways communities are responding politically, aesthetically, and culturally.

Our aim is to add to the ongoing conversation and to address the nuanced experiences of LGBTQ lives, to push us to think critically and move us in different directions when thinking about queer, gender variant, and trans communities. Given that we are in transmovimientos always, we present an anthology that fills voids but also creates new questions, creates visibility, blurs lines, and tells stories without obfuscating others. In *Transmovimientos*, we see trans and queer bodies and frameworks that move us, moving into a necessary future, critically and unapologetically.

References

Alexander, M Jacqui. 2005. *Pedagogies of Crossing: Meditations on Feminism, Sexual Politics, Memory, and the Sacred*. Durham NC: Duke University Press.

Alvarez, Eddy Francisco, Jr. 2019. "Finding Sequins in the Rubble: The Journeys of Two Latina Migrant Lesbians in Los Angeles." *Journal of Lesbian Studies* 24 (2): 77–93.

Cárdenas, Micha. 2012. *The Transreal: Political Aesthetics of Crossing Realities*. New York: Atropos Press.

Crawford, Lucas. 2016. "'I'll Call Him Mahood Instead, I Prefer That, I'm Queer': Samuel Beckett's Spatial Aesthetic of Name Change." In *Trans Studies: The Challenge to Hetero/Homo Normativities*, edited by Yolanda Martinez-San Miguel and Sarah Tobias, 47–64. New Brunswick NJ: Rutgers University Press.

Cuevas, T. Jackie. 2018. *Post-Borderlandia: Chicana Literature and Gender Variant Critique*. New Brunswick NJ: Rutgers University Press.

DiPietro, Pedro Javier. 2016. "Of Huachafería, Así, and M' E Mati: Decolonizing Transing Methodologies." *TSQ: Transgender Studies Quarterly* 3 (1–2): 65–73.

Galarte, Francisco J. 2014. *Aztlan: A Journal of Chicano Studies* 13 (2): 118–39.

Green, Kai M., and Treva Ellison. 2014. "Tranifest." *TSQ* 1, no. 1–2 (May): 222–25.

Johnston, John, Dante Alencastre, and Roland Palencia. 2013. *Transvisible: The Bamby Salcedo Story*. Directed by Dante Alencastre.

La Fountain-Stokes, Lawrence. 2011. "Translocas: Migration, Homosexuality and Transvestism in Recent Puerto Rican Performance." *E-Misférica* 8 (1), https://hemi.nyu.edu/hemi/en/e-misferica-81/lafountain.

Latino Media Collective. 2018. Honduran Migrant Caravan: Fact vs. Fiction. https://latinomediacollective.com/2018/11/16/nov-16th-2018-honduran-migrant-caravan-fact-vs-fiction/.

Martinez-San Miguel, Yolanda, and Sarah Tobias, eds. 2016. *Trans Studies: The Challenge to Hetero/Homo Normativities*. New Brunswick NJ: Rutgers University Press.

Padrón, Karla M., and Bamby Salcedo. 2013. "TransVisible: Transgender Latina Immigrants in U.S. Society." TransLatin@ Coalition. https://www.translatinacoalition.org/.

Quesada, Uriel, Letitia Gomez, and Salvador Vidal-Ortiz, eds. 2015. *Queer Brown Voices: Personal Narratives of Latina/o LGBT Activism*. Austin: University of Texas Press.

Rivera-Servera, Ramón H. 2012. *Performing Queer Latinidad: Dance, Sexuality, Politics*. Ann Arbor: University of Michigan Press.

Rodríguez, Juana María. 2003. *Queer Latinidad: Identity Practices, Discursive Spaces*. New York: NYU Press.

Rodríguez, Richard T. 2006. "Queering the Homeboy Aesthetic." *Aztlan: A Journal of Chicano Studies* 31 (2): 127–37.

Rodriguez de Ruiz, Alexandra, and Marcia Ochoa. 2016. "Translatina Is About the Journey: A Dialogue on Social Justice for Transgender Latinas in San Francisco." In *Trans Studies: The Challenge to Hetero/Homo Normativities*, edited by Yolanda Martinez-San Miguel and Sarah Tobias. New Brunswick NJ: Rutgers University Press.

Roque Ramirez, Horacio N. 2007. "'Mira, yo soy boricua y estoy aquí': Rafa Negrón's Pan Dulce and the Queer Sonic Latinaje of San Francisco." *CENTRO: Journal of the Center for Puerto Rican Studies* 19 (1): 275–313.

Sandoval, Chela. 2000. *Methodology of the Oppressed*. Minneapolis: University of Minnesota Press.

Stallings, LaMonda H. 2015. *Funk the Erotic: Transaesthetics and Black Sexual Cultures*. Champaign: University of Illinois Press.

Stryker, Susan. 2017. *Transgender History: The Roots of Today's Revolution*. 2nd ed. Berkeley CA: Seal Press.

Stryker, Susan, Paisley Currah, and Lisa Jean Moore. 2008. "Introduction: Trans-Trans or Transgender." *WSQ: Women's Studies Quarterly* 36 (3–4) :11–22.

"Symposium: Funk the Erotic: Transaesthetics and Black Sexual Cultures." 2017. *Syndicate*, https://syndicate.network/symposia/literature/funk-the-erotic/.

TRANSMOVIMIENTOS

Twenty-First-Century Student Movements

Triunfando con o sin papeles

Muxerista y jotx-historias of DACA-mentation
and Activism in Las Vegas

JOANNA NÚÑEZ, JASMINE RUBALCAVA-CUARA, AND ANITA TIJERINA REVILLA

In December 2005 the Border Protection, Antiterrorism, and Illegal Immigration Control Act of 2005 (HR 4437) passed by a majority vote in the U.S. House of Representatives. The bill sought to further criminalize undocumented immigrants and anyone accused of aiding them with felony charges.[1] HR 4437 passed in the House, but because of the unexpected uproar and activism from the undocumented community, in particular high school students, it never gained the support of the U.S. Senate and did not become law. Las Vegas, Nevada, activists played an important role in resisting the criminalization of immigrants and rallying for a comprehensive immigration reform at a time when mass immigrant marches were still new in many parts of the country. "It was unheard of for Latina/o students in Las Vegas to walk out of school by the hundreds" (Revilla 2012, 97), and we were lucky enough to be among those who led those protests as both participants and leaders.

With the DREAM Act and immigration reform being debated in Congress for over two decades, the 2012 Deferred Action for Childhood Arrivals (DACA) program offered much-needed relief, even if it was incredibly limited.[2] August 15, 2020, marks the eight-year anniversary of the implementation of DACA. Over the years, recipients and their advocates have experienced an emotional and political tug-of-war. They are forced to apply every two years and endure constant threats of the elimination of the program as politicians use the program and the recipients as pawns in a political game. As recently as June 18, 2020, we were still uncertain about the future of the program.[3] The Supreme Court decision to restore the 2012 Obama administration DACA policy in full was again a welcome temporary relief. While the beneficiaries of this program are still considered to be undocumented, the risk of being deported is minimized as long as the recipient continues to meet the guidelines or until federal officials decide to end the program.

Although DACA had the potential to include more people in the undocumented community, it closed the doors to anyone who arrived to the United States after the age of sixteen and was over the age of thirty-one on June 15, 2012. It denied access to applicants who were not in school or had not obtained a high school diploma or GED. It rejected applicants who have a "criminal" history as little and insignificant as a misdemeanor; what is considered to be a significant misdemeanor has yet to be clarified. Along with the strict guidelines, there are other barriers that need to be overcome in order to apply. The applicants had to prove that they met the guidelines with documentation that showed physical presence in the United States since June 2007. This requirement does not take into account that the lack of immigration status in any nation often purposely necessitates an invisibilized experience with a limited paper trail.[4]

Legality versus Illegality

Historically, language has been used to dehumanize and marginalize muxeres, people of color, queer and trans people, immigrants, and anyone who resists hegemonic expectations and parameters. Discriminatory language not only creates an environment of hatred but also has the power to inform laws that deny access to those who lack structural power. When one refers to an immigrant as "illegal" because they are without documentation or status in the United States, it is both dehumanizing and a misnomer.[5] While the act of being in this country without documentation may be deemed "illegal," the human being is not "illegal." Revilla and Evelyn Rangel-Medina's research further adds that this phenomenon is fueled by a practice called "citizenism," which is "the ideological practice of inherent citizen superiority, the [belief in the] right to dominance of citizens over noncitizens, and a system of unearned advantages and privileges based on citizenship granted at birth" (2011, 168).[6] Alternatives to "illegal" that are commonly used by social justice activists are "undocumented," "economic refugees," and "unauthorized." In Spanish, we also say "sin papeles," which translates to "without papers." For the purpose of this research, we use "undocumented" or "DACA-mented," which implies that a person is protected under the DACA program.

Undocumented youth activists, many of them queer or "undocuqueer," continue to be at the forefront of (re)framing legality, "DREAMer" or DACA-mented identity, and migration narratives through their activism, artwork, and scholarship (Negrón-Gonzales 2014; Ochoa 2016). One notable moment in the fight for the liberation of immigrants in this country and full recognition of their humanity was when undocumented youth stepped out of the shadows in the spring of 2010 and declared that they were "undocumented and unafraid" (Cisneros 2018).[7] This act challenged the mainstream media and policy makers' conditional acceptance of DREAMers as "exceptional immigrants" while villainizing and criminalizing the majority of immigrants, and it demanded that all immigrants be free from fear of deportation.

Migration as Survival

The decision to migrate to the United States is not made as an isolated or spontaneous incident. People's decisions to migrate are intimately connected to their struggle to survive under global capitalist trends, including free trade agreements, wars and military occupations fueled by economics, privatization, and other forms of economic displacement. In an effort to create lucrative economic gains, the United States put in place very intentional and strategic laws and regulations that led to the exploitation of immigrant labor and a limitation of the migration process. This issue expands far beyond the United States and is, in fact, a global phenomenon. Immigrant criminalization and labor exploitation in this country are directly linked to the 1994 North American Free Trade Agreement (NAFTA). Patricia Fernandez-Kelly and Douglas Massey (2007) illuminate the consequences of the passage of this policy. They argue that the purpose of NAFTA was not to facilitate trade and open markets but rather to expand opportunities for capital investment. This led to the free exchange of business; however, it eventually led to the criminalization of laborers at the border. NAFTA omitted workers' rights and free mobility within trade zones to prevent Mexican workers from migrating to the United States. As a result, immigration from Mexico into the United States has grown in rapid numbers, partly because this treaty has pushed Mexican immigrants from their country as economic refugees. Immigrants and their families have settled permanently in the United States to avoid the dangers of leaving and reentering. This policy not only created inequalities in immigration policy but also led to massive discrimination and racism, which still remain with us today.

Although immigration law is drafted by the federal government and executed in the same manner by all states, each state has the right to create policies within its jurisdiction. As Irma Aboytes explains, "The Supreme Court was the first branch of the federal government to talk about the situation of undocumented students within the educational systems. The Supreme Court determined in the 1982 ruling on *Plyler v. Doe* that states cannot deny undocumented students access to free public education in elementary school, but it failed to extend the same right to post-secondary education" (2009, 581). Therefore, federal financial aid is only provided to legal residents and citizens of the United States. However, as of 2019, seven states in the United States have provided some form of state financial aid, in addition to in-state tuition eligibility for undocumented students in nineteen states.[8] Governor Brian Sandoval signed a bill in May 2013 that allowed undocumented immigrants residing in the state of Nevada to obtain driver authorization cards, valid for four years. Although many are calling this a triumph for the undocumented community because this bill allegedly prohibits the Department of Motor Vehicles (DMV) from sharing applicants' information with the U.S. Immigration and Customs Enforcement (ICE), the authorization cards are not valid as an official identification to board commercial flights or enter federal government buildings. Latinx community members questioned the intentions behind this bill, and legal advocates discouraged people from applying for driver authorization cards because they suspect that immigrants' statuses were indeed being disclosed by the DMV to ICE.[9] Evidence of this is apparent in the high number of raids connected to people who have applied for the driver authorization cards. Nevada requires proof of legal status in the country to obtain a standard and real ID license.[10] Although this was believed to be a significant step for Nevada, having state identification still does not allow undocumented people to obtain a Social Security number or many other benefits inherited by legal permanent residents and citizens. Nevada was the eleventh state to offer driving privileges to undocumented immigrants (National Conference 2020).

Deferred Action for Childhood Arrivals (DACA)

U.S. Citizenship and Immigration Services (USCIS) is required to report the number of applications being received, approved, or denied. Based on USCIS data from as far back as 2012, when the government began accepting applications for DACA, a total of 825,439 applications were initially approved. The Migration Policy Institute suggests that "this number is the maximum of people who have ever held DACA status at one point or another during the life of the program." In total, USCIS granted 91 percent of the initial applications while denying 9 percent (which equaled 81,768).[11] A lack of monetary and legal resources delayed the ability of many undocumented Latinxs to apply at the outset of the program. Questions of safety and risk were also cited as the main factor in delayed application for all of the participants in this study. Participants held a distrustful view of the government, specifically the Obama administration, because they were intimately aware of the record-setting number of deportations that were taking place. Participants in this study waited to receive confirmation from legal experts and advocates that the information they provided in their DACA applications would not be weaponized to track and deport their family members. DACA was viewed by active members of the immigrant rights community as a band-aid approach to the malpractices of the U.S. immigration system, a fact that was later confirmed through research studies that demonstrated it barely scratched the surface in providing temporary protection for eligible recipients. The Migration Policy Institute found that only a small number of the undocumented population met the requirements to qualify for DACA because of the many restrictions.[12] In 2013 Mexican immigrants made up the majority of applicants at approximately 75 percent but only accounted for 57 percent of those who were approved. Applicants from Jamaica, Honduras, Guatemala, El Salvador, and Venezuela were also approved for DACA at lower-than-average rates.[13]

Von Diaz (2013) offered a snapshot of the stories of DREAMers and their complex feelings and political responses in the immediate aftermath of the program's implementation. Our findings echo Diaz's exposé and expand upon her initial findings. Our participants expressed an equally wide range of emotions and political concerns in response to the process as they simultaneously considered how their gender, race, class, and sexuality figured into their experiences. In Diaz's article, one applicant's reaction was positive, while another participant shared feeling disappointment and shame from having his application denied. However, the most telling reaction was embedded in the deep political conflict a third participant, Sonia, shared. Although Sonia qualified for DACA, they chose not to apply for the program because they were critical of the fact that only they qualified, while their family did not. Sonia added that DACA also "created divisions within the undocumented youth movement." Our participants' counterstories revealed a similar critique of DACA because it excluded their parents and countless undocumented people who had also arrived as children in this country.

Oscar Ramos's (2009) research illustrates that the impact of being an undocumented immigrant is so far-reaching that it even impacts their U.S. citizen children's educational development and self-identity. When Ramos asked citizen children to discuss their awareness of their parents' struggles as undocumented immigrants and the extent of the relevance of those struggles to their own educational experiences, Ramos found that citizen children tended to develop identities that identified with their parents' struggles. Our project showed a direct correlation between students' educational outcomes and their career aspirations with their immigrant parents' undocumented status. We chose to include two parent interviews within our study to further investigate the link between parents' identities and their children's academic outcomes.

Migrant and jotería Intersections

Muxerista and jotería undocumented activists from Las Vegas voice a critical awareness of how their gender and sexuality are racialized and stigmatized to perpetuate xenophobic, homophobic, and transphobic policies.[14] They apply what Juan Ochoa (2016) conceptualizes as a "Jotería analytic" in their activism, as is reflected in Xuanito's and José's jotx-historias.[15] Queer migration studies and the concept of a jotería analytic are useful in understanding the continued exclusion of both migrant parents and their jotx, trans, and nonbinary children from the nation. Queer migration studies scholar Eithne Luibhéid asserts that heteronormativity is central to the production of a range of marginalized or "subaltern groups, including lesbians, gay men, trans people, poor and racialized parents, interracial couples, sex workers, migrant and colonized sexual subjects, and others" (2018, 305). Heteronormativity exclusively privileges a sexuality and intimacy that is connected to childbearing by married cisgender male/female couples of the dominant ethnic/racial and class group. Undocumented jotxs and their migrant parents are targeted precisely because in one way or another they both represent a threat to whiteness, patriarchy, middle-class status, and (neo)colonialism (307). Their legality and the possibility of their exclusion or admission into the nation will always hinge on the intersection of these factors (Luibhéid 2008, 295). As a participant astutely asserted in 2020, "We may be DACA-mented, but we are still undocumented." Despite the set of protections that DACA offers, undocumented jotería and their families remain vulnerable to deportation, violence, and displacement.

The legalization of same-sex marriage in 2015 created a pathway for DACA-mented jotería to adjust their status through a process that was previously closed to them. For the majority of our participants' lives, status adjustments through marriage were not an option, nor were they a viable option at the time when DACA was announced. Approximately 68 percent of legal residents in 2016 obtained their residency through family sponsorship or marriage, which demonstrates how unjust it was that queer couples were excluded from this benefit.[16] Having the right to have his queer marriage recognized and for his partner to petition him proved monumental for one of our participants who has since become a legal resident. Though our participants hold a critical view of marriage as a sexist, heteronormative institution, they acknowledge that their critique coexists with a desire to create a semblance of security for themselves and their family.

Research Methodology

We use two primary research methodologies in this project, muxerista action research and testimonios (Márquez 2019). Muxerista action research is akin to participatory action research and community-based participatory research (Deeb-Sossa 2019); however, it is rooted in the muxerista and jotería tenets outlined in our previous work (Revilla 2004; Revilla and Santillana 2014). Immigrant rights research conducted in Las Vegas by our collective has always involved action outcomes in which the researcher and the research participants work in partnership for those outcomes. At the center of our relationships, researchers and research participants build community and trust, dismantling hierarchies of power within research, and working toward social transformation.[17] Another aspect of the partnership between us and our participants was that as a result of Jasmine's eleven years of employment as an immigration law assistant, she was able to help all five of the participants, as well as dozens of others within our community, fill out and submit their DACA applications. She worked personally on hundreds of local immigration cases, experiencing pain, disillusion with immigration laws, failed attempts, and victories.

The interviews for this study took place in 2014, 2017, and 2020, and we have been in community from 2006 to the present. We have known each other for over ten years. As such, this is both a historical snapshot and a longitudinal study. The researchers and participants were first and foremost friends and coconspirators who built a muxerista and jotería community. We are also fellow colegas who were formerly in student-teacher relationships at the University of Nevada, Las Vegas (UNLV). As muxeristas and jotería researchers, we know that the lives of our communities are often not validated within our society nor within academia. We find ourselves fighting for a place and voice for women, queer and trans people, immigrants, and children of immigrants because so many of our experiences are dismissed in mainstream culture. "Testimonios provide a gateway into the lives of a largely marginalized population, legitimizing their experiences by highlighting collective and individual forms of resistance" (Márquez 2019, 94). Generations of legal exploitation, institutionalized racism, patriarchy, homophobia, transphobia, and citizenism have stripped much of our communities' humanity. We share these testimonios to give insight into our lives and theirs. These testimonios document the resiliency and strength of jotería and muxeristas who have existed as undocumented activists who eventually attained temporary legal status through DACA. Furthermore, the interviews we collected tell jotx-historias that challenge heteronormative and xenophobic majoritarian stories.

The Setting

Many people are not aware of the large immigrant presence in Las Vegas. Most people are blinded by the glitz and allure of "Sin City." Many people go to Vegas to escape their realities. In fact, the city has capitalized on the idea that "what happens in Vegas stays in Vegas," indicating that there are no consequences for illicit misbehavior for the guests of the city. However, local activists have challenged this perspective, remarking that the phrase upholds rape culture and enables people to leave a metaphorical and actual mess behind them as they travel back to their homes after their visit. As Vegas locals, we know that what happens in Vegas has deep consequences for the people who live there. The Latinx immigrant population has grown tremendously in the past two decades largely because the city became one of the fastest-growing cities in the nation, and thus both the construction and service industry have thrived. The parents of the participants of this study were largely drawn to Las Vegas because they were in search of jobs and affordable housing. Many of their family members and community members have worked in both the casino and construction industries. Thus, they are responsible for building and sustaining Las Vegas while also cleaning up after the people who go there and have little regard for the impact they have on communities that live there.

Beginning in 2013, we conducted six in-depth interviews lasting one to two hours. These interviews were one-on-one. In 2017 we recruited an additional participant who gave us insight on being DACA-mented in Las Vegas during the Trump administration, bringing our total number of participants to seven. Finally, we conducted a focus group, taking the form of a plática, following the Supreme Court decision of June 18, 2020, which upheld DACA, with five participants from our study.[18] Of the seven participants, five were DACA-mented, and two were parents of the students interviewed. The interviews were conducted in the language the participant chose, either English, Spanish, or Spanglish, because so often we are told to censor our language or "speak English only." We view this method as essential to storytelling, trust, and keeping our tradiciones alive in the midst of so much violence against our culture.

The participants' ages ranged from twenty-three to sixty-three, and they are all of Mexican origin. Four of the participants identified as Chicana/o/x, and one of them identified simultaneously as a mestizo feminist. Three of them identify as muxeres, two as men, one as gender queer, and one as nonbinary. Four of them identify as queer/jotería, two as fluid, two as heterosexual, and two as gay (participants were allowed to choose more than one sexual identity). Although the parents did not disclose their sexuality, they have been in a heterosexual marriage for the majority of their lives. When asked what their immigration status was, they all used the term "undocumented" and rejected the terms "illegal" and "DREAMer." As one of the participants stated, "I only identify as a DREAMer when it comes to tactical essentialism." As scholar-activists, we believe it is fundamental to any research project to identify ourselves in terms of our positionality. Positionality includes but is not limited to

our race, class, gender, sexuality, citizenship, and ability categories. Thus, we have included our positionalities in appendix A at
the end of this chapter.

Muxerista y jotx-historias

José

José was born in Chihuahua, Mexico. He immigrated to the United
States when he was two years old and grew up in Phoenix, Arizona.
The same year José graduated from high school in 2010, Governor
Jan Brewer introduced SB1070, a law that legitimated discrimination and racial profiling against undocumented people in Arizona.
José's parents were concerned for him and ordered him to leave town
to pursue his college degree. José graduated with a bachelor's degree
in women's studies and acknowledges that without DACA, life after
college would be drastically different: "I had many cousins that graduated from school and [the] university and many cousins that had
college degrees, but before DACA they were working at restaurants
or doing whatever they could because they were undocumented,
although they had degrees. . . . In that sense I think it's very useful . . . now that I'm looking to graduate, the things that I'm prob-
ably going into, the jobs that I'm going to apply for are all because
of DACA. Otherwise, I would've never, never been able to apply."

José is a son, a brother, and an uncle. During our plática, José
shared that being undocumented and having the threat of deportation consistently hanging over his family have contributed to shaping how he performs his gender and sexuality within the space of
his family's home. He recalled watching a news story where the
pain of deportation and family separation was on full display, a
common practice by the mainstream media that he critiques for
being exploitative. In it, an undocumented father who was being
deported tells his thirteen-year-old son, "Take care of your family.
Be a big boy." As José recounted the story with tears in his eyes, his
voice broke as he told us that when deportation is always on the
table, he also feels like he has to be a "big boy." At a very young age,
he knew that if his parents were deported, he would have to step

1. Our love has no borders. Photo taken on May 1, 2013, by José Manuel Santillana.

in to be responsible for his siblings as the eldest son. Furthermore, he believes that regardless of his jotx identity, he may never be able to share his jotería with his father. He will always have to perform masculinity and heteronormativity in a way that will ease his family's pain, particularly his dad's anxiety.

I have to show my dad that if anything were to happen, I can take care of it. As far as gender and sexuality goes, I identify as gender non-conforming, but when I'm home, when I'm with my dad, when I'm with my family, I'm not that, and that's something I've had to come to terms with. . . . I don't think that my experience with my dad will be like a Disney moment, where I sit down and we hug about me being gay, and maybe later on, it will be. And a lot of it has to do with the fact that I want him to know that I've got it.

He went on to say, "How many other little boys are experiencing deportation and are then thrown into manhood? So much of their queerness or sexuality or gender expansiveness just goes out the window. Because now you are thirteen, and you're 'the man of the house.'" For José, his jotería and his undocumented status are inextricable, but so is his ongoing responsibility to his family.

Maria

Maria de La Salud was born in Michoacán, Mexico. She immigrated to the United States at the age of nine with her sister, Karina, and brother, Hugo. They arrived in East Los Angeles to meet their father, and a week later their mother arrived. The family moved together to Las Vegas. Maria graduated from UNLV with a bachelor's degree in hotel management and a minor in women's studies. She is a queer Chicana feminist, a muxerista, and has been an activist since her first march in 2008, when she advocated for the DREAM Act. When we asked Maria if she felt that activism helped pass DACA, she replied:

I think all those sit-ins, with all the undocumented youth, all the protests, everything has brought a different level of knowledge to the community. . . . So the sit-ins and other different news outlets have helped bring out the actual stories of undocumented youth. It has helped bring a human aspect to what's really going on and how being undocumented affects us on so many different levels. I think that bringing the stories and what we really go through has helped bring Deferred Action, because now the legislators and president [Obama] are actually reading our stories. They can see that it's not something that we just want, it's something that we need.

Maria notes that the news outlets she is referring to are not mainstream outlets. She believes that alternative media outlets and social media provide a more comprehensive and critical immigration narrative.

When DACA was introduced on June 15, 2012, Maria was hesitant to apply. There was very little information available about the risks of applying, and this was the first time since she arrived to the United States that this type of access had been available to any undocumented people. When she first heard the announcement, Maria said that she was skeptical: "I was like, how is this going to work? I wasn't happy right away.... Is it going to help everyone? Is it going to help me? . . . my brother? . . . my sister? I wasn't right away happy.... There were a lot of questions and also a little bit of fear." Maria is the daughter of Esperanza and Orlando, both of whom are also undocumented and do not have any immigration benefits. Like millions of undocumented people, Maria's parents do not qualify for DACA. When we asked her what she felt about it, she said, "It's so unfair, just because I went to school, now I have Deferred Action, but they work as hard as I have" (interview conducted in 2014). This is a sentiment that other undocumented children echo about their parents not being protected under immigration laws or reform. By excluding certain segments of the community, DACA further marginalizes the undocumented community and places certain people in a position of privilege that can never be attained by others. Maria explains:

> Even in the undocumented communities, certain people have privilege. For example, me. I have an education. I have a four-year degree that places me way above a lot of undocumented people because, obviously, I have that privilege of education, but that doesn't mean that I deserve immigration status more than anyone else. There [are] so many families, undocumented people that work really hard, but they didn't have the resources to get an education, but they're providing the same amount. They provide so much for this country, as much as I am, but the majority didn't have the opportunity to go to college.... And [they] are seen like they don't deserve immigration status because they're not smart enough or they're not providing for the country. (Interview conducted in 2013)

Maria's voice started to break and her eyes welled up with tears when Jasmine asked her if having a work permit has changed her life. She admits that before she got a work permit and a Nevada driver's license, she felt embarrassed and ashamed of showing her matrícula in public places because they would not always accept it.[19] She recalls these experiences as dehumanizing. She says that having a "work permit just gives you so much confidence. . . . Before, I knew I had those skills. I knew I had all the good things to get a better job, but because I didn't have a work permit, I didn't try" (2013). Maria's story demonstrates the value our society places in having "proper" documentation. As she testifies, documents and document holders alike are scrutinized when it comes to determining someone's legality and human dignity. Documents such as a driver's license, Social Security card, and work permit are gateways to access and safety. Today, Maria is working for an immigration law firm and plans to continue working in the field of law.

Xuanito

Xuanito was born in Aguascalientes, Mexico. He immigrated to the United States at the age of thirteen with his grandmother, who was his main caretaker, to reunite with his mother, who had already immigrated to the United States to work. He remembers his elderly grandmother telling him she could no longer take care of him because she had to take care of herself. Xuanito identifies as a teacher who is led by social justice and attributes his spirit of activism to his grandmother and mother. In regard to his commitment to social justice, Xuanito said, "My grandmother was very political, and I think I inherited that from her, that unwillingness to settle, that unwillingness to stand still and let things be and not question things. I learned that from her from an early age, and it just felt normal, like how do you not question things? I learned that from her and my mother" (interview conducted in 2017).

When asked about his process of becoming politically conscious, Xuanito reflected on his life-long commitment to activism: "I gave my youth to organizing" (2017). At an early age, Xuanito became involved in political campaigns to register members of Latinx communities to vote, and as a high school student he started the first gay and straight student alliance in Vegas. He now sees his place as a change agent in spaces of teaching and learning. He also believes he has a right to heal, to create security for himself, his partner, and his community.

> Is the political process important? Yes. Obviously, it is, you know, but I think there's enough people there that are doing that work, but probably not enough of us in the classrooms and in the student movements. And to me that's where my space is. If I have to go volunteer, make a phone call, whatever, you know, I think there are enough people doing that. I feel like my difference is in the classroom, in my community, and I happen to get paid for it . . . by being a teacher. Some people will say, "Oh, you're being lazy." No, I feel like I gave my youth to activism, and I deserve to have health insurance. I deserve to be able to afford my medicine, my food and live an okay life and travel and do shit that I've been wanting to do for many years, but it's okay. I'm not gonna feel guilty about it. . . . "If I change myself, I change the world." And, like, we are nobody's sacrificial lambs. (Interview conducted in 2020)

He added that student organizing taught him he had to stop relying on the government to validate his humanity. Xuanito earned two associate degrees, two bachelor's degrees (in women's studies and English), and a master's in education. In the fall of 2020 he will begin his doctoral program at UNLV. When we joked that he liked degrees, Xuanito became serious and said that he believes that he pursued education to overcompensate for being undocumented. He both internalized the need to be an "exceptional immigrant" in order to be deserving of humanity and rejected it: "If you push people, anybody can be exceptional. If our survival depends on exceptionalism. It's not that DREAMers are better than anybody, it's that willingness to survive and to thrive. I think it's what drives so many of us" (2020).

With regard to being queer and undocumented, he stated, "I certainly think that there's a correlation between queerness and the undocumented and how we learn to organize, how we use our bodies as a tool for organizing" (2020). We agree that it makes sense that queer people are the leaders of these movements, including the immigrant rights movement, the LGBTQ movement, and even the Black Lives Matter movement. There are queer people at the head of these movements. Queer and trans people also fight to be free and authentic, and they demand human dignity. Hence queer, trans, Black, and Indigenous immigrant people of color are inevitably catapulted into these struggles, and they often have the vision to be our leaders.

DACA allowed Xuanito to teach, get his driver's license, and travel more freely in the United States. Though he has been a resident for almost a year, he has had a difficult time shaking the feeling that his permanence in this country can still be taken away at any moment. This is not far from the truth, given Trump's threats of stripping residents and new citizens of their status. Xuanito said, "We carry a lot of trauma from being undocumented." This was starkly evident in all of the interviews we conducted. In fact, when we asked them whether DACA had a mental and spiritual impact on them, all of the participants acknowledged the attempted spirit murder they had experienced, noting that it was primarily their activism that preserved their mental and spiritual health. "Spirit murder" is a term coined by legal scholar Patricia Williams (1991). She argues that spirit murder takes place when people experience dehumanizing acts of racism. We believe racism is one dimension of spirit murder, and immigration status, gender, sexuality, and ability add more levels of vulnerability to these attempted acts of spirit murder by the state.

Esperanza

Esperanza was born in Michoacán, Mexico.[20] She immigrated to the United States twenty-two years ago after her husband, Orlando, and their three kids had all made it across the border. Like many other immigrants who leave Los Angeles for Las Vegas, they went in search of jobs, which are plentiful in the service and construction industries, and they went for affordable housing. Esperanza is the mother of Maria, Karina, and Hugo. We asked Esperanza how she felt about the belief that parents are to blame for the unauthorized migration of their children. She responded with the following:

> No, yo pienso que tiene que haber para todos. . . . No es culpa de nadie. Osea que ni los niños tienen la culpa, porque uno se los trae chicos, y nosotros tampoco, porque pos asi se acostumbro que asi se venía la gente para aca y aca podía trabajar. Por eso los demás se atrevían a venir porque ya sabían que si se podia y pos ay vinimos todos para aca. (Interview conducted in 2014)

> [No, I think it has to be for everyone. . . . It is no one's fault. In other words, it's neither the children's fault, because we bring them young, or ours, because it was the custom for people to come here to work in that way. That's why others dared to come, because they already knew that it was possible, and so we all came here.]

Esperanza obtained her primary education as an adult in the United States and was taking English classes at the time of the interview. When we asked Esperanza whether or not her children had suffered in the United States due to their immigration status, she had the following to say:

> Yo más he sufrido porque no puedo ir a ver a mi familia, a mis hermanos, a mi papá que tu sabes que ya falleció. Y eso era lo que más me preocupaba a mi. En diciembre yo ya me había decidido ir, pero mi papi, él mismo, me dijo que no fuera porque el sabia que al ir iba a dejar a los muchachos y iba a dejar a mi esposo. Entonces, el dijo que no fuera, pero a mi antes eso era lo que me preocupaba más. Al ultimo yo me decidí que pues tenia que pasar lo que pasara, yo tenía que estar tranquila porque este, ¿si uno le hace caso pos adonde va a parar? Pos al hospital y el hospital no lo cura gratis a uno. (2014)

> [I have suffered more because I cannot go see my family, my brothers, my dad, who, you know, has already passed away. And that was what worried me the most. In December I had already decided to go, but my dad himself told me not to go, because he knew that by going I was going to leave the kids and my husband. So he said not to go, but that was what worried me the most before. Ultimately, I decided

that what had to happen would happen. I had to be calm, because if we listen to everything, where are we going to end up? Well, to the hospital, and the hospital does not cure you for free.]

She indicated that she suffered tremendously because of those she had left behind, including her father, who passed away without her being able to see him. She decided to stay in the United States rather than go to Mexico to see her dying father both because she and her father believed it was too much of a risk for her to leave and because she needed to stay to support her family. She shared that her father reminded her of the cost of leaving and clarified for her that when she made the decision to leave it would have to be alone.

Cuando él supo que yo iba ir en diciembre el me dijo que no fuera pues por que no tenía papeles y que el ya sabia que al ir yo me iba a estar allá ya no iba a pasar por que pos tan peligroso que está ya y ya el me dijo eso. Y yo me creí y ya no fui . . . Y ahorita digo si no hay ninguna solución, pues si quiero ir a ver a mis hermanos pos necesito ir así y con el fin que ya me voy a quedar allá y yo sola porque los muchachos aquí están estudiando y mi esposo esta trabajando y me tengo que prevenir a las consecuencias a quedarme allá sola. (2014)

[When he knew that I was going in December, he told me not to because I did not have papers, and he already knew that by going, I was going to stay there, and I was not coming back because it is so dangerous, and, well, that is what he told me. And I believed him and didn't go. . . . And right now I tell myself that if there is no solution, because if I want to go see my siblings, I need to go like this [without papers] and knowing that I'm going to stay there by myself, because the kids are studying here and my husband is working, and I have to face the consequences of staying there alone.]

Esperanza is steadfast in her dream of reconnecting with her family in Mexico and refuses to accept the possibility of one of her siblings passing away while she is in the United States, like their father did, without her there to accompany them. She exemplifies the multiplicity of emotions that undocumented immigrants are forced to carry. She knows that returning to Mexico means her undocumented husband and children will not be able to visit her, but she will not ask any sacrifices of her family, because she supports them in their educational and career advancements.

Where Are They Now?

On June 28 and 29, 2020, we interviewed five of the participants. It was a powerful experience to be on the same call with all of them seven years after the first interviews were conducted. All of them have graduated and begun their career trajectories. When we started the interviews, their futures were tenuous and uncertain. They reflected on the past seven or eight years of having DACA. Today, one is a teacher and a doctoral student, another is a designer and architect, another is an accountant and project manager at a casino, two have aspirations of practicing law (one is already in law school, and the other is an immigration legal assistant). All of them are providing economic support for their parents and siblings, four of them have purchased houses, four are married and seeking legal residency, and all of them remain deeply committed to challenging the social and legal institutions that continue to discriminate against immigrants from around the world.

Despite the achievements they have reached, the stability and safety of the participants were still under attack as of June 2020. One of the participants stated:

> Of course, materially life is better with DACA. Access is better to institutions, and that really matters. A couple weeks ago, when we weren't sure what was going to happen to DACA, I found myself thinking, like, what's going to happen? People were expecting DACA to go away, it was pretty certain. And so I was kind of just like, "Fuck, DACA's about to go away. I just started law school. I'm probably not gonna be able to practice. What does that mean for me?" It was really, really terrifying, but I don't feel like I was defeated. I definitely was chillando when they fuckin' announced it. I was like, thank god. But that reassurance, that I think that people and you three and everybody on the call sort of gave me and we gave to each other, it's what brought me back to mind. (Interview conducted in 2020)

These words resonated with all of the participants on the group call. They refused to depend emotionally and spiritually on DACA for their sense of worth and survival. Each of them recounted that they were all surviving without DACA. They pointed to their muxerista and jotería activist community as the source that gave them self-worth, determination, and strength—it served as a space of spirit restoration and defense. They agreed that, regardless of DACA, it was their organizing and activism that gave them the foundation on which they stood.

Conclusion

The decision to migrate to the United States is not an isolated event in someone's life. The decision involves more than one person and often includes an entire family and community. It is important to understand that one of the rippling effects of migration is the long and deep spiritual wounds it creates and leaves. Historically, undocumented Latinx immigrants have sought refuge in the United States from armed conflicts, poverty, gender and sexual violence, or political persecution in their country of origin. In accordance with several studies and our own findings, we affirm that Latinx undocumented students often experience multiple socioemotional and psychosocial challenges that significantly impact their academic, physical, and spiritual well-being.

We found that the DACA program is a band-aid and offers only temporary relief to DACA-eligible recipients and their families, *and* it is simultaneously one of the few programs that has offered opportunities for immigrants. While the students have fierce critiques of DACA and of the exclusions and limitations of the program, they acknowledge that DACA has opened doors for them that would have otherwise been closed. The interviews with the parents showed that they were fully aware of the extreme sacrifices they were forced to endure for the sake of their children's academic access and, hopefully, their success. They chose to forgo their own goals not only for their economic survival but also for the opportunities afforded to their children. All three of Esperanza and Orlando's children have now graduated from the university. All three have received DACA

2. Queer immigrant, and here! Photo taken on May 1, 2013, by José Manuel Santillana.

and are finally able to pursue careers of their choice, for which they received academic training. Still, they are highly critical of and disappointed with the inequalities that their parents and communities have inherited due to the extreme citizenist laws in place. They continue to work to raise people's awareness and to demand a more just immigration process.

NÚÑEZ, RUBALCAVA-CUARA, AND REVILLA

Some members of our youth activist community were ineligible for DACA. They were ineligible because they aged out of eligibility or arrived in the United States after their sixteenth birthdays. Their experiences were strikingly similar to the experiences of the participants who were DACA eligible, but merely because of timing and the arbitrary age limits that were set, they were denied the opportunity to live in this country without fear of deportation. Their ineligibility and the impact it had on their lives further illustrate that the age limits and exclusions structured into this program are a detriment and missed opportunity. Although DACA is useful and has changed many people's lives in drastic ways, it has also served to further marginalize millions of others.

Furthermore, this program has created a false category of young people who are considered to be "perfect DREAMers." This concept is critiqued by undocumented students, youth, and activists across the nation. In fact, many undocumented student activists consciously chose not to take advantage of DACA because they did not want to contribute to the notion that there is such a thing as the "perfect immigrant" or "deserving immigrant." As Xuanito indicated, "I never liked the term DREAMer. It implies passivity. It implies not questioning things. I waited a year or so to apply for DACA because I was already working, already surviving" (2017). Participants were already feeling supported by their community because of their activism, and they resisted DACA because of the inequalities it presented against youth and adults who did not qualify. Further, they did not trust that the government would not use their DACA applications against them and their parents. While they acknowledged that their professional positions after college necessitated legal status, they were clear that their human dignity and self-respect originated in their homes and communities. They contend that they all deserve an equal and just path to citizenship, and they will continue to strive for it. As José indicated, "Even before DACA was announced, I was still moving around the world in a way that was maybe more freeing than people would expect because we had blueprints. We had people before us who were doing it." He was referring to his fellow activists, Kari, Hugo, and Mari, whom he had not seen in many years. He continued, "I think that's where my spirit was most nourished. It wasn't through an announcement by the president. It was through the organizing that we did in Las Vegas. We have these communities who we're building on top of each other and pushing each other forward. And I think that that's the biggest takeaway for me from the DACA experience" (2020).

Xuanito ended his interview with a statement that resonated with the collective spirit of our participants' struggle: "I want to take a minute to honor all of the undocumented people who have transitioned waiting for a system to validate their humanity. I want to honor all the family members that died without watching their loved ones come back home. I want to honor the pain that we've been through as a collective. You deserve to heal. Do not feel guilty about living your best destiny, because you deserve it." We offer Xuanito's words, the words of all of the participants of this project, and the energy and strength of our muxerista and jotería community. Among us there are healers, teachers, and activists who are spirit restorers and defenders. We lift up their words, their struggles, and their triumphs, and we offer Xuanito's message to us over the years, "¡Jota triunfa!" This phrase has layered meanings. Literally, it means "Queer, triumph!" It is a gender-inclusive use of the word *jota*, and the call to triumph is a rejection of the attempted and actual spirit murder that so many immigrants and queer and trans people experience. The phrase calls upon us to reclaim our joy, to heal, and ultimately to triumph in the face of generations of pain and struggle.

Appendix A

Jasmine's Positionality

My mother immigrated to the United States when she was thirteen years young, more than forty-two years ago, at a time when the immigration laws and Border Patrol were not as violent as they are now. Mi ama y tía were sleeping passengers said to be US citizens and were waved through the border with a coyote my grandparents had paid. Patricia Cuara, mi ama, was born in Purepero, Michoacán, Mexico, and is the eldest of nine siblings.

In 1986 the Immigration Reform and Control Act was passed and allowed my mom and our family to obtain documentation only three years before my birth. I was born in Long Beach, California, and was raised by resilient immigrant muxeres. My life is guided by matriarchy. My mother has worked sunup to sundown, as immigrants are often forced to do in this country. At a very young age, I developed a strong determination to change the world because I wanted a better life for my family and community. I learned that people that look like us are pushed to the margins and suffer injustices daily. In 2007, at the age of seventeen, I organized a march for the DREAM Act, and I knew that I had found a home in community organizing. Simultaneously, I began working at an immigration law firm and immersed myself in the immigrant rights movement in Las Vegas. It was through this journey that I met my jotería familia. It is important to note that the relationship with the participants of this research project extends far beyond these interviews. Over the years we have organized, marched, loved, grown, and worked toward our collective liberation together. I am honored and humbled by their continued trust and can only hope that our work does justice to their struggle.

I am a queer muxerista, first-generation Chicana striving for social change. My hope is that research like mine offers a platform for social justice with a jotería and muxerista consciousness. I hold a bachelor of arts degree in women's studies from the University of Nevada, Las Vegas (UNLV). I am currently pursuing a master's degree in social work at Northeastern Illinois University. This project originated as my feminist undergraduate capstone project in 2014.

Joanna's Positionality

I am a queer, feminist, first-generation Chicana from San Jose, California, with joint roots in Las Vegas, Nevada. Las Vegas was home during my most formative years; it was there that I became a student activist and organizer in the movement for immigrant, queer, trans, and feminist liberation. My connection to immigrant rights organizing and investment in activist-scholar research begins with my family. My parents were undocumented at the time of my birth, and to this day my extended family is mixed in status. This reality made me hyperaware as a child of how borders, police/immigration officers, and immigration policies directly contributed to fracturing and displacing families and are emblematic of a regime of violence and domination.

Growing up as a daughter of immigrants also taught me about the enduring spirit of freedom and resistance that lives in those who have had to migrate to survive. After my mom gave birth to me, she refused confinement in the United States as an undocumented person. She returned to Mexico three times and crossed the border back to the United States by foot until she got her papeles in 1993, shortly after she birthed my second sibling. My family continued to organize for family members to cross the border, reunite with their children, and strategize to avoid the migra at the border and in their workplaces. My family taught me to be critical of a world with borders and instilled in me a disdain for borders, prisons, and nation-states. Their resistance inspired me to become involved as a young person in the fight for the DREAM Act, against the criminalization and detention of immigrants, and for the uncompromising legalization of all undocumented peoples. It is in this movement that I met many of the participants in this research project. As a queer young person, I chose fellow queers and feminist student organizers in this movement to be my chosen family. We constantly worked to document our organizing work, knowing that the narratives of immigrants, youth, queers, women, and femmes are often co-opted and silenced. Our passion for unapologetically telling our stories and for shaping narratives on national and transnational levels is what led me to pursue a PhD as a feminist researcher. I continue to be fired up by the truths that my undocuqueer and feminist familia have to share, and I remain grateful to be a part of documenting their stories. My involvement with this project began when Jasmine and Anita invited me to conduct follow-up interviews and revisions of the original project, initiated by them in 2014.

Anita's Positionality

I am a third- and fourth-generation Tejana, raised by a single widowed mother, Delia. My father died when I was eight years old.

He was thirty-one years old and already dying of cirrhosis of the liver. My mother was thirty years old when he died, and she raised three small children on her own. She had a limited education. She had been pushed out of school when she married my father as an eleventh grader. There was a policy that did not allow married people to attend the same school, so as the young woman in the relationship, she was the one who was expected to leave school. We grew up in extreme poverty, struggling with a lack of money, mental illness, domestic violence (we inherited my father's pain and wrath), spiritual trauma, and all of the other unnamed institutional barriers we faced. Still, my mom was determined to support me in my education. She was convinced that I would go to college, and she did everything possible to make it happen. She sold BBQ plates to pay my way to a summer program in Washington DC in middle school, again for a program at Brandeis University my junior year in high school, and a last time for my trip to New Jersey when I got into Princeton for undergraduate school. Since then, I have been racing through education and activism to ensure my family's survival and my community's access to higher education. For this reason, I have committed myself to working with my students and comrades and immersing myself in these movimientos. I served as Jasmine's advisor and collaborator on this feminist capstone project, completed in 2014. This work is an extension and expansion of the research that I was simultaneously conducting between 2005 and 2019. I met both Jasmine and Joanna when they were completing high school (different years), becoming leaders of the Las Vegas immigrant rights movement, and entering UNLV. I was a professor of women's, gender, and sexuality studies at UNLV between 2004 and 2019, and they both became majors in the department and thus were also my students. The research participants of this study were also fellow activistas and former students. Since then, all of them have graduated, and we continue to build upon our muxerista and jotería community spanning multiple states, including but not limited to Las Vegas, Minnesota, California, and Arizona.

Notes

1. See "H.R.4437—Border Protection, Antiterrorism, and Illegal Immigration Control Act of 2005," congress.gov, https://www.congress.gov/bill/109th-congress/house-bill/4437.

2. The DREAM (Development, Relief, and Education for Alien Minors) Act was introduced in Congress in 2001. It would have granted legal status to some undocumented immigrants who arrived in the United States as children and went to school in the United States. It never passed. Luis Miranda, "Get the Facts on the DREAM Act," The White House—President Barack Obama, December 1, 2010, https://obamawhitehouse.archives .gov/blog/2010/12/01/get-facts-dream-act.

3. See https://www.supremecourt.gov/opinions/19pdf/18-587_5ifl.pdf.

4. We use the term "immigration status" as opposed to "legal status" because we reject the illegal versus legal dichotomy that abounds within the immigration discussion. We contend that immigration law is unjust and discriminatory. Therefore, the "illegality" of people's presence in this country without authorization is largely due to institutional citizenism, classism, racism, sexism, homophobia, and xenophobia. For this reason, we consciously choose not to adopt the federal definition of "illegal" versus "legal" citizenship status.

5. See ColorLines campaign to "Drop the I-word" (2010), https://www.youtube.com /watch?v=v6GcPft7mqU&feature=youtu.be.

6. Citizenism is a global system founded on the legal and social subordination of noncitizens. It is social, economic, political, and legal discrimination against undocumented immigrants across the globe. Specifically, it is a system of legal advantages that unfairly privileges (U.S.) citizens and reinforces unearned and unjust citizen privileges. It is the belief in and practice of citizen superiority and results in the dehumanization of immigrants around the world. It intersects with racism, classism, sexism, ableism, and heterosexism but is specific in its targeting of people who were not born citizens of the nation in which they reside.

7. See the work of artist Julio Salgado (https://juliosalgadoart.com/) and writer Yosimar Reyes (http://yosimarreyes.com/) for excellent examples of work that has helped catapult undocumented and queer people out of the shadows and into the national dialogue demanding their human dignity.

8. Accessed from "States Offering Driver's Licenses to Immigrants," National Conference of State Legislatures, https://www.ncsl.org/.

9. We use the term "Latinx" to signify gender inclusion, including men, women, and nonbinary people in the community. To learn more about this practice, see Alan Pelaez Lopez, "The X in Latinx Is a Wound, not a Trend," colorbloq.org, https://www.colorbloq .org/the-x-in-latinx-is-a-wound-not-a-trend.

10. See "Nevada Real ID," Department of Motor Vehicles—Official Website of the State of Nevada, https://dmvnv.com/realid.htm.

11. See Jeanne Batalova, Brittany Blizzard, and Jessica Bolter, "Frequently Requested Statisitcs on Immigrants and Immigration in the United States," Migration Policy Institute, February 14, 2020, https://www.migrationpolicy.org/article/frequently-requested -statistics-immigrants-and-immigration-united-states.

12. See "Deferred Action for Childhood Arrivals (DACA) Data Tools," Migration Policy Institute, April 1, 2020, https://www.migrationpolicy.org/programs/data-hub/deferred -action-childhood-arrivals-daca-profiles.

13. See Nicole Prchal Svajlenka and Audrey Singer, "Immigration Facts: Deferred Action for Childhood Arrivals (DACA)," Brookings Institution, August 14, 2013, https://www .brookings.edu/research/immigration-facts-deferred-action-for-childhood-arrivals-daca/.

14. Muxerista, like the term "muxeres," is an alteration of the word *mujeres*, or "women," in Spanish. The terms "muxerista" and "jotería" are fluid, living identities with changing definitions. Muxerista was originally coined in 2002. To see earlier definitions of the term, see Revilla (2004). Today, we define muxerista as a nonbinary, gender-inclusive, gender-fluid, trans, queer, and/or sexually inclusive Chicanx and Latinx identity that honors our multiple intersecting identities and communities while uplifting our radical commitment to personal and collective liberation. Embedded in a muxerista identity is a jotería politic. We are all contributors to and cofounders of the Association for Jotería Arts, Activism, and Scholarship (www.ajaas .com). Jotería refers to queer and trans Latinx people and communities. The word "jota/joto/ jotx" has been used as an insult toward lesbian, gay, bisexual, transgender, intersex, and queer people, but today it is reclaimed by many members of the Latinx queer and trans community.

15. A jotería analytic is informed by multiple genealogies of activism and theory, including Chicano gay men's and Chicana lesbians' cultural productions, women of color feminisms, Chicano studies, and queer of color theory. This mode of consciousness and critique is employed to challenge power, subjectivity, and citizenship (Ochoa 2016, 184, 188). "Jotahistoria, Joto-historia, [jotx-historia], and Jotería-historia are terms that we use intentionally to indicate the absence of Queer history from traditional academic spaces. They refer to a process of reclaiming and documenting our personal testimonies and experiences" (Revilla and Santillana 2014).

16. See "Fact Sheet: Family Based Immigration," National Immigration Forum, February 14, 2018, https://immigrationforum.org/article/fact-sheet-family-based-immigration/.

17. For more examples of muxerista action research within this Las Vegas activist community, see Joanna Nuñez (2019), Briceida Hernandez-Toledo (2020), and Santillana in this text.

18. See Department of Homeland Security v. Regents of the University of California (2020).

19. A matrícula consular de alta seguridad (MCAS) is a consular identification card (CID) issued by the consulate offices of Mexico. It is offered to nationals living outside of Mexico.

20. Due to the sensitive nature of this research and the risks that undocumented people generally face in this country, Esperanza was highly skeptical of the research and almost refused to participate. However, because of the trust and close relationship she had with Jasmine, who conducted the interview, she agreed.

References

Aboytes, Irma. 2009. "Undocumented Students and Access to Higher Education: A Dream Defined by State Borders." *Journal of Gender, Race, and Justice* 12 (3): 579–601.

Anzaldúa, Gloria. 1987. *Borderlands / La Frontera: The New Mestiza*. San Francisco: Aunt Lute Books.

Cisneros, Jesus. 2018. "Working with the Complexity and Refusing to Simplify: UndocuQueer Meaning Making at the Intersection of LGBTQ and Immigrant Rights Discourses." *Journal of Homosexuality* 65 (11): 1415–34.

Deeb-Sossa, Natalia. 2019. *Community-Based Participatory Research: Testimonios from Chicana/o Studies*. Tucson: University of Arizona Press.

Department of Motor Vehicles, State of Nevada. 2020. Proof of Identity and Residency. https://dmvnv.com/dlresidency.htm.

Diaz, Von. 2013. "Three Faces of DACA: Colorlines." Applied Research Center. https://www.colorlines.com/articles/three-faces-daca.

Fernandez-Kelly, Patricia, and Douglas Massey. 2007. "Borders for Whom? The Role of NAFTA in Mexico-U.S. Migration." *Annals of the American Academy of Political and Social Science* 610 (1): 98–118.

Hernandez-Toledo, Briceida. 2020. "'There's Life beyond the Strip': Immigrant Rights Activism and Spatial Resistance in Las Vegas, Nevada." Master's thesis, University of California, Los Angeles.

Luibhéid, Eithne. 2008. "Sexuality, Migration, and the Shifting Line between Legal and Illegal Status." *GLQ* 14 (2–3): 289–315.

———. 2018. "Heteronormativity: A Bridge between Queer Migration and Critical Trafficking Studies." *Women's Studies in Communication* 41 (4): 305–9.

Márquez, Lorena. 2019. "Recovering Chicana/o Movement History through Testimonios." In *Community-Based Participatory Research: Testimonios from Chicana/o Studies*, edited by Natalia Deeb-Sossa, 91–110. Tucson: University of Arizona Press.

National Conference of State Legislatures. 2020. "States Offering Driver's Licenses to Immigrants." February 6. https://www.ncsl.org/research/immigration/states-offering-driver-s-licenses-to-immigrants.aspx.

Negrón-Gonzales, Genevieve. 2014. "Undocumented, Unafraid and Unapologetic: Rearticulatory Practices and Migrant Youth 'Illegality.'" *Latino Studies* 12 (2): 259–78.

Núñez, Joanna. 2019. "¡Mi mamá me enseño! Teaching and Learning *Mexicana* and Chicana Feminisms in the Home." PhD diss., University of Minnesota, Minneapolis.

Ochoa, Juan D. 2016. "Shine Bright Like a Migrant: Julio Salgado's Digital Art and Its Use of Jotería." *Social Justice* 42 (3–4): 184–99.

Pérez, William, and Richard Douglas Cortes. 2011. *Undocumented Latino College Students: Their Socioemotional and Academic Experiences*. LFB Scholarly Publishing LLC.

Ramos, Oscar. 2009. "U.S. Citizen Children, Undocumented Immigrant Parents: How Parental Undocumented Status Affects Citizen Children's Educational Achievement." Master's thesis, University of California, San Diego.

Revilla, Anita Tijerina. 2004. "Muxerista Pedagogy: Raza Womyn Teaching Social Justice through Student Activism." *High School Journal* 87 (4): 80–94.

———. 2012. "What Happens in Vegas Does Not Stay in Vegas: Youth Leadership in the Immigrant Rights Movement in Las Vegas, 2006." *Aztlán: A Journal of Chicano Studies* 37 (1): 87–115.

Revilla, Anita, and Evelyn Rangel-Medina. 2011. "Las Vegas Activist Crew and the Immigrant Rights Movement: How We Transformed 'Sin City.'" In *Marching Students: Chicana and Chicano Activism in Education, 1968 to the Present*, edited by Margarita Berta-Ávila, Anita Tijerina Revilla, and Julie López Figueroa. Reno: University of Nevada Press.

Revilla, Anita, and Jose Manuel Santillana. 2014. "Jotería Identity and Consciousness." *Aztlán: A Journal of Chicano Studies* 39 (1): 167–80.

"Undocumented Student Tuition: Overview." 2019. National Conference of State Legislatures, September 19. https://www.ncsl.org/research/education/undocumented-student-tuition-overview.aspx.

Williams, Patricia. 1991. *The Alchemy of Race and Rights*. Cambridge MA: Harvard University Press.

2

Somos jotería

UCLA *Chicanx Latinx Student Activists Fighting for Social Justice*

JOSÉ MANUEL SANTILLANA

"¡Que viva la jotería!" screamed a friend of mine as we walked among thousands of people during one of the biggest immigration marches in U.S. history. "¡Si, que viva la jotería!" people replied enthusiastically. On March 25, 2006, several UCLA queer Latinx and Chicanx student activists decided that they needed to show their presence at the immigration march in downtown Los Angeles. The jotería committee, along with other queer Latinx organizations, gathered together at the march to show that queer people were part of the struggle too. Rainbow banners streamed through the streets with slogans supporting immigration rights. It was a powerful day for all of the organizers of the jotería conference and one of the driving forces to create a specific jotería space.

This essay examines the experiences of nine queer Latinx and Chicanx student activists who participated in the 2006 immigrant rights marches in Los Angeles and the organizing of the 2006 jotería conference hosted at UCLA. It explores the involvement of these students in social justice movements at the university and in their communities. This is a qualitative case study of a group of students (the jotería conference committee) who eventually formed La Jotería de UCLA, a queer Latinx and Chicanx student activist group that initialized in 2006. Race, class, gender, immigration, and sexuality discrimination were major topics within their lives and proved to be the driving force of their activism. By exploring the lived experiences of queer Latinx and Chicanx student activists, I examine the way they perceive and respond to the intersections of multiple forms of oppression and how these factors affect their commitment to social justice. As a member of the jotería conference committee myself, I have interchangeably played the role of the researcher and the participant observer, meaning that I was fully invested in the organization. Using interviews, surveys, document examination, and day-to-day observations, I have captured the participants' insights about identity, activism, injustice, and liberation. The organizing of the 2006 UCLA jotería conference played a significant role in the lives of the participants. It provided its membership with a specific queer Latinx and Chicanx space that fostered their activism.

In 2006 millions of people participated in protests nationwide over a proposed change to U.S. immigration policy. The protests began in response to HR 4437, the Border Protection, Anti-terrorism, and Illegal Immigration Control Act of 2005; the bill attempted to raise penalties for undocumented immigrants and classify immigrants, as well as anyone who aided them, as felons.[1] The bill's continued effort to criminalize undocumented immigrants sparked national debate and motivated millions of people to stand up to xenophobia and racism. On March 10, 2006, an estimated one hundred thousand individuals stood in protest in Chicago, while on March 25, over five hundred thousand people marched for immigrant rights in downtown Los Angeles. By May 1, 2006, the national boycott El Gran Paro Estadounidense (the Great American Strike) had been organized. People were encouraged to boycott schools and businesses to demonstrate that immigrants were a powerful force.

A large number of members of the jotería committee, along with members of MEChA de UCLA (Movimiento Estudiantil Chicanx de Aztlán), helped do security for the May 1 protest, while many more attended the March 25 protest of 2006. Over twenty jotxs from UCLA took part in the actual March 25 protest and queer contingent. As members of the coalition, we felt that it was important to take part in the national efforts to support immigrant rights. Since many members came from immigrant families or were immigrants themselves, they recognized that these issues affected them as queer people of color. In one of the regularly scheduled meetings, members organized a sign-making party to make protest signs that reflected their politics and concerns as queer Latinxs. The hand-painted rainbow signs included slogans that read "Queers Are Immigrants Too," "Jotería Unida," "Jotería Presente," "We're Queer & We're Here," and "Queer Rights Are Workers' Rights." When the day came, everyone was prepared and ready to take action.

During the historic march, over a hundred people marched with the queer Latinx contingent, which included Bienestar's Transgéneros Unidas and queer Latinx students from UCLA and CSUN.[2] The jotería committee brought their signs, as well as Mexican and United Farm Workers flags. While Transgéneros Unidas led chants like "No somos criminales, somos transsexuales!" (We are not criminals, we are transsexuals), others chanted, "Que viva la jotería, que viva los immigrantes" (Power to the queers, power to immigrants). Pilar recalled: "I remember Transgéneros Unidas having a huge white banner identifying themselves among the crowd. Although they had traded their high heels for sneakers, all the glamour and fierce pride the transgender community was known for was still present. There was mixed responses from the crowd around them. Some marchers would smile, others would stare, but the majority of the participants kept on marching along with them, side by side." The unity and pride among the jotería community that day brought feelings of accomplishment and challenged the larger Los Angeles community in viewing immigration as a heterosexual issue. It provided queer Latinx visibility in the immigrant rights movement, which often excludes queer issues.

The jotería committee's vision for social justice and revolution came from the need to define who they were. The following is the mission statement that was written by the committee and serves as a manifesto for their queer Chicanx and Latinx identity.

We are Jotería. We are lesbian, gay, bisexual, homosexual, transgender, intersex, sexually defiant, fluid, downe, queer and many other sexual expressions. We are womyn, men, transgender and people who defy gender categories. We are Raza of the Americas, de Nuestra America, Latina/os and Chicana/os. For the time being we are students although historically we are of working class and lower middle class. We are a community from different nations and our existence defies both the physical and social borders that have been imposed. Our community is also made up of those that still cannot publicly join us in the struggle because they are going through their own internal struggle. We fight so that one day they have the opportunity to join us.

Despite the range of categories within the community, all of these identities are consolidated into a single word: Jotería. Although the word "Joto" initially emerged as an insult, we have appropriated this word because our identity is not shameful. Jotería is the plural form of Joto and also includes Jotas, or queer mujeres. When we are criticized as different we reply: Y que?

The contradiction of our struggle is that it is very complex yet at the same time it is very clear. The object of our liberation is to end all forms of oppression and exploitation: social, ideological and economic. We must be clear that we are actively fighting a capitalist empire that continues to globalize not only its capital and free market trade agreements but also its institutionalized forms of sexism, homophobia, racism, xenophobia, heterosexism, and gender discrimination.

The constant attacks on our communities demand that we become organized, obtain collective demands and continue with the struggle. We are committed to bringing awareness about Jotería issues to our communities and our allies because this affects everyone.

We are fighting because we have witnessed the continual marginalization of our Jotería from our community and political/social organizations. As Jotería, we feel it is necessary for us to have safe spaces where harassment due to one's race/ethnicity, gender, class, sexuality, and culture is nonexistence.

The varied gender and sexual expressions represented in the mission statement are a shift in some activist organizations to have more inclusive politics. In its initial development, the jotería committee considered the multiplicity and range of its members' identities. They wanted to make sure that people were being represented in the best way possible. Therefore, they used terms with both gender and sexual fluidity.

This essay is a reflection of the conversation with the jotería committee and an attempt to document and conceptualize the organizing of the 2006 UCLA jotería conference. Modeled after Anita

Revilla's (2004) mujerstorias, the following is a collection of queer Chicanx stories and conversations to which I refer as Latinx and Chicanx queerstorias. They are personal narratives, collective narratives, and interviews, written, oral, formal, and informal.

My research found that the jotería committee was dedicated to exploring the complexity of their identities. When speaking about queer Latinx and Chicanx gender and sexualities, we must be able to consider the various identities that exist in the fabric. Similarly, other scholars have found value in understanding the complexity and fluidity of gender and sexual identities (Revilla 2004). Luz Calvo and Catriona Rueda Esquibel argue that "research should be attuned to the diversity of identities claimed by queer Latinas and the specific terms and words that this population uses" (2010, 229).

By choosing to identify with varied but specific identities, the jotería committee began to carve out a specific space for themselves and define what jotería meant to them. They sought to include everyone within Latin America, as well as Latinxs and Chicanxs living in the United States. They also situated themselves as both students and members of the working class. It was important for them to vocalize that although some members were "out" about their queer sexuality, others who remained in the closet were part of the larger struggle. As queer Latinx and Chicanx activists, they claimed an anticapitalist agenda that actively sought to work against homophobia, patriarchy, classism, xenophobia, racism, and gender discrimination. The jotería committee vision in this way coincided with the vision of raza womyn muxeristas at UCLA (Tijerina-Revilla 2009).

In the following section I will discuss (1) how the jotería committee members developed a distinct collective jotería identity/consciousness, (2) how they created a new radicalized space for their social justice vision, (3) how their activism created familia, visibility, and change both on and off campus, and (4) how their identities/consciousness informed their vision of movement building.

The Formation of a Collective Identity

The usage of derogatory words has long existed in our society. People have used them to lessen the merit of not only individuals but also groups of people. Specifically, but not limited to the United States, there has been a long history of homophobic terms that have targeted anyone who does not identify or conform with society's gender and sexuality norms. If one does not submit to their assigned gender role as "woman" or "man," they are viewed as outcasts. Similarly, if they defy the heterosexual standard, they are often marginalized as the other (Pharr 2007). Words such as "faggot," "dyke," "sissy," "queer," and "tomboy" have been used to dehumanize individuals on the basis of sexuality and gender expression. They continue to manifest themselves harshly in schools, religious institutions, work environments, and homes. Although these words have affected people across racial lines, every community has distinct experiences with such insults. For many queer Chicanxs and Latinxs living in the United States, other words have been used to dehumanize their existence. Terms such as "maricón," "marica," "marimacha," "joto," "puta," and "puto" have also been used to oppress individuals. These terms are believed to have originated in Latin America. There are a few theories surrounding the meaning and roots of these words, which I will discuss further.

The term "joto" has a strong presence among many Mexicans and Chicanxs in the Southwest. In "Domination and Desire: Male Homosexuality and the Construction of Masculinity in Mexico," Annick Prieur (1996) contends that the possible meaning of joto is that it is derived from the Spanish dance where men move in ways that are perceived as feminine. She also claims that the root of the word is connected to the Mexico City federal penitentiary, where prison authorities at one point attempted to isolate overtly homosexual inmates in cell block J (pronounced "jota" in Spanish), while maricón is believed to be the male-gendered version of María, a common female name in Mexico and Latin America. Most if not all of these words continue to be used to marginalize and silence people. However, many individuals who have been harmed by these words have time and again reclaimed them as words of empowerment. The participants of this study are part of that group that has challenged oppressive language by using it as a tool for resistance and liberation. They have redefined what it means to be jotx by choosing to identify themselves as such.

Queer communities have used jota, joto, and jotería across Latin America in multiple ways. My research focused on how queer Latinx and Chicanx writers and student activists have used and defined these terms. In 1987 Gloria Anzaldúa made reference to jotería in *Borderlands / La Frontera: The New Mestiza*, and in 1993 Cherríe Moraga's *The Last Generation: Prose and Poetry* referred to jotería as a Chicano term for "queer" folk. Since then, other artists and activists have been embracing the term. UCLA's La Familia has been using the term interchangeably since the early 1990s to refer to the queer Chicanx community.

Alex, a member of the jotería committee, recalled when he first heard the term "jotería" and the reason that he embraced it:

> The first time I heard it being mentioned was in Cherríe Moraga's book. I remember her starting to talk about Aztlán and how Aztlán was a homeland for Chicanas and Chicanos. She talked about the need for Queer Aztlán, a need for a homeland that included jotería. A homeland for us. To me that was cool because it embraced jotería. And I embrace it because I see myself as part of my community, a community that I come from being queer, working class, Chicano, and immigrant parents. Like many other jotas y jotos, queers, I know it's not that easy to separate our identity from our queerness and our jotería.

As student activists at UCLA, many of the jotería committee members were exposed to Chicana lesbian literature through Chicanx studies and women's studies courses and by recommending the books to one another. This literature played a pivotal part in the forming of their identity because Chicana lesbians like Gloria Anzaldúa and Cherríe Moraga were talking about their experiences in dealing with sexism, racism, and homophobia in all sectors of their lives. Alex identifies with Moraga's struggle and usage of Queer Aztlán and jotería because these terms were able to reflect his multiple identities. The concept of Queer Aztlán, a Chicano homeland for all its people, including its jotería, was an attempt to name and envision a movement free from all oppression (Moraga 1993). This was critical because Alex felt that separating his identities limited his being. To him, jotería was an identity that encompassed being queer, working class, Chicano, and immigrant. This was powerful because Alex was contributing to the definition of jotería; not only was he coming out as queer, he was coming out as an activist, Chicano, queer, immigrant, and working-class person. He was making a political statement with his identity and had agency in building language that essentially unifies being Brown and queer.

Lupe explained why he felt empowered by the usage of jotería during a planning meeting for the conference:

> I remember Gloria Anzaldúa saying "Listen to your jotería." To me, that empowered me because someone was validating my existence. Someone was carving a space out for me in the Chicana and Chicano movement to say it's okay for you to be queer. More importantly, now I could be raza and queer and many other things. It's hard, because even when we created the space lots of people were resistant because not many people were trying to fight class, race, gender, sexuality, and issues of globalization. The power of jotería is that you can be queer and also retain all other identities and all other movements that you are following.

In search of finding himself, Lupe was looking for a place that could speak to all of his experiences. As we have learned from the various movements of the 1960s, 1970s, and 1980s, many movements failed to address issues of intersectionality (Alaniz and Cornish 2008; García 1997). Still today this is one of our greatest challenges. Lupe felt that Anzaldúa was able to address this in her vision; she was calling for the inclusion of queer Chicanxs and other queer people of color. This vision motivated him to continue developing the concept of jotería. Just as Anzaldúa carved a space for him, Lupe was also continuing the legacy of creating this vision.

"Cruz" (a pseudonym) asserted why jotería suited her best and included both of her identities as a Chicana and a lesbian:

> The first time I heard it was by Cherríe Moraga. It's not just joto, it's not gendered. When I first came out I would go to West Hollywood a lot, which was all middle-class white folk. I didn't really feel that I belonged to that group. So I didn't just see it as let's queer up our

community but rather let's show the queer community that we are here too. Let's show them that we're here as Chicanas and Chicanos and Latinas and Latinos and that there is other queer people too. It seemed to me that the jotería embraced themselves that way too.

For many queer Latinxs living in the Los Angeles area, West Hollywood (WeHo) was one place where they could go to be themselves, to be queer. However, Cruz's experience with West Hollywood was that she did not identify with the white queer culture. She was not able to connect with white middle-class queers because her culture was different. The power of jotería was that it included her culture coming from a working-class family, as well as her queerness. In that way she was able to feel at home with others who identified with jotería.

As Cruz explains, jotería has the advantage of not coinciding with one specific gender but rather embracing multiple genders, unlike the term "joto," which only referred to males. Angel further explained why it was important for him to make that connection: "The first time I heard it, it was being used in Cherríe Moraga's Queer Aztlán. I didn't understand it at first but slowly understood it as an array of queerness. At the same time [I was] using the word "joto" and taking it away from being gendered, as a gender connotation. Also, taking it away from being derogatory. It's hard to take it away from the word "joto," being gendered. But at the time, the people that were using it were lesbian Chicanas." Angel felt it was important to have a queer Latina Latino Chicana Chicano term that connected multiple genders. Although he felt that the term "jotería" was often too associated with "joto," he believed Chicana lesbians were redefining the term to include mujeres. The way that Chicana lesbians were embracing jotería empowered him to use it.

Pilar echoed experiences similar to those of Angel: "The first time that I heard this term was my first year at UCLA, and that is also the first quarter that I started to go to La Familia. The first time I heard it was from Delia, a raza womyn at a student fair. . . . I remember raza womyn would use jota with an *x*. Delia would say, 'Yeah, I'm a xota.' I remember thinking that it was weird, because I had only heard it as a male term. So that to me opened up my mind to use the term." Queer Chicana mujeres have been at the forefront of embracing jotería as an identity in the United States. While Angel first heard the term being used in Cherríe's Queer Aztlán, Pilar heard jota for the first time from a queer raza womyn.

In seeking to define jotería, "Trinidad" (a pseudonym) stated the following in a survey: "Jotería is a political identification among queer Raza. An understanding that gay culture ignores our unique struggles, and thus cannot be used as a way to identify ourselves. Jotería presents the diverse struggles of Raza who not only struggle for acceptance and to end homophobia within our families and communities, but also fight to end racism in Amerikkka and the gay-rights movement." The jotería committee has been unable to be part of gay culture and gay and lesbian movements because of the deep embedded racism that exists in them. Similarly, other Chicana scholars have addressed the racism within mainstream gay cultures and movements (Anzaldúa 2007; Moraga and Anzaldúa 2002; Moraga 1993, 2000). Trinidad further illustrates his critique of racism with his usage of the term "Amerikkka," which is a combination of the United States and the white supremacist group the Ku Klux Klan (KKK).

The term "jotería" also provided a space for allies to explore their own sexuality and define what it really means to be a partner in the struggle. "Norma" (a pseudonym), a self-identified "ally/straight but not narrow" individual, shared why she chooses to identify with the term:

> I first heard the term in college from my friends and roommates. I identify with the term because jotería to me means it is encompassing of things that are gay and are related to being gay. Although I do not identify as gay, I am very close and comfortable with my gay friends who are Mexican and of Mexican descent. Maybe it's the openness and the consciousness that my gay friends and I share that brings us together. I also identify with the term because I have an uncle who was gay and who was probably one of the first Latino gay men to die of AIDS. I also had gay and transsexual babysitters growing up.

Being gay, and I use the term broadly, is not outside of what my perception of the norm is. I have been encompassed by jotería for as long as I can remember. I sometimes wonder if a part of me is a gay man.

Norma explains that her identification with jotería is rooted in her experience with her family and surrounding community. She has been around so many jotxs from an early age that she has come to understand that being jotería is part of who she is. Maybe not in a sexual way, but in a political way it has shaped her way of thinking and viewing the world. Her uncle, babysitters, and friends are symbols and gateways into that politicization.

Still, not all participants fully embraced the term. While some were not out, others were in the process of exploring their sexuality. Alma, a self-identified "Fluid/Explorative" Centro Americana, explained how she has yet to embrace the term:

I don't identify with jotería not because I don't like the word but because I have yet to embrace it. I like the word, I like its playfulness and feel it is very inclusive of many sexualities and also has a cultural, ethnic aspect, for lack of a better word, but I felt my understanding of my own sexuality came after this word was introduced to me. I, somehow, still related it more to gay males of color, even though it has not been exclusively portrayed as so. I think I have a difficult time with identifying myself with a strong "queer" term because my sexuality has often been contested by others, and so I've been unable to define it for myself—partly because it is so fluid, and partly because others tend to want to define it for me and even disempower my sense of agency over it, partly because a strong identity is intimidating and scary in a sense, and partly because I don't necessarily want to adhere to a particular identification.

Although Alma does not identify with the term "jotería," she leaves an open space for its embracement. She believes that the term is inclusive. However, as a woman, she feels that it is still too connected with maleness. Many often connect jotería solely with the masculine/joto aspect of it without considering the feminine/jota counterpart. This can possibly be because the term "joto" is more commonly used than "jota" in the Latinx community. Alma also expresses that any queer term confines her sexuality. For many across the queer spectrum, identifying with any one term boxes them into one category.

The interviews and surveys suggested that a collective identity/consciousness—jotería—was formed because it was inclusive of their multiple identities and consciousness as queers, feminists, Latinxs and Chicanxs, working class, men, women, nonconforming genders, and immigrants. The jotería committee felt that the term embraced them in ways that queer and Latinx and Chicanx did not. Chicana lesbian scholar-activists like Gloria Anzaldúa and Cherríe Moraga also played a large role in the participants' perception about jotería because many of the organizers felt empowered and validated by their writings. Still, one of the organizers remained skeptical of the term because she felt it was more male-oriented than female-oriented.

The participants of my study were able to construct jotería spaces through their activism, which garnered critical consciousness about their multiple identities as queers, feminists, Latinxs and Chicanxs, working class, men, women, nonconforming genders, and immigrants. Similarly, other scholars have found that student activists engage in meaningful acts of pedagogy through their collective action and conversations (Berta-Ávila, Revilla, and López Figueroa 2011; Covarrubias and Revilla 2003; Revilla 2004). While some of my findings may coincide with those of other scholars, there are distinct experiences and lessons to be learned from these participants' involvement and thought processes as queer Latinx and Chicanx activists at UCLA.

Discontent with Campus Organizations

The majority of the participants expressed that the reason for the unity of all the organizers came out of their disillusionment with on-campus organizations at the time. Many of them felt that raza organizations and queer organization did not represent them and the type of activism they wanted to do. While queer student organizations solely focused on queer issues, raza student organizations did not create space for jotería. Pilar remembered feeling frustrated with all the organizations he was part of:

> I remember thinking that La Familia wasn't for me. In La Familia there was some WeHo [West Hollywood] boys and some political people, but every meeting we were fighting about what to do. . . . I could have stayed, but it was too attached to the queer alliance. Other queer people of color groups were being shut down. La Familia was using money to go to TJ [Tijuana] to party. They were wasting money on useless events which had not much of a purpose. It was disappointing. I can also relate to that. I went through being disillusioned with La Familia and then being disillusioned with Conciencia Libre. That same year I was pushed out of the directing track from theater. I was too radical for many organizations.

In college, many students engage themselves in self-discovery and building a political consciousness. For some of the participants in the study, this process was a result of learning about their radicalized, gendered, classed, and sexualized identities (Revilla 2004). The majority of the participants were women's studies, Chicanx studies, political science, and lesbian, gay, bisexual, and transgender (LGBT) studies majors. However, many of them also engaged in the same process through their participation with activist student organizations. So it was important that they felt comfortable in respective organizations. While Pilar joined La Familia, he did not stay for long, because he felt that part of its membership represented "WeHo boys," which he connected to "white superficial" culture, to which he felt no connection. Perhaps Pilar's dissatisfaction with La Familia spending money on trips to Tijuana reflected his varied identities as a working-class gay Chicano. His deep concerns were focused on his communities and the fact that money was not being spent to advance queer Latinxs. At the same time, he realized that Conciencia Libre failed to include sexuality in its work and vision for justice: "I have experienced many forms of discriminations for being part of the jotería community, such as people judging me wrong and excluding me from political processes because of who I am. I have been asked, such as when I was in Conciencia

Libre and one of the leaders asked me to choose between the Chicano and gay community because I couldn't successfully do both." For Pilar, both La Familia and Conciencia Libre were pushing him out. They were forcing him to choose the identity that mattered to him the most. Important to note is that Pilar's experiences are age-old dilemmas: many Chicanas within the Chicano movement felt that they had to choose between being a woman and being a Chicana (García 1997). It is essential to understand how new and old issues are being dealt with among queer Latinx and Chicanx student activists. Pilar's conflict with both organizations affected his political consciousness because those spaces were not able to provide safe environments that garnered critical consciousness and development. Dealing with these issues also affected his schoolwork. Pilar felt he did not have a good support system and instead was further marginalized within groups that were supposed to cater to him.

For Lupe, it was his previous experiences with student organizations that pushed him away from wanting to even organize before the jotería conference:

The organizing of the conference was very important to me because I was extremely traumatized about what had happened to me my second year, because the space that I was able to belong to pushed me out, it was La Familia. . . . I was really disillusioned with UCLA and students coming together with certain spaces. I felt that, one, I was pushed out of La Familia, and two, I felt how difficult it was to advocate for LGBT issues and raza issues. And being questioned on the type of work I did over and over again. I wanted to talk about trans issues as well as academia. I felt very much silenced and disillusioned, traumatized with everything that was going on.

Lupe was able to find a space among the jotería committee where he did not have to compromise his identity. Many underestimate the power of creating safe environments. For queer Latinx and Chicanx student activists who have often been silenced both at home and in community spaces, being able to create such spaces contributes to their survival in academia. Additionally, student activism has historically been a tool of resistance and transformation for many students across higher education who are discontented with a particular aspect of society and their educational institutions (Revilla 2004). Lupe's frustrations with UCLA student organizations were connected to his struggle to try to advocate for multiple issues within one organization. Lupe felt limited in the development of his consciousness because he felt he was being silenced; therefore, he was not able to advocate issues that were important to him, such as trans issues. "Trans" has been used as a more inclusive and encompassing term for those who would be included under the umbrella term "transgender" but do not necessarily fully identify with the term. The term is being used more frequently among trans communities in an explicit effort to acknowledge that there is a multitude of trans identities (Galarte 2011).

La Familia's male-dominated membership discouraged other jotería committee members from joining the only queer Latinx group on campus. Cruz recalls her years as an undergrad: "Personally I got involved because I was not involved as an undergrad. I didn't join La Familia because it was boys planning on what they were going to do in WeHo that weekend." While La Familia was supposed to provide a space for both women and men, Cruz felt that the organization was geared more toward men and a socializing agenda. Although La Familia was originally created to bring together queer Latinxs and Chicanxs at UCLA, it failed to maintain its appeal to many student activists who wanted to discuss multiple issues, at least during the period in which this research was conducted. The disappointment with student activist organizations on campus ended up being one of the driving forces to create a new space among jotería. The jotería committee ultimately succeeded in forming a new radicalized space that nourished its membership and allowed for many of them to put forward their multidimensional vision of social justice.

Creating Familia, Creating Visibility, Creating Change

For the organizers of the jotería conference, it was much more than a project. Although they had first come together to make the conference a reality, many participants expressed that the process created familia, visibility, and change for queer Latinxs and Chicanxs at UCLA. "Rosario" (a pseudonym), a second-year transfer student, discussed what motivated her to seek social change:

Well before the conference, I had never been a part of a group such as la jotería. It was my opportunity. Joining the group helped me in my own coming-out process, it allowed me to be able to have the courage to speak to my small siblings and familia. I already know some of them are [queer]. I had a couple of people who have come out in my family, and they didn't accept them, and so then I seen how they struggled with that. I had an uncle that was gay and had AIDS, and no one talked about it, and now I have another uncle that has AIDS. It really affected me to see my uncle not have support and die alone. I mean, yes, we were there, but no one was supportive with him having AIDS and him being gay. I am always hearing my aunts and uncles say derogatory things about my uncles. It needs to be addressed. So I am a part of the AIDS Walk, and I try to take and teach my siblings about different issues. So now I am creating those safe spaces, so now I am here.

Rosario's primary reason for joining the jotería committee had to do with her experiences at home. Her uncles having AIDS affected her deeply, and in return she wanted to make sure her siblings had a safe space to talk about different issues, including sexuality. Building support systems was vital to her understanding of survival. Her activism therefore took place on two fronts, at home and in the community. Ultimately, being part of the jotería committee provided a space for her coming-out process (Revilla 2009).

For Cruz, that change meant the inclusion of women as equal partners in the organizing of the conference:

The dynamic that was created in la jotería group was that different people from different orgs came with different mindsets. One of the most important things was that everyone listened to each other, and that is something that I didn't experience before. People were actually listening to each other and supported each other, and there [were] a lot of women. And the men were listening to the women, and to me that was huge, because I was use[d] to men talking, and the women

were doing things, and "yay, we had a conference." It's what motivated me to organize the conference.

The majority of the jotería committee self-identified as feminists and
aligned themselves with both the academic and activist work that
feminists did, specifically, queer Chicana feminists. Their activism
therefore reflected these politics, which essentially allowed them to
transform the spaces. While many queer organizations often failed
to make the necessary connections with feminism, the jotería committee successfully advocated a feminist agenda at the forefront.
They further organized themselves in a nonhierarchical structure
that allowed collective decision-making among all its members.

Angel, a fourth-year student, for example, felt like he made it
through the year because of the familia that was being built in the
jotería committee: "The reason that I did it was because I needed to
be part of that space. I was motivated to do the work, and the work
in return kept me in school. The jotería kept me going and helped
me finish school. Having you all building this family. It was a collective, we had an equal play in it. Everyone in there wanted to be
there and wasn't out to join for individual reasons. My education
was not about school, it was about my activism." The jotería committee was able to provide its membership with a space that encouraged healthy queer relationships. Angel felt it was important to be
part of something where individuals' voices could be heard, where
he was an equal contributor to the "family," like everyone else. He
found a community among the jotería committee members that not
only had this but also helped him navigate the university system. As
a marginalized student, he found a space that did more than accept
him. The jotería committee embraced him through love and activism. This, in return, motivated him to push forward. Angel indicates that his jotería activism was a leading force in keeping him in
school. It was through his involvement in on- and off-campus student
organizing that he found meaning in his education (Revilla 2004).

Similarly, Trinidad, a fourth-year student at UCLA, expressed how
jotería was making more than a conference happen, it was also organizing, creating visibility, and forming safe spaces for queer Chicanxs:

In coming out, I wanted to do work! I wanted to go to other raza orgs and tell them, you need to address homophobia and other queer issues in your organization. And to me, all of these things were important. So I wanted to do the conference, but then other things slowly came. We had the Queer Aztlán workshops for parents and youth at the raza youth conference. It was amazing. We also had the protest! It was more than just the conference. I wanted to work with other jotería, I wanted that space. That's why I join[ed].

Trinidad's motivation to organize the conference is a reflection of his continued struggle in addressing homophobia. His experiences reveal how student activists often are burdened by having too much on their plate, specifically, organizing and navigating the university system. As a result, many student activists within predominantly white institutions experience racial battle fatigue, stress and anxiety caused by constantly dealing with both overtly racist actions and subtle references to one's race (Smith, Hung, and Franklin 2011). In coming out, he wanted to make sure that activist organizations were providing students with a type of space that could protect individuals' identities. He did this by organizing with the committee members around jotería issues. His experiences reflect how some marginalized students begin creating academic and social "counterspaces" that challenge, establish, and maintain a positive collegiate racial climate (Solórzano, Ceja, and Yosso 2000). In Trinidad's case, these spaces also include gender and sexuality.

Pilar shared how he and other organizers were queering up different organizations at UCLA by closely working with them:

I also liked working with the community in UCLA 'cause we were asking them if they wanted to sponsor the conference. And if they were going to sponsor it, they had to change their mission statement to include queer issues. We got Conciencia to do it, MALCS [Mujeres Activas en Letras y Cambio Social], La Gente, and we got LASA [Latin American Studies Association] to consider it, RGSA [Raza Graduate Student Association] declined it. So I really like that, because it was concrete sponsorship. We pushed them to sponsor in concrete ways, MEChA changed it, in Xicachli even got a queer workshop out of it. . . . And in return they went to the high school groups and worked with them on queer issues. . . . We opened it up to everyone. I really enjoyed that. We were putting pressure on everyone because we had many of us. We confronted organizations like RGSA. We pushed people to dialogue with us.

The jotería committee's frustrations with activist student organizations allowed them to take militant stances on issues of homophobia, sexism, and racism. While the word "militant" has many layers and implications, I use it to describe how the jotería committee was aggressively active in pushing queer Latinx and Chicanx politics on and off campus. They demanded that different groups actively fight against sexism and homophobia by having them change their mission statement, schedule meetings with the jotería committee to discuss the marginalization of women and queer people, add gender and sexuality components to their organizations, and continue the cosponsorship of queer/feminist events. Not only were they building a familia among themselves, they were going back to their organizations and talking to them about how they were marginalizing others on the basis of race, class, gender, sexuality, and immigration status. They were a powerful group because they had numbers, they had support within various student organizations they were already part of. If an organization rejected the jotería committee's suggestions, other organizations pressured them to rethink their position.

The jotería Movement

The jotería committee was able to accomplish much-needed unity among many student raza organizations that were actively fighting racism, sexism, xenophobia, gender discrimination, and homophobia. They created spaces that both challenged and transformed what it meant to be a queer Latinx and Chicanx. They were able to do so because they were part of a legacy of many queer Latinxs and Chicanxs who fought physically, intellectually, and spiritually for their existence. From the queer people of the Americas to the queer Latinx and Chicanx communities of the United States, la jotería has existed. This recognized ancestral past is part of an ongoing movement that is based on radical jotx love. It was through their resistance that many jotería committee members began exploring new ways to love and exist among themselves. Their jotería consciousness allowed them to continue finding dignity and self-worth. The notion of radical jotx love comes from a collective effort to root queer Latinx and Chicanx love in activism and a multidimensional consciousness. Perhaps the most important aspect of the jotería committee is that they were constantly fighting for social justice and envisioning new possibilities. They were part of a jotería movement.

As Lupe explained excitedly, "Yes, there is a jotería movement! Although it hasn't been explicit, I am not going to say that it doesn't exist. . . . Cherríe and Gloria have fought for it. . . . It has been an ongoing movement, and I'm not going to measure it with ourselves." From this research, we saw that many queer Latinxs and Chicanxs have struggled to find and locate themselves among different movements and organizations. They have often felt rejected in spaces that were supposed to cater to them as queers or Latinxs or both. By acknowledging that there is a jotería movement, Lupe recognizes that we have a history, as well as a contemporary movement and vision, and that we have spaces where we can be both queer and Latinx and Chicanx. Although we cannot clearly define this movement, we know it is ongoing and growing.

Alex further defined what he thinks the jotería movement to be:

I understand a movement as an organizing effort to resist oppression. So, yeah, there is one. But I understand that it is developing and quiet. We are talking about movements developing that are from privileged folks that are learning about theory, so we become these little nerds. And, well, not everyone is privileged to have access to all of this theory and books. So I understand that is why the jotería movement is not strong in South-Central LA, where poverty is increasing and there is violence. . . . Survival there is different. They are struggling because the cops are harassing them, the queens, because everyone harasses them. A queen resisting to get off a bus is a part of the movement. It's hard to organize when you have all these things working against you. When you have things like 209 [Proposition 209, passed in 1996, prohibits the consideration and use of race, sex, and ethnicity in state governmental institutions] working against you. We are not getting retained like we used to. All these issues affect us.

For Alex, the jotería movement encompasses queer Chicana/o intellectuals and queens from South-Central Los Angeles. He also understands this movement to be happening simultaneously from one location to another. While many acknowledge that there has been a gay rights movement, women's liberation movement, Chicano movement, Black liberation movement, and now an immigrant rights movement, very few have acknowledged the possibilities of a jotería movement, partly because it cannot be pinpointed and credited to specific groups or specific time frames. However, to not acknowledge the historical presence of a jotería movement is to not acknowledge the resistance of queer Latinxs and Chicanxs throughout time. We have existed and still exist in all radical social movements. The jotería committee's ability to engage in the conversation of movement building reflects their vision of liberation.

The organizing of the first annual jotería conference allowed the jotería committee members to develop a safe space to discuss issues important to them. They engaged in meaningful jotería discourse and analysis that considered multiple identities and positionalities. Through their activism, they were able to push forward their vision for social justice.

Notes

1. I consciously use the term "undocumented" instead of "illegal" to stay away from oppressive language. The term "illegal" is both misleading and dehumanizing when speaking about immigrant and migrant populations.

2. Transgéneros Unidas was established in 1996 to provide services to the Latina transgender community. The group caters specifically to the needs of Latina immigrant transgender women.

References

Alaniz, Yolanda, and Megan Cornish. 2008. *Viva la Raza: A History of Chicano Identity and Resistance*. Seattle WA: Red Letter Press.

Anzaldúa, Gloria. 2007. *Borderlands / La Frontera: The New Mestiza*. 3rd ed. San Francisco: Aunt Lute Books.

Berta-Avila, Margarita, Anita Revilla, and Julie López Figueroa. 2011. *Marching Students: Chicana and Chicano Activism in Education, 1968 to the Present*. Reno: University of Nevada Press.

Calvo, Luz, and Catriona Rueda Esquibel. 2010. "Latina Lesbians, BiMujeres, and Trans Identities: Charting Courses in the Social Sciences." In *Latina/o Sexualities*, edited by Marysol Ascencio, 217–29. New Brunswick nj: Rutgers University Press.

Covarrubias, Alejandro, and Anita Revilla. 2003. "Agencies of Transformational Resistance: Dismantling Injustice at the Intersection of Race, Class, Gender, and Sexuality through Lat Crit Praxis." *Florida Law Review* 55 (1): 459–77.

Galarte, J. Frank. 2011. "Notes from a Trans* Chican@ Survivor." *Mujeres Talk*. https://mujerestalk.org/tag/j-frank-galarte/.

García, Alma. 1997. *Chicana Feminist Thought: The Basic Historical Writings*. New York: Routledge.

Moraga, Cherríe. 1993. "Queer Aztlán: The Re-formation of Chicano Tribe." In *The Last Generation: Prose and Poetry*, 145–74. Brooklyn NY: South End Press.

———. 2000. *Loving in the War Years: Lo que nunca paso por sus labios*. Brooklyn NY: South End Press.

Moraga, Cherríe, and Gloria Anzaldúa. 2002. *This Bridge Called My Back: Writings by Radical Women of Color*. 3rd ed. Berkeley: Third Woman Press.

Pharr, Suzanne. 2007. "Homophobia as a Weapon of Sexism." In *Race, Class, Gender in the United States: An Integrated Study*, edited by P. S. Rothenberg, 168–77. New York: Worth Publishers.

Prieur, Annick. 1996. "Domination and Desire: Male Homosexuality and the Construction of Masculinity in Mexico." In *Machos, Mistresses, Marias: Contesting the Power of Latin American Gender Imagery*, edited by Marit Melhuus and Kristi Anne Støle, 83–107. New York: Verso.

Revilla, Anita. 2004. "Muxerista Pedagogy: Raza Womyn Teaching Social Justice through Activism." *High School Journal* 87 (4): 80–94.

Smith, William A., Man Hung, and Jeremy D. Franklin. 2011. "Racial Battle Fatigue and the Miseducation of Black Men: Racial Microaggressions, Societal Problems, and Environmental Stress." *Journal of Negro Education* 80 (1): 63–82.

Solórzano, Daniel, Miguel Ceja, and Tara Yosso. 2000. "Critical Race Theory, Racial Microaggressions, and Campus Racial Climate: The Experiences of African American College Students." *Journal of Negro Education* 69 (1–2): 60–73.

Tijerina-Revilla, Anita. 2009. "Are All Raza Womyn Queer? An Exploration of Sexual Identity in a Chicana/Latina Student Organization." *NWSA Journal* 21 (3): 46–62.

Reading Performance and Performativity
from Cuba to Los Angeles

3

Working Trans in Jaime Cortez's *Sexile/Sexilio*

CARLOS ULISES DECENA

> There is a woman—an American woman. She's waiting for me.
>
> Está una mujer, una mujer americana. Ella está esperándome.
>
> —JAIME CORTEZ, *Sexile/Sexilio*

Adrift at sea between Mariel Harbor, Cuba, and the United States, drowning in gloom and not yet lifted by expectation at the beginning of the second phase of her odyssey, Adela Vázquez, protagonist and testimoniante in Jaime Cortez's *Sexile/Sexilio*, sits with the wounds and heartbreak of Cuba, the homeland that curtailed her possibilities of becoming someone she could love, the patria that expelled her and visited violence on her body to make clear Adela's nonbelonging. Days before the scene where she utters the words above, Adela paid a taxi driver to get her to the stop where a bus would take her to the Mariel port, where she would join thousands of Cubans leaving the country in the early 1980s. While she is waiting for that bus at a Cuban military base, an army official persuaded her to get on a truck that would take her to the port instead of waiting for the Mariel bus.

It was a trap. Una vil mentira. Before she was let go, the doors of the truck opened to a mob that treated Adela to violence and physical assaults for "betraying" a Cuba that did not want her, the home that exempted her from serving in the armed forces. A home undergoing a revolution determined to reject not just the queer body but also the queerness of its citizenry, old and new. Having survived this blind and near date with brutality and after finally hopping

59

on the bus that would get her to Mariel harbor, Adela throws out of a window a wad of Cuban pesos her mother gave her when they touched for the last time before Adela's departure. Refusing the currency of Cuba in that moment, Adela Vázquez begins to share with her shipmates and fellow Cubans in the uncertainty of their journey. At this point in the narrative, hope is still a scarce commodity, barely discernible through Adela's wounded eye. When a mate asks Adela if she has family in Florida. "No," she says. "My family stayed back in Camagüey. But there is a woman—an American woman. She's waiting for me."

The mate, who volunteers a fantasy about the beauty of this woman and wonders if she has a sister, learns from Adela that "there is only one like her." He gives up on the pursuit of the woman Adela calls Beautiful. La niña de sus ojos. Beautiful is his, the man surmises as he looks at Adela, incapable of imagining that the apparently male interlocutor will one day become a woman and that the woman awaiting is not doing so for her Ulysses. Adela names the woman to herself, for herself, through the screen of retrospection. She may not have a name yet, but Beautiful will do to name Adela's potentiality beyond her mate's heteroerotic desire.

A Body I Owe Myself

A graphic novel published in 2004, *Sexile/Sexilio* was created by Jaime Cortez in collaboration with trans activist and testimoniante Adela Vázquez as part of a series of initiatives developed by the Institute of Gay Men's Health, Gay Men's Health Crisis, and AIDS Project Los Angeles.[1] Many of these initiatives featured and drew upon the experiences, insights, and theorizations of queers of color (who themselves drew inspiration from earlier anthological work by feminists and radical lesbians of color) in publications such as *Corpus*, *Think Again*, and *To Be Left with the Body*. Many of these collections and assemblages of materials draw on philosophical premises that have been crucial to addressing HIV/AIDS in communities of color.[2]

Sexilio narrates the story of Adela Vázquez, a trans Latina immigrant activist who arrives in the United States as part of the Mariel

3. "I gave them back to Cuba." From Jaime Cortez, *Sexilio/Sexile*. The Institute for Gay Men's Health, 2004, 27. Used with permission.

boatlift. The epic story of how Adela "leaves what she loves to become what she loves" (from Patrick "Pato" Hebert's foreword to *Sexile/Sexilio*, iii), the novel is set against the backdrops of U.S.-Cuba relations, the Mariel boatlift itself, and the early days of the AIDS crisis. It is a love story, but one framed as a quest for the love of self, the love that allows one to pursue the elsewhere, the mas allá, to become other than what one has been given or promised by parents, by leaders, by nation-state projects, revolutionary or not. It is important to find one's queer body as a place worth dwelling (and loving) in. Thus, *Sexilio* attends to sexual exile in the geographic and geopolitical sense as it also narrates the struggle of its main character as a struggle to overcome multiple exiles, including exile from the notion that her cuerpo raro (freak body) is worth loving.[3] Subsequently, this is a novel that hangs not on the promise of the American Dream of the husband, the picket fence, or the peace of the work table or Virginia Woolf's "room of one's own." Homonormative respectability does not register as a viable horizon here, nor does the Cuban exile dream of a different Cuban society. The finitude of a telos of trans identity is not the end here either: notice how Adela's "arrival" is in the moments when she loves her queer body *in the present*, not in the future. Maybe those interventions are necessary, but they do not stop the quest for love of self in the here and now; it doesn't end futurity. The reconciliation desired in this text is of self with self, a transitive and never final operation.

I am interested in *Sexilio* as one important text because it demands that we move and think with it. As an artifact, *Sexilio* is a text not content with just telling us a story. I will argue here that *Sexilio* operates as an apparatus that helps push at the very boundaries of how we think about borders and boundaries. *Sexilio* is not satisfied with illustrating boundary crossing or cultural hybridity. It is a text that itself acts as constative and performative evidence of its operations. In other words, it both describes a world and performs it at the same time.

As a text, *Sexilio* is not a border text. One might say, instead, that all kinds of borders cross it, and it is for this reason that I am interested in thinking of it as a text of roce, or a text that reveals intimate encounters involving friction and exposure. A roce can be roughly translated as a brush, as in the frottage of skin on skin—the kind of proximity that thrills uncomfortably, an epidermal reaction that might welcome the all-too-proximate other in its experience of the fear and delight of rapture and literal rupture, the fear of the skin that, on the self, might tear.

In Cortez's novel, language is deployed to signal and point toward the histories of coalition and struggle to make sense of selves and worlds not by ever settling but by arriving, becoming, and doing so awkwardly. Or maybe these are just provisional arrivals. Read as a text of roce, *Sexilio* indexes the violence, discomfort, and uneasy accommodation of unequally situated actors in contact zones. Thinking of it in this way becomes necessary now, precisely in a moment when queers of color are often in positions of control to produce critique and activism and to lay claims on insights and experiences of subjugated knowledges. Although raising these questions might be uncomfortable, the labor of decolonizing our imaginations resides not only in "exposing" heretofore-ignored experiences and insights. I believe very strongly that we must account, as fully and as honestly as we can, for the often-awkward yet productive ways in which some of us find ourselves speaking for others, often despite our best efforts not to represent anyone other than ourselves, often knowing fully that our ability to speak is a function of the forms of privilege we enjoy but still being placed in structurally overdetermined loci of enunciation. In other words, despite our best efforts to speak only for ourselves, some of us are invariably expected to speak for others. How do I speak with and not for Adela Vázquez?

i.

Adela Vázquez desires the body of a woman, yes. However, she desires it because this is the body she has promised herself, the woman she owes herself. Heteroerotic, not heteronormative. Or perhaps heteronormative, but with a twist: the body being fashioned here is not only in the process of becoming for a male erotic gaze; it is a becoming by and for the self being fashioned. This is the self that will be born, the capullo that will bloom into the butterfly she will become, a self made of love of self, against all odds and despite all signals that one's life and one's beauty are not worth living, not worth discovering and enjoying, not worth beholding, not worth the fight. Beautiful is the woman Adela Vázquez will become, the narrator who faces her history, her listeners, and her readers as she looks back at her life, "beautiful like everything I ever wanted but never thought I would have. You gonna be beautiful, girl. Like revolution in the flesh. Like hope" (Cortez 2004, 35).

An American woman is waiting. La americana está esperando. But she is not like Godot, who leaves us all in anticipation, diving into fanciful bits of stage business to while away our boredom as time slithers by. Adela's americana is like hope, in a transformed and insurgent flesh, and not like the Lady Liberty greeting immigrants, her arm held aloft with Olympian flames of leadership for a mass of the impoverished and the exhausted. She is not like the nice Cuban ladies, with their coiffed hair and the noblesse oblige of middle-class first-generation respectability, greeting the poor and tired marielitos at the end of their journeys. Revolution in the flesh, in other words, does not look like an other to love. It looks like loving myself. There may be a lot of suitors out there, but I make and unmake a quilt for the one I love, the self I become when I direct love to myself. For someone like Adela Vázquez, this self-love is not a given, a birthright. It is an act of defiance against the conditions stacked up against her, a fierce act from which those engaging her text have a lot to learn. It is in this way that Jaime Cortez's *Sexilio* signals an epic journey toward loving oneself.

> I was swimming, swimming, swimming,
> I had the fear like before
> And then I knew
> All the in-between spaces are my home
> This beautiful freak body is home.
> And every day I love it . . .
> I arrive. (65)

Perhaps this is a moment to offer a friendly amendment to Marlon Riggs's resonant dictum at the end of his pioneering documentary *Tongues Untied*: it might be revolutionary for a black man to love another black man, but revolution also resides in the possibility of the queer brown subject who loves her own body. As a narrative of estrangement and a queer reimagining of revolution, *Sexilio/Sexile* puts pressure on the implications of revolution to the sexually nonnormative and on the intrajection of the body politic in the human body itself, on the racialized body, no less. The real revolution is not just one staged through rallies, coups d'état, and policy transformation. Revolution involves how we imagine our own bodies, how standing notions of self require stretching and change to accommodate the I, the you, the we. In this sense, then, Adela Vázquez's narrative is a text shaped strongly by a revolutionary consciousness that extends the conviction of the necessity and urgency of social change to the human body.

As a Cuban testimoniante of the promise and perils of revolution, Adela Vázquez is not the first one to point to the edges of its ethos, to the asphyxiating machismo, sexism, and heteronormative rigidity that made many lives difficult and several impossible. Indeed, narratives of queer Cuban revolutionaries turned dissidents have abounded before and after the Mariel boatlift. Perhaps the most visible example of all these cultural workers and exposed lives is that of writer Reinaldo Arenas, who engaged in the exhilaration of revolutionary fervor only to find himself persecuted, his work banned, and ultimately himself severed from Cuba and from the Cuban American community. But there were several texts circulating internationally that sought to critique and (in some cases) discredit the revolution precisely by adopting or co-opting the views of sexual dissidents such as Arenas—I am thinking here, specifically, of the 1984 documentary film *Improper Conduct*, made by Néstor Almendros and Orlando Jiménez Leal. Arenas himself makes an appearance in this film. The homophobia and persecution of homosexuals in the early years of the revolution came back to bite the state in the international arena, as the denouncement of concentration camps and the obstacles placed in the lives of queer (mostly) male writers and artists became yet another means to criticize and discredit the Cuban state project in the 1980s. But other texts were written by Arenas himself: his fiction and, perhaps most notably, his autobiography, *Antes que anochezca* (1992), made into the memorable 2000 film *Before Night Falls*, directed by Julian Schnabel and featuring actor Javier Bardem playing the part of the writer.

Important scholarly work has also helped offer a complex picture of the specific conditions of the Mariel boatlift, itself a very distinct moment in U.S. history and in the history of Cuban populations in that country. It is important to highlight, for instance, that marielitos were themselves discredited by the Castro regime before they arrived in the United States and that their racial and class profiles were viewed as suspect and distinct from those traditionally associated with the first wave of Cubans who fled the revolutionary takeover in the late 1950s and 1960s. As the work of scholars such as Susana Peña has also shown, not only has sexuality played an important role in the experience of populations specifically affected by persecution in Cuba and settlement in the Miami area before and after Mariel, but it has also operated as a contradictory and dense transfer point between the U.S. and Cuban nation-states. One remarkable feature of Peña's work is that she suggests not just that sexuality operates as a Foucaultian "transfer point" but also that discourses of sexuality became in some cases the literal pivot that facilitated particular movements between Cuba and the United States during this period. The figure of the effeminate homosexual male, as Peña explains, has become a particularly vexed image and site of intense surveillance and investment in multiple ways in the Cuban and in the U.S. sides. This is clearer in the Cuban case, as elements identifying someone as a "loca" were generally used in formal and informal protocols to designate improper revolutionary subjects eligible for departure during what would become Mariel. The workings of the image of the effeminate homosexual are much less clear in the U.S. case, as the morality of the whole Mariel population was cast as suspect but where homosexuality itself was not at the center of the understanding and profiling of specific immigrant populations. What is remarkable about this scholarship is how it manages to illustrate the politicization of marginalized identities and positionalities within state-sponsored projects of population expulsion and reception while avoiding the reification of categories of sexuality (such as codes associated with the specific image of the effeminate homosexual).

But Adela Vázquez, even given this particular history of articulate political dissidence and of scholarly engagement with it, stands firmly on her own in a distinct place in comparison to many of the testimonios that are available, not just because of the fact that she is a woman of trans experience—though that is, itself, something that sets her apart from many a Cuban testimoniante. The dimension that interests me in this essay has more to do with the mediations and negotiation that produce *Sexilio* as a text in the service of a specific kind of activism as it engages directly with cultural work produced in the time of AIDS in the United States. Unlike other cultural products engaging the Cuban American and the Cuban immigrant experience (often distinguished from U.S.-Latin@ narratives as a story of exile), *Sexilio* presents an individual experience of resistance and critical engagement with transformations in Cuban society not simply to denounce these conditions and show the violence they visit on bodies like Vázquez's. This is a text produced very explicitly in the context of the AIDS crisis by Latin@s in the United States and for Latin@s and other queers of color with the specific aim of engaging the crisis to impact the way other trans-identified Latinas and queer men and women see themselves, their histories, and their identifications.

If I may borrow and play queerly with Juan Flores's coinage, *Sexilio* may be properly called a "trans-Latina" text. While Flores's invocation of "pan-Latino, trans-Latino" addresses more centrally the question of different U.S. Latino transnationalisms and their link to the question of panethnicity, I want to weave "trans-Latina" into a reading of this text that invokes the multiple ways in which it moves with the notion of "trans." My use of "trans" attends to trans identification, as well as to the densities of history, movement, and evolution evident in the text. One may claim *Sexilio* as a trans studies text, and one would be correct in doing so. However, *Sexilio* is also saturated by the specificities of the Cuban immigrant experience and the immigrant activist experience in San Francisco. So I would try and open trans here not to deflate the crucial political impulse of trans studies but to attend to the manner in which a multiplicity of histories and forms of knowledge coalesce in this text.

Sexilio does not operate within circuitries of production, dissemination, and consumption similar to those of other texts produced by and for Cuban Americans and Cuban immigrants in the

United States. Unlike several well-known and widely publicized texts produced by and for Cuban exile and Cuban American populations, *Sexilio* is produced for a wider audience, an audience that includes Latin@s other than Cubans and African Americans and other minorities. The graphic novel's production by AIDS Project Los Angeles and Gay Men's Health Crisis situates it not only as a Cuban American or Cuban immigrant text but, most importantly, as a text embedded and drawing from Chican@ and Latin@ traditions of queer of color critique. It is also a text caught in the challenges of that kind of collaborative production, and that is a central concern of the analysis that follows here.

I am interested in exploring how *Sexilio* both describes and enacts the confluence of various cultural forces. Through interactions and conversations with some of the workers who collaborated on the development of this text and through reading the various texts connected with it, I have learned that its development was an arduous labor requiring a lot of negotiation. However, it will be up to other scholars to carry out the work of mapping the specific conditions for the development of *Sexilio*, admittedly important labor that might help us grasp important dimensions of what we might learn from the professionalization of queers of color in the HIV/AIDS sector. What I want to suggest throughout this text is that one need not recount these negotiations to gather that putting together *Sexilio* was a rather complex undertaking. I believe that the text itself indexes those fraught negotiations, and it is for this reason that I believe that reading some dimensions of it closely yields important insights about the perils and possibilities of queer of color activist praxis. What I seek to show is how the way in which the text seeks to carry out its work is itself indicative of the fractures and fissures that shaped its production.

While not being dismissive of this history and its import, my argument here positions this reading of texts like *Sexilio* at the crossroads of interests that have begun to be articulated and become imaginable, given the AIDS crisis. I view the epidemic here as prompting community mobilization, as well as helping to set discursive limits and possibilities for unequally situated social actors (artists, activists, and academics). My desire to highlight the confluence and potential conflict among different forms of interest does not discount the value and ideational possibilities that texts like *Sexilio* help us envision, but it does help us better grasp the forms of mediation and the different forms of becoming that coalesce in a collaborative text like this novel. I see my critical engagement with *Sexilio* as a means to help highlight and build on a text that deserves to circulate widely not just within the preventionist and community circles where it has circulated but also in classrooms as an essential component of how we might think about populations of color in the United States. Moreover, by "thinking of populations of color," I seek to place value at the door not just of stories of survival and ultimately transitive success like Adela Vázquez's. In fact, I love that narrative is transitive to the degree that we do not know at the end of the story if biomedical intervention is the ultimate genital telos of her journey. However, this is a story about that movement and that incompleteness, and my aim throughout this reading is to highlight the messiness of that mediation as a condition of possibility and a richness of this remarkable text. In other words, understanding incompleteness as a strength.

ii.

Sexilio was developed as part of the efforts of organizations like Gay Men's Health Crisis and AIDS Project Los Angeles to create cultural products in the context of HIV/AIDS education and prevention. This context lends an important nuance to the production and dissemination of *Sexilio*, as it mobilizes the genre of the graphic novel to do consciousness raising around Adela's history and the form of activist practice she embodies. This makes *Sexilio* an expressive artifact crafted in the service of activist practice. As artivism, it places aesthetics in relation to an activist project that is not merely documentation, not just making visible something previously invisible, and not just using art to reveal or estrange an audience from the quotidian dimensions of daily life. The goal here is to place artistic practice in the service of enacting concrete results in the world, prompted by the reflection that the audience of the novel may come to as a consequence of engaging with it.

Thus, there are "collateral" yet crucial dimensions of the development of research projects in HIV, particularly in relationship to queers of color. Projects like *Sexilio* emerge at that particular confluence of desires and needs: the desires of scientists to have their research validated to obtain the cooperation with the communities they seek to engage and the additional interest that activists and other community workers might have in finding a measure of legitimacy and validation to work that they tend to carry out for the health and well-being of their communities. The confluence of desires and needs is further reflected in the mutual need and opportunity provided by standing funding structures for the career advancement of some, the creation of incentives for participation in research projects, and both validation and capacity-building that turn out to be life-altering for community workers. These are accomplishments that would not stand a chance before a panel evaluating the "effectivity" of such projects, but they are nevertheless crucial to the important community-building and professionalization work carried out by these projects.

Sexilio has also helped refocus scholarly inquiry often too centered on an almost functionalist explanation for what motivates immigrants to go from one place to another. An immigrant finds himself out of work and having to sustain a family; getting a whiff of the elsewhere where work lies, he (traditionally) or she (more recently acknowledged) decides to embark on the journey. Some accounts suggest that the imbalance in resources between sending and receiving locations is restored through the sending of remittances. However, this thesis has been contested widely, with others suggesting that the transnationalization of social relations, spawned by asymmetrical relations at the macrostructural level, only deepens the dependency produced through the addition of remittances to the sustenance of individuals, families, and communities. The traditional focus on economic imperatives as push and pull factors, for instance, has increasingly been shown as unhelpful for grasping the complex reasons that may drive someone to make the life-changing decision to move from one place to another, especially given the increased state policing of borders and the increasing dangers of crossing them. Still, the appeal of stories like that of Adela Vázquez does not reside exclusively in the qualitative complexity that they add to our often quantitative understandings of immigration questions. Her story illustrates that operationalizing what it is about sexuality and gender formations that renders them excessive and incompatible with state-sanctioned forms is not always fully legible and that mobilizing categories such as "sexuality" in relation to immigration might run the risk of oversimplifying how it is that Adela's project of becoming moves through gender and sexual dissidence but does not stay there. This is a project of becoming and quest, at least in the way it is told in *Sexilio*, to reconcile the self with the self.

Looking at it this way, the immigration narrative stages a separation of the body from the body politic, a severing of self from the isle of the social, or, to be more precise, a separation of one's sex from the isle of the social (sex-isle). There is a severing of individual self from nation in the moment of Adela's departure from Cuba, but the story of *Sexile* is, importantly, a story about the severing of Adela's self from her ideations of her own becoming. She tells us, early on, the following: "I couldn't wait to grow up because I knew that when I turned 10 . . . my dick would fall off my pussy would grow and finally I'd become a complete girl" (10). That this transformation does not take place is never made a problematic point in the narrative, yet it is clear by the end of the story that finding love in Adela's "freak body" is about loving it despite how much it becomes like that of a woman—though not quite, in the end of at least the story as told in *Sexilio*. Thus, the word "sexile" throughout this novel has various meanings that are worth considering alongside one another.

This is a question that Cortez and the GMHC/APLA team wrestle with in ways analogous to other cultural workers who have debated these questions before. At this point, it is useful to review briefly the history of various efforts to represent the other, the testimoniante other, in this instance. Perhaps the most famous of these cases is that of Nobel Peace Prize winner Rigoberta Menchú and her autobiography, *I, Rigoberta Menchú*. Like other narratives emerging in this same historical period, Menchú and interlocutor/mediator Elizabeth Burgos engaged in a "guided conversation" that was itself an important, influential, and extremely uncomfortable yet productive cultural encounter to produce the text that readers ultimately engage, a text full of disclosures and secrets, and a text that fostered a rather complicated set of debates about truth, secrets, and the question of representative "native" informants.[4] Though it must be pointed out that such debates have been the stock in trade of disciplines such as anthropology, it is also important to highlight just how unusual it was, at least at the time, for culture broker Burgos to mediate between her assumed First World audience and a figure of the stature of Menchú, whose fame and ability to speak for herself transcended the mediation of the interviewer. It was also quite unusual to question the veracity of someone like Menchú.

The nuances of that particular debate are relevant here but transposed to the U.S. queer of color context, as the issue in these communities is partly veracity but, most importantly, the questions of who gets to speaks for whom and who gets to do the "representing" that is needed in these communities. And in this regard, no text has been as impactful in terms of that discussion, as generative of debate, influential, and problematic, as Jennie Livingston's *Paris Is Burning*. At the beginning, much of the debate around the text concentrated on the queens themselves as "pseudowomen" or "women wannabes," a framing of the problematic nature of the debate that engaged cultural theorist bell hooks and philosopher Judith Butler, among others. The debate shifted in nuance over time as critics began to pay attention to Livingston's positionality and her absence in the text as narrator and as the white female body in the context where so many queer male and trans bodies proliferated. How do we account for the presence of a Jewish lesbian who "found" the children of the houses in Washington Square Park, filmed them, and then made a movie about them that became an art house film sensation, garnering enough money and attention that the queens (all of whom died either during or after the film's release) sued Livingston for a cut of the profits and lost? Cultural theorists such as Philip Brian Harper, mobilizing a critical Marxist lens, explained that the relations of exchange that obtained for the queens were radically different from those available to Livingston, whose possession of the testimonies utilized, as well as the signed consent forms from her informants, guaranteed that the film actually constituted her standing as "author" or "filmmaker" at the expense of the utilization of the queens' perspectives. This was a film, Harper explained, that helped constitute Livingston's "voice" socially to the degree that it was tied to the possession of the voices and filmic expressions of the bodies of others to constitute it. Toward the end of the essay where he offers this particular view and critique of Livingston's film, Harper suggests that it will not be until the queens control the conditions of the production of their own film (or other cultural artifacts) that they will be fully empowered as cultural producers.

The debate about *Paris Is Burning*, after being the important and foundational cause célèbre that it was, aged into the kind of useful pedagogical instrument for introductory queer studies courses. The passing of all of the men (including the late Willi Ninja, of Madonna and "Vogue" fame) made the questions raised by this debate yet remain strangely dormant in the literature. But I have sat with Harper's insight for several years and wondered out loud about what might need to happen in order for queens like Adela to control the conditions of the possibility for their own production or to control their own production, particularly in contexts where cisgender queer males tend to be the ones who are better situated structurally to do the image producing.

Another text that poignantly revisited that particular set of questions is Arnaldo Cruz-Malavé's *Queer Latino Testimonio*. In his preface to Juanito Xtravaganza's testimonio, author Cruz-Malavé talks about the conditions that not only brought him together with but also separated him from the testimoniante. How to listen and narrate the proximal, queer other? "What if I was," writes Cruz-Malavé, "assuaging someone's guilt, my own included, about living, just living or going about one's daily life while entire populations were being reconnoitered and targeted?"

What is important to highlight here is that engaging a text like *Sexilio* and the various mediations and uncomfortable negotiations

that helped construct the text returns us to terrain that is recognizable both within the Latin American tradition of the testimonio and
in the incipient discussion on queer critique and the conditions for
queers of color to speak for themselves and for one another. What
might it mean for queers of color to have control over the conditions of the production of their own voices? Does it change matters radically that the inequalities being negotiated within narratives
such as *Sexilio* are inequalities among queers of color? How do we
grapple, for instance, with the fact that this narrative of the journey of a woman of trans identity is being produced in the context
of HIV/AIDS prevention work for queer (and mostly cis) men and
that queer or otherwise gay male-identified workers are the ones in
charge of the various parts that make up this particular intervention?

The section that follows identifies and discusses briefly two examples of *Sexilio* as a text of roce to suggest the concept's potential to
help us grasp the unease with which Latinx artivism becomes possible through negotiations and tensions that cannot be subsumed
under the view of it as a border text.

iii.

A discussion of this excerpt from the Spanish and English versions
of the text helps illustrate the challenges and possibilities of thinking of *Sexile/Sexilio* as a text of roce (Cortez 2004, 9). What follows suggests that moving from Spanish to English reveals histories
of vernacular exchange among communities of color but that the
question of intelligibility across languages and debates around gender, sexuality, and coalition benefits from continued discussion of
the conundrums this text presents.

It is no secret that translation is a challenge in *Sexilio/Sexile*, as
one might quickly glean from the way in which "there's a woman"
gets translated into "está una mujer" instead of a possible "hay una
mujer." This is an awkwardness that is characteristic of scientific and
expressive production among HIV preventionists, where the exigen-
cies of translations and back translations (to comply with institutional review boards) produce consent forms with sometimes odd or
even bizarre locutions in both English and Spanish but most often

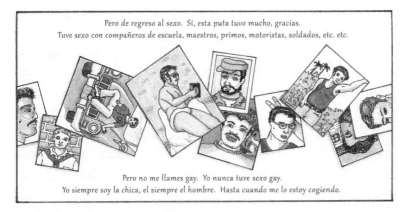

4. Pero de regreso al sexo. From Jaime Cortez, *Sexilio/Sexile*. The Institute for Gay Men's Health, 2004, 9. Used with permission.

5. But back to the sex. From Jaime Cortez, *Sexilio/Sexile*. The Institute for Gay Men's Health, 2004, 9. Used with permission.

in Spanish as the result of the work of second-generation and/or community translators.

Even given these circumstances, translating the word "mama" to "puta" might seem startling to bilingual ears. "Mama," as used in this section, would certainly not translate literally to the Spanish "madre" but perhaps more adequately to the word "mujer" (woman). But "puta," which can mean "slut," "bitch," or "whore," might be a stretch here, unless we take note that the movement between languages in *Sexile/Sexilio* is not between received standard English or Spanish but from one vernacular English locution mobilized in queer and trans communities of color (mama) to what might be an equivalent in Spanish. Whether the translation "works" or not is an open question and might require a better sense of the context in which the locution is used, though the Spanish-language audience for the word "puta" would be mostly made up of U.S.-based Latinx populations.

A further source of consideration in relation to this section and the limits of intelligibility in translation lives not so much in questions concerning language use but in the conceptual grid of gayness we need to challenge on the basis of how Adela Vázquez understands her embodiment and her own experience. This is illustrated most clearly in Vázquez's emphasis that although she has had plenty of sex, her interlocutors (and readers) "do NOT call me gay. I never had gay sex. Never will. I'm always the girl, he's always the man. Even when I'm fucking him." At first sight, one might immediately note this as a pointed critique of the utilization of "gay" as *the* grid of intelligibility for manifestations of sex among superficially cisgender bodies without a substantive critique of the "hegemony of gayness" (Guzmán 2006) from the vantage point of gender presentation.

Still, there is something else at work that should be discussed more substantively in future engagements with *Sexilio/Sexile* but that suggests the elastic operations of "trans" that must be negotiated when we engage a text that is trans gender, trans national, and trans-lated. "Gay sex" might be cast as sex between two cisgender subjects who self-identify as "gay." We might not be talking, strictly speaking, about "gay sex" standing in for any sex between men irrespective of how they self-identify. Might it be possible to think here that the homoerotics are double: not only do you have "gay sex" by having a cisgender man have sex with another cisgender man, but both of those men must self-identify as "gay"? We land in the terrain of same with same, with the requirement of that self-identification of sameness.

When Adela Vázquez claims that "gay sex" is something she does not have, she might be rejecting the facile reading of the biological cis body, but part of what she's occupying and challenging is the mise-en-scène of heteroerotic desire: "I'm always the girl, he's always the man. Even when I'm fucking him." Two important operations are performed here: first, Adela casts the players as "girl" and "man" irrespective of the work of genitalia in the sexual exchange; second and most crucially, Adela invokes a scene cast as encounters between others, not two men, a man and a woman, but a "girl" and a "man."

My allusion to these two aspects of translation in this excerpt suggests that there is much to be theorized about the relevance of *Sexile/Sexilio* to trans and queer communities of color, and I close with a final note regarding translation in one of the more complex and challenging pages of the text. Page 60 in Spanish and English features a display of our protagonist's naked body as Adela narrates her process of transitioning. The titles of the page are "Womanizing" and "Afeminándose" in English and Spanish, respectively. Language purists on all sides might balk at the literal inadequacy of either term, but I contend that something productive might be gleaned from seeing the terms used not as "mistakes" but as indexical marks of the proximities *Sexilio/Sexile* illustrates. "Womanizing" might read as the pursuit and conquest of women, among other definitions, but what is curious about "afeminándose" is that it means to elaborate attributes considered feminine on a male body. More precisely, it means to "effeminate," if such a verb exists. It is worth considering at some length why these bodily changes are narrated in the way that they are in this particular graphic moment, but the awkwardness of the terms suggests problems and tensions that are not resolved but rendered graphic by the novel.

Future readers of *Sexilio/Sexile* should take up such moments of uncomfortable and charged proximity. Thinking of queer of color futures together may be pursued through such intellectual and activist labor not so much to resolve or undo differences but to cultivate and grow theoretical work with the agility to apprehend and work through complexity.

Notes

1. Vázquez also collaborated in another approach to telling her life history through collaboration with Uriel Quesada, Letitia Gomez and Salvador Vidal-Ortiz. See Vázquez (2015).

2. The anthological work in question was carried out as part of efforts developed through a collaboration, in the Institute for Gay Men's Health, of New York's Gay Men's Health Crisis (GMHC) and AIDS Project Los Angeles (APLA).

3. The original coinage of the term is by Manolo Guzmán (1997).

4. An important collection of interventions in this debate is Arias (2001).

References

Arenas, Reinaldo. 2013. *Antes que anochezca.* Madrid, Spain: Planeta Publishing.

Arias, Arturo, ed. 2001. *The Rigoberta Menchú Controversy.* Minneapolis: University of Minnesota Press.

Before Night Falls. 2005. Directed by Julian Schnabel. Grandview Pictures.

Butler, Judith. 1993. *Bodies That Matter: On the Discursive Limits of "Sex."* New York: Routledge.

Cortez, Jaime. 2004. *Sexilio/Sexile.* New York: Institute for Gay Men's Health.

Cruz-Malavé, Arnaldo. 2007. *Queer Latino Testimonio, Keith Haring, and Juanito Xtravaganza: Hard Trails.* London: Palgrave Macmillan.

Flores, Juan. 2000. *From Bomba to Hip Hop: Puerto Rican Culture and Latino Identity.* New York: Columbia University Press.

Guzmán, Manolo. 1997. "'Pa' la escuelita con mucho cuida'o y por la orillita': A Journey through the Contested Terrains of the Nation and Sexual Orientation." In *Puerto Rican Jam: Rethinking Colonialism and Nationalism,* edited by Frances Negrón-Muntaner and Ramón Grosfoguel, 209–30. Minneapolis: University of Minnesota Press.

———. 2006. *Gay Hegemony / Latino Homosexualities.* New York: Routledge.

Harper, Phillip Brian. 1999. *Private Affairs: Critical Ventures in the Culture of Social Relations.* New York: New York University Press.

hooks, bell. 1996. *Reel to Real: Race, Class and Sex at the Movies.* New York: Routledge.

Improper Conduct. 1984. Directed by Néstor Almendros. ComeVista Video.

Menchú, Rigoberta. 2010. *I, Rigoberta Menchú: An Indian Woman in Guatemala.* New York: Verso.

Paris Is Burning. 1992. Directed by Jennie Livingston. Fox/Lorber.

Peña, Susana. 2013. *Oye Loca: From the Mariel Boatlift to Gay Cuban Miami.* Minneapolis: University of Minnesota Press.

Tongues Untied. 1989. Directed by Marlon Riggs.

Vázquez, Adela. 2015. "Finding a Home in Transgender Activism in San Francisco." In *Queer Brown Voices: Personal Narratives of Latina/o LGBT Activism,* edited by Uriel Quesada, Letitia Gomez, and Salvador Vidal-Ortiz, 212–20. Austin: University of Texas Press.

4

Wonder Woman, Pancho Villa, and the Shifting Rio Grande

Transnational jotx Identity, Desire, Pleasure, and Death on the El Paso / Juárez Border

OMAR GONZÁLEZ

What was I thinking? I shudder when I think about the outfits I wore to the Old Plantation, the largest and most popular gay bar in El Paso. I actually felt like a queer Chicana superhero—the joto reincarnation of Wonder Woman. Like Wonder Woman's buttoned-down alter ego, Diana Prince, I had to dress conservatively in public because of the heteropatriarchal praxis of my hometown, El Paso, and my family home environment, which included my Protestant stepfather. That notwithstanding, my best friend would pick me up; we made up stories about heterosexual bars for our parents—particularly our mothers—about our destination. We were destined for a clandestine location. We were headed to the "bar." No one dared utter the name of the "bar" in public. This is one of the strategies of negotiating a jotx existence in El Paso. Everyone in the city affectionately known as El Chuco, queer and heterosexual, is familiar with the Old Plantation club, or O.P., for short. (In a recent stand-up comedy show, the Chicano comedian Gabriel Iglesias performs in El Paso and says that after getting drunk he came to consciousness at the O.P., described as an "alternative nightclub." The crowd hooted and hollered—they got the punch line.) The "bar," along with the few other gay nightclubs in El Paso, was situated less than a mile north of the U.S.-Mexico border in a run-down industrial area of downtown. The El Paso Police Department straddled the west side of this queer space, yet I never felt completely safe because of its presence. We would always park in a dark alley, away from the sex workers, substance abusers, and homeless people. We needed some semblance of privacy for our transformation. My friend and I would strip and complete our emergence from the static safety of heteronormative performativity (based on our dress and "straight-acting" speech and mannerisms) into a liminal state of jotería identity performance. We dressed in spandex neon-colored hot pants or very, very short denim shorts, a body-defining shirt (or a vest with no shirt), and combat boots. We were as scantily clad as Wonder Woman herself emerging from the relative safety of her Diana Prince drag. We strutted from the alley to the club, the rhythmic house music beckoning us, imploring us to shed our Catholic guilt and join the debauchery of this space. Once my friend and I crossed the threshold of the "bar," we knew we had entered into a queer transnational space, however ephemeral, where the heteropatriarchy of the church could not punish/absolve our sins (desire) and the bourgeois legal system was powerless to imprison our bodies (pleasure). The praxis of our queer desire and pleasure intersected through our transnational identity as Chicano border jotx straddling the First and Third Worlds where nothing and no one remain constant beneath a veneer of humble stasis. Border jotx thus negotiate a transnational queer identity on the El Paso / Juárez frontera while traversing the dangerous social and physical terrain while disguising their homoerotic desire, pleasure, and identities with a heteronormative mask.

Social and physical violence stalk the border, manifested most conspicuously and brutally by the twenty-year reign of murders of mostly Indigenous women working in the maquiladoras and the more recent spree of drug cartel–related killings in Juárez, illustrated in numerous cultural productions, such as the 2005 Alicia Gaspar de Alba mystery novel, *Desert Blood: The Juárez Murders*; the 2001 Lourdes Portillo documentary, *Señorita Extraviada*; the 2006 Jennifer Lopez vehicle, *Bordertown*; and the 2000 alternative rock song and music video, "Invalid Litter Dept." by the group At the Drive-In.[1] Juárez held the dubious title as the world's most violent city from 2008 to 2010, according to Lee Moran (2012) of the *New York Daily News*, but has recently slipped to second. (San Pedro Sula, Honduras, claims the crown of the most violent city.) Conversely, according to a study conducted by the FBI, El Paso ranks as the safest large city in the United States (Borunda 2010a). Although the Sun City's crime statistics are drastically lower than in cities of a comparable size, the title of "safest city in the United States" belies the rate of hate crimes against lesbians, gays, bisexuals, and transgender people in El Chuco. In 2012 crimes against LGBT persons constituted two of the three bias crimes reported to the authorities, according to the *El Paso Times* (Borunda 2010b). An El Paso–based gay rights group claims that victims of hate crimes often do not report them to the authorities; thus, these crimes are underreported. Jonathan Kennedy, chairperson of the gay rights group Rio Grande Adelante, states, "We know there is more than three or four a year. Those who are harassed or victims of hate crimes are afraid [to report] because of the stigma from mainstream society" (Borunda 2010b). Many of the victims may be reluctant to report a bias crime for fear of disclosing a secretive sexual identity to an unsuspecting social network.

Transgressing gender roles south of the border attracts unwarranted punishment, as evidenced by the unsolved femicides of Juárez. Unknown men punish the women of Juárez for transgressing their patriarchal-driven roles of daughter and mother by working outside the home at one of the numerous maquiladoras. Are queer Chicanx being targeted and punished for transgressing heteronormative roles? Is heteropatriarchal violence crossing the border in a transnational nature? Do queer practices (identity, desire, and pleasure) migrate in a transnational manner as well? I will attempt to explore these questions in this chapter.

Sexuality on the border is as fluid as the Rio Grande once was. The Treaty of Guadalupe Hidalgo established the Rio Grande as the official border between the United States and Mexico. However, according to Jeffrey Schulze (2012) in his article "The Chamizal Blues: El Paso, the Wayward River, and the Peoples in Between," the shifting nature of the Rio Grande caused a liminal rupture between the two nations in 1864 when the river overflowed and left a trail of destruction on both sides of the border. Between 1864 and 1868 (when the ink on the Treaty of Guadalupe had just dried), the Rio

Grande transgressed its colonial masters and carved a new path into the terrain (Schulze). Thus, the unresolved border initiated a dispute that would not be resolved for a century. During these hundred years, what became of the citizenship status of the inhabitants of this border region? Although my maternal grandmother's family lived a stone's throw from the Rio Grande, the shifting river (and international border) did not affect their day-to-day realities. At that historical moment, the people who lived in close proximity to the border lived relatively similar lives. My grandmother's family, all born in the United States, suffered from the poverty and indignation of having their ancestral land seized by a white settler, forcing them into migrant farmwork. Although a geopolitical framework may define this space along the border as the United States or Mexico, the residents of this liminal space know their realities defy such categorizations. They are living in a third space, one that is neither here nor there—they live, love, and sometimes perish on Gloria Anzaldúa's (1987) "thin edge of barbwire." The U.S. government has established concrete embankments in the Rio Grande and has militarized the border; however, the apparent fixity belies the fluid, transnational practices of the area's queer Chicanx inhabitants.

These queer practices are located on both sides of the border, and LGBTIQQA Chicanx are able to draw from both multiple cultures—El Paso, Juárez, tejana/o, Chicanx, Anglo, and the hybridization of some and all of them. I examine the lived experiences of border jotx from the El Paso / Juárez area in order to demonstrate that transnationalism encompasses more than the unfettered distribution of people, capital, and goods and service. Emma Pérez's essay "Decolonial Border Queers: Case Studies of Chicana/o Lesbians, Gay Men, and Transgender Folks in El Paso/Juárez," in the anthology *Performing the U.S. Latina and Latino Borderlands*, edited by Arturo J. Aldama, Chela Sandoval, and Peter J. García, provides the lived experiences of people negotiating a transnational third queer space. Pérez offers an analysis of twenty-five LGBTIQQA people from the El Paso / Juárez area. From the start, her essay problematizes the situation of Chicanx, Latinx, mexicana/o, fronterizx, and Hispanic border queers. The interviewees' self-ethnic/racial categorization is another factor to explore in terms of how they negotiate their sexual identity. For example, are LGBTIQQA border dwellers who identify as "Hispanic/mexicana/o" more closeted than those who claim a "Chicanx" identity? This is a research question for another study. In Pérez's study, the majority of the interviewees identified as Chicana/o, Mexican, or Hispanic.

Sociohistorical Revolutionary Context of the El Paso / Juárez Region

On the surface, El Paso appears to be a sleepy appendage of its more violent half, Ciudad Juárez, but a revolutionary past that percolates El Paso's seemingly static nature belies its revolutionary history. My ancestors are from the Tiwa (also known as Tigua) tribe, a splinter of the Pueblo Indigenous family. In 1680 Po'pay, an Indigenous leader, and the Pueblos instigated the first American uprising against a European colonial force—the Spanish—and were successful in driving them out of what is now central New Mexico. However, the confederation of tribes allowed the Spaniards to enslave a group of Tiwa from the village of Isleta. With only the sacred drum and few other ceremonial items, the Tiwa marched south to the young Spanish settlement of El Paso del Norte (present-day Juárez). Po'pay's successful, though short-lived, revolution attempted to decolonize the Puebloan peoples from Spanish hegemony. According to the website Architect of the Capitol, New Mexico presented a statue of Po'pay to the National Statuary Hall Collection in Washington DC in 2005. The website credits Po'pay for the organization of the Pueblo Revolt, which "helped to ensure the survival of the Pueblo culture and shaped the history of the American Southwest" ("Po'pay"). The Spanish ultimately regained control of the region, but the revolutionary spirit of Po'pay continues to inhabit the ideologies and practices of marginalized groups, such as the queer Chicanx of the El Paso / Juárez region.

Further historical context is necessary in order to begin to understand the risks that Pérez's interviewees and I undertook willingly and regularly. During the Mexican Revolution, women often transgressed their traditional roles, prescribed by the dictates of marianismo, the gender codes based on traditional Catholicism. The

Chicanx and mexicanx inhabitants of the El Paso / Juárez region are very familiar with the female soldiers of the Mexican Revolution, known as las soldaderas. The image of one of the soldaderas, Adelita, is ubiquitous in the region. In fact, traditional mexicanas/os and Chicanx use the name Adelita to describe young girls who transgress conventional gender roles based on marianismo. My paternal grandmother labeled one of my sisters as an Adelita because of her habit of playing with boys, disobeying orders, and performing handstands and somersaults while wearing a dress. She uttered the name Adelita in a similar fashion as some mexicanas/os spew the name Malinche. Both represent Mexican women who changed the course of Mexican history through their revolutionary actions.

Teresa Urrea, the folk healer saint of the Mexican Revolution, is another woman who violated traditional gender roles and is relatively familiar within a Mexican historical context. However, another woman not necessarily connected with the Mexican Revolution deserves mention: Carmelita Torres. Who is Carmelita Torres? David Dorado Romo, author of *Ringside Seat to a Revolution: An Underground Cultural History of El Paso and Juárez, 1893–1923*, discusses her at length:

> *The El Paso Times* described the leader of the Bath Riots as an "auburn-haired Amazon." She sparked an uprising against a policy that would change the course of the history in El Paso and Juárez for decades. Some even consider her a fronteriza Rosa Parks, yet her name has been mostly forgotten. The "Amazon" was Carmelita Torres, a 17-year old Juárez maid who crossed the Santa Fe International Bridge into El Paso every morning to clean American homes. At 7:30 a.m. on January 28, 1917, when Carmelita was asked by the customs officials at the bridge to get off the trolley, take a bath, and be disinfected with gasoline, she refused. Instead, Carmelita got off the electric streetcar and convinced 30 other female passengers to get off with her and demonstrate their opposition to this humiliating process. By 8:30 a.m., more than 200 Mexican women had joined her and blocked all traffic into El Paso. By noon, the press estimated their number as "several thousand." (2005, 225)

What is more amazing is that the women placed their bodies on the tracks to prevent the trolleys from advancing further. They wrestled control of the trolleys away from the operators, who, of course, were all men. The women fought off soldiers from the local army base, Fort Bliss, *and* those fighting for Francisco Murguía, the anti-Villa Carrancista general. Soldiers from both countries were powerless against the mob of women. This act of sheer bravery and courage transcends transnationalism. Although the women represented a transnational labor force, they became, as Dorado Romo describes, "fronteriz[a]s, people who live on the border, . . . unclassifiable hybrids. They are not exactly immigrants. Immigrants don't cross back and forth as much. Border crossers are a people on the margin. Not real Americans. Nor real Mexicans for that matter" (2005, 11). Las soldaderas, Teresita Urrea, and Carmelita Torres and her cohorts established an ethos of gender transgression in the El Paso / Juárez region that I argue border jotx are embodying in their daily queer praxis. The revolutionary spirit of the Mexican Revolution lives on in the experiential realities of border jotx.

Linking history with the life experiences of ordinary people evokes a public memory, one that contests the master narrative of a certain people or region: "Memory is life. It is always carried by groups of living people, and therefore it is in permanent evolution. It is subject to the dialectics of remembering and forgetting, unaware of its successive deformations; open to all kinds of use and manipulation. . . . History is the always incomplete and problematic reconstruction of what is no longer there. Memory always belongs to our time and forms a lived bond with the eternal present; history is a representation of the past" (Saldívar 2006, 11). Thus, the memories of ordinary people fill in the gaps of "official histories" and provide a richer context to explain contemporary phenomena, for example, queer identity on the border. This is what makes the case studies of Emma Pérez's essay so crucial. Pérez is documenting the muted voices of ordinary people living extraordinary lives, similar to Carmelita Torres and her compañeras, whose names we shall never know. Chicanx jotx negotiating the El Paso / Juárez terrain possess a "border knowledge" that Ramón Saldívar argues is subaltern and therefore "excluded from rationality and validity, and hence, from history" (2006, 54). Perhaps this is the reason why few know of Carmelita Torres; she inhabits the same space as border jotx, a "transnational imaginary," a phrase used by Saldívar to describe the works of the pioneering scholar Américo Paredes. Saldívar cites Walter Mignolo as arguing that border knowledge constitutes new epistemologies; the "transnational imaginary" is the new center of knowing instead of a traditional reading of transnational for Mexico and the United States.

Therefore, are the border queers of Pérez's essay or I any different from the transnational imaginary figure of Francisco Villa? A folkloric figure, Villa is as transnational as one could get, as he traversed the border north when the Mexican authorities sought him and transgressed the southern border when the U.S. authorities attempted to capture him. Many El Paso families have some story mythologizing or demonizing him. One of my paternal great-grandmothers, Eva Archuleta, ran off with a Villista after the death of my great-grandfather, as the story goes. One of my father's tías is the progeny of this union, a scandal at the time, as she was born out of wedlock. I have heard other people tell stories of their connection to Villa, a figure definitely embodying Saldívar's "transnational imaginary" ideal. The revolutionary spirit of the Mexican Revolution invigorated the spirit of the women on the trolley in 1917; it remains evident with the strategic queer practices of LGBTIQQA Chicanx.

Besides ethnic self-identification, another issue needing interrogation is that of their sexual self-identification. One of the women in Pérez's essay does not identify as gay or lesbian, even though she has lived with her female partner for over fifteen years. One may be tempted to scoff at her apparent "denial," but the situation is more complicated than it seems. For many queers of color, the "alphabet soup" labels of LGBTIQQA, however inclusive and encompassing, connote a middle- or upper-class whiteness that is not culturally relevant to the lived experiences of many people of color. For example, some queer Black people have replaced the labels of LGBTIQQA with the phrase "same gender loving." Part of the reason for the reluctance of people of color to identify with the mainstream LGBTIQQA movement is the media representation of the community. The overwhelming construction of the LGBTIQQA community in the mainstream media is of white middle- or upper-class men, which is often nothing more than a stereotype. Ironically, one of the few representations of a queer Latinx in a major Hollywood studio film was in the biopic *Milk*. This film attempted to present the life story of the openly gay city supervisor of San Francisco in the 1970s, Harvey Milk. Dan White, another city supervisor, assassinated Milk in his office shortly after resigning. The film portrayed one of the protagonist's love interests as a pathetic and possessive Latinx who ultimately commits suicide.

Although Chicanx border queers of El Paso may have been disappointed with one-dimensional representations presented by the U.S. mainstream media, they have rich queer representations from el otro lado: the recently deceased chanteuse Chavela Vargas, the inimitable Juan Gabriel, and the hilarious psychic Walter Mercado. Did the aforementioned Chicana "lesbian" look south toward a queer personage with whom she could identify when she could find no one from el norte to model? What is interesting is that neither Juan Gabriel nor Walter Mercado have ever officially announced a nonheteronormative sexual identity. In addition, Chavela Vargas, one of Frida Kahlo's many lovers, only "came out" with the release of her autobiography in 2002. Pérez's Chicana "lesbian," therefore, is modeling her identity on the cultural signifiers that she recognizes. Although her family may be reticent to state the obvious regarding the sexualities of said celebrities, there is a knowing look among El Paso Chicanx when deejays play the music of Juan Gabriel or Chavela Vargas or watch the dramatic horoscope readings of Walter Mercado.

In Pérez's essay, she highlights the story of a tragic hate crime that occurred on the El Paso / Juárez border. Pérez cites an article in the *El Paso Times* on the murder of Hector Arturo "Arlene" Díaz: "At home in Sunland Park [a New Mexico community that straddles El Paso and the U.S.-Mexico border], he was the baby boy of a hard-working mother, the sibling of nine brothers and sisters. At night, the 28 year old man dressed in women's clothing and became 'Arlene,' a fixture of the gay scene in Downtown El Paso" (2012, 197). The media racialized the murder of Arlene Díaz, Pérez argues, because of their lack of attention, certainly unlike the sensationalized hate crime murders of Matthew Shepherd and Teena Brandon. It is not surprising, however, because Juárez is the site of hundreds, perhaps thousands, of murders of women. An irony most likely unbeknownst to Díaz's killer is the desolate location where he dumped her body, Anapra Road, which is the notorious neighborhood of Juárez where many corpses of raped women have been found. Fortunately, the judicial system has brought Arlene's killer to justice. Authorities apprehended Justen Grant Hall one month after Díaz's murder, yet the jury convicted him on a previous murder charge. The judge sentenced Hall to death, but he never stood trial for Díaz's murder. Arlene received no justice.

Although danger constantly lurks on the El Paso / Juárez border, this does not stop border jotx from their queer praxis. Yolanda Leyva, another of Pérez's border queers, recalled that "going to bars 'made me really aware of how dangerous it was to be a gay person in El Paso' in the 1970s" (2012, 200). Queer Chicanx had to contend with constant police raids and harassment from "heterosexual" men who waited in the parking lot of the bar to bully patrons. Regardless of the dangers, Leyva and other border queers did not let the potential violence prevent them from expressing their sexual identities. Leyva "even cross-dressed sometimes, and her mother would help her dress in men's suits, declaring, 'Mija, you look so handsome, the women are really gonna love you'" (200). Her mother's support belies the stereotype of the homophobic Chicanx family. However, it is interesting that Leyva, a college professor, would negotiate the butch of the butch/femme dichotomy. The butch/femme dichotomy *sometimes* mimics heteronormativity and all of its issues. The butch/femme binary is, from my anecdotal experience, very common in the El Paso queer Chicana community.

Leyva's experience of familial support contrasts with that of Pepe Porras, a queer Mexican born in El Paso but raised in an affluent family. His family belonged to the prestigious campestre, the country club, in Ciudad Juárez, and he attended boarding schools. However, his father expelled him from the home and disowned him when he caught Pepe in bed with another man. When he returned for his clothes the next day, his parents had burned all of his possessions. The familial ending is tragic; his father granted him an allowance with the understanding that he would never have to see Pepe again. Pepe has reconciled his identity as a gay mexicano, but the contradictory practices of the border once again surfaced when he declared that "queers who are too open are the cause of violence against them. He concluded: 'I don't see color, I don't see sexuality, I'm just me'" (Pérez 2012, 203). One would think that Pepe, after being the victim of such familial violence, would harbor more understanding for those who "flaunt" their queer identity. His apolitical stance toward race and sexuality makes him a complicated figure, which is typical of border queer identity. Porras fails to realize that he will always be a target of homophobic violence, regardless of how well he may "pass" for straight, particularly if his mask of heteropatriarchy falls off at an inopportune moment. One may wonder, Why would border queers risk their lives to venture to these sacred sites (the bars) to practice their fragile identities, express their desires, and experience fleeting pleasures? I often wonder what drew me to walk those unsafe streets of central El Paso, nearly nude, at all hours of the night. For me and other border queers, desire and pleasure overcome the fear of potential violence.

Next, I turn to the violence-stricken Juárez. According to the *El Paso Times*, the murder rate numbered over three thousand in 2010. That number dropped to less than eight hundred in 2012. Although the violence seems to be ebbing, the drug war remains, with no end in sight. One might conclude that the queer community in Juárez would keep a low profile because of the violence toward the women of the maquiladoras and those who dare to challenge the supremacy of the cartels. However, in 2009 the queer community of Juárez organized and participated in a gay pride parade. This event was the fifth annual gay pride parade held in Juárez. Several thousand people participated in and viewed the parade. Several Juárez-based LGBT organizations, including the main organizer, Juárez Diverso, had banners displaying their brand of queer pride. I find this act to be extraordinarily brave, political, and transgressive. These queer people are not organizing within the safe confines of a "gay ghetto," such as San Francisco's Castro District or Los Angeles's West Hollywood. These people are marching in the current murder capital of the world. A video clip of a news segment on YouTube entitled "Marcha Gay Ciudad Juarez (2009)" illustrates the bravery of these queer activists. Drag queens, scantily clad men, and other queers marched on one of the main avenues of Juárez without fear or trepidation. The Mexican army looked on with interest. The news clip even shows several soldiers taking videos and pictures of the parade with their cell phones. Carlos Morales, one of the principal organizers, granted an interview and stated that participation in the gay pride parade has doubled every year and that they expect over three thousand people to march. Other participants showed no fear and consented to an interview, including a drag queen named Virginia Jam. This act is as revolutionary as those of Carmelita Torres and Pancho Villa. They are risking their lives not for bourgeois rewards of marriage or military participation; instead, they are marching for visibility. They want to exist. In the words of a Mexican lesbian named Jessica Salais, "Queremos ser libres" (We want to be free). Is this not the sentiment of the Mexican Revolution?

Queer activism is present on both sides of the border. In 2006, the nonprofit organization Rio Grande Adelante organized a gay rights parade in El Paso. This organization defies the neoliberal notion of arbitrary borders. On its website, the organization states, "We are committed to serving the LGBT community of West Texas, Southern New Mexico, and Northern Chihuahua. Adelante is a 501(c) (3) non-profit organization aimed at educating and empowering our LGBTIQQA community through social events, educational programs, political awareness, and spiritual guidance." Rio Grande Adelante embodies the transnational spirit and practices of the El Paso / Juárez region. The United States Border Patrol may have militarized the border, and crossing may be more bureaucratic, but the people and their spirit will continue to act in a transnational manner. The gay rights parade committee invited critically acclaimed queer Chicano author John Rechy to deliver the keynote address. He gave a truncated but passionate queer history and civics lecture to the crowd. Rechy connected social movements: "Too often, we gay people separate ourselves from signals of dangers when they appear to involve others. Yet those who scream out for violence against 'illegals' are the same who scream out against 'faggots.' Those who turn 'Support Our Troops' into a cry for their deaths are the same who deny us equal rights" (2006). Rechy concluded his speech by highlighting unknown queer activism in El Paso:

I prefer to end my talk tonight by recalling a few instances of courage and pride exhibited by individuals here in El Paso long, long before Stonewall [the bar in New York City where drag queens rioted against police abuse in 1969; it is considered the "birth" of the modern gay rights movement] or the Black Cat riot [a Los Angeles gay uprising in 1967], decades ago. Barely a teenager [Rechy was born in 1934], I used to cross San Jacinto Plaza on my way home from the public library. There, almost nightly, a bleached blond queen held court, brash, assertive, unashamed, unfazed by heckling and routine harassment by cops. She sat proudly on the stone ledge like the queen of the alligators that lazed then in a pond. She was a symbol of bleached defiance, a revolutionary tromp[e] l'oeil. With her boldness, she inspired others less identifiable to shed their shame, an act that required much less courage than hers. I remember two women ate regularly at Luby's Cafeteria. They wore their hair smartly short, they wore suits. When they entered, there were often sniggers. They walked in—sometimes they marched—with squared shoulders and a steady pace, undaunted. That was individual courage equivalent to that shown collectively at Stonewall. I remember two men, always together, slightly effeminate, in the same cafeteria. . . . The two could not have escaped the overt and covert looks of disdain, the leering smiles, and, not infrequently, a not-too-whispered reference to "queers." They never lost their dignity as they invaded—yes, at times with an added arrogant swish—what must have seemed to them a minefield of derision. That manifestation of courage matched that of those who defied the cops in riots. Rather than brand those men, those women as stereotypes, as they now so often and so sadly are, I would call them stalwart pioneers who proclaimed their difference: "I am not what you want me to be." (2006)

The events to which Rechy alluded must have occurred in the late 1940s and early 1950s in El Paso. As Rechy stated, these were acts of *revolution*. They went unrecorded by history, as so many events on the border go unrecognized, but given the dynamic nature of the El Paso / Juárez border, I am not surprised. Queer activism on the border, therefore, is transnational.

The jotx participating in the parade contradicted the testimony of the somewhat closeted Pepe, who does not agree with "flaunting one's sexuality." To reiterate Rechy, the "stereotypical" jotx has effected real social change in terms of LGBTIQQA visibility and activism.

Along with queer activism comes the transnational nature of machismo, unfortunately. Two of the men from Pérez's case studies shared traditional views of gender and sexual identity as it relates to queer pleasure. In Mexico and Chicanx communities in the United States, the sexual position a man occupies is crucial to his identity. Pepe states, "In Mexico, if you're the top [the active partner], then you're the male, hence not gay. But if you're on the receiving end, then you're the gay one. In Juárez, lots of married men have sex with other men" (Pérez 2012, 203). This is an archaic treatment of gender and sexuality, yet it is an attitude that endures on the border. Sexuality, like the Rio Grande, is much more fluid than it seems. In my experiences on the border, the majority of married men I met desired the passive position. I doubt that these men considered themselves "women"; they merely knew what gave them pleasure. I have never met a man who refused penetration because of this arbitrary categorization. Therefore, pleasure is transnational as well.

The practices of machismo also affect women. One of Pérez's case studies, Myrna Avalos, a Chicana lesbian, believed that machismo harms women via "drunkenness, womanizing, and battering" (2012, 203). Myrna commented that machista attitudes affect lesbian relationships negatively via the practices of butch lesbians. According to Pérez, Myrna "observed that butch women in lesbian bars exhibit territorial behavior that she does not like. She said she used to go to You Got It, a lesbian bar that closed down around 1996 because the police had to break up fights between lesbians too often. 'I mean

GONZÁLEZ

these women would literally fight. Throw bottles at each other. I mean, territorial . . . with their women. This is my woman; you leave her alone, Bop!' She named their territorial behavior a 'butch pussy stance' and refused to engage in the type of restrictive role-playing that was anti-feminist" (2012, 203). Myrna displayed the same revolutionary Third World women feminist attitude as Carmelita Torres and her compañeras on the trolley.

Queer visibility is another transnational trait of border jotx. Similar to the border queers in Juárez who participated in the gay pride parade, twenty-one-year-old David Andrew Rubalcava, who identifies as a gay Hispanic male, believes in the power of visibility, as well as the activists from Juárez and El Paso. A student at the University of Texas at El Paso, David wrote a play entitled *A Piece of Mind*. David believes that coming out can help educate people and challenge stereotypes, which will help overcome homophobic attitudes. He holds a similar attitude to the queer martyr Harvey Milk, the assassinated San Francisco supervisor who encouraged all LGBTIQQA people to "come out." David, like Milk, believes that queer people must eschew the closet "to educate heterosexuals who hold stereotypes about queers" (Pérez 2012, 204). Although I believe "educating" heterosexuals is akin to "acceptance," I applaud his courageous stance as an out Hispanic gay man negotiating his identity on the border.

Religion, particularly Catholicism, plays a major role in the lives of Chicanx and mexicanas/os on the border. The majority of people in the region claim Catholicism, although a fair number also adhere to curanderismo and other Indigenous spiritual and healing practices. My family was devoutly Catholic and believed in the local Indigenous practices. When I was fourteen, I subtly came out to my confirmation teacher, a kindly older Chicana. I felt that she would offer me a sympathetic ear. However, she glared at me and proclaimed that homosexual desire was an abomination. She then opened her King James Bible to Leviticus 18:22 and read aloud, "Thou shalt not lie with mankind, as with womankind: it *is* abomination." She then stated that I would *burn* in hell if I ever acted on my desires. The following weekend, I attempted suicide. I have since reconciled my relationship with Catholicism, but David holds a much more radical attitude: "Fuck that, I'm not gonna listen to this bullshit because who are they to say who I can fall in love with, who I can have sex with, what kind of sex I can have, if I can use birth control or not, if I can make decisions about my own body" (Pérez 2012, 204). David holds a liberatory perspective regarding organized religion.

Similarly, there is activism in Juárez against the proliferation of organized religion, particularly Catholicism, into public spaces, such as public schools. The strict separation of church and state has a long history in Mexico, and members of the Lay Mexico Civic Forum are working to uphold this tradition. Members of the then-ruling party, the PAN, supported a reform that "guarantees the right to practice religion in 'public as well as private' places" (Paterson 2012). To some anticlerical activists, however, this reform seems like an end run around the Mexican Constitution's separation of religious and civic spaces. Kent Paterson of the New American Media writes, "On a recent day in Ciudad Juarez, members of the Lay Mexico Civic Forum gathered on the downtown plaza to pass out leaflets and collect signatures on letters calling on the Chihuahua State legislature to reject the constitutional reform" (2012). Some activists believe that the proposed reform is a calculated measure for the Catholic Church to regain hegemony over Mexico. In El Paso, David espouses anti-Catholic sentiment because of his sexual identity and desires. In Juárez, a public educator shares David's feelings: "A career public educator, [Armide] Valverde endorsed secularism as one of the pillars of the Mexican educational system. 'There's no reason for [religion] to be part of education,' Valverde said. 'That's why the Church exists'" (Paterson 2012).

Though the El Paso / Juárez region is steeped in Catholic history (the Spanish first established a mission here in the 1600s), there exists a deep current of anti-Catholicism traversing the area. The mask of Catholicism does not fully represent the Indigenous spiritual practices on both sides of the border. The art of Indigenous folk healing, curanderismo, is another transnational practice. Anyone could find a trusted curandera in the El Paso / Juárez region.

Interestingly, I never heard of a curandero in El Paso; my family labeled men who dabbled in the supernatural as brujos. I predict, however, that Catholicism will survive any protests and remain the dominant religion of the region, particularly as it is embedded in the local spiritual practices of the region's Indigenous inhabitants, particularly the Tigua Indians, who celebrate a feast day to San Antonio, and the Tarahumara Indians, who live in the mountains of Chihuahua just beyond Juárez.

For nearly two hundred years, the cities of El Paso and Juárez were one unified community that represented a strategic geographic location for Spain during the colonial period. Because of the outcome of the Mexican-American War, the Treaty of Guadalupe Hidalgo dissected the city into frontiers of two countries destined to take radically different developmental trajectories. Despite the proclamation of the treaty, Mexicanas/os and Chicanx continued to migrate north and south in a normal fashion. Both cities shared common histories, language, culture, and people. The border was nothing of consequence until the 1990s, with President Clinton's infamous Operation Gatekeeper. Still, people moved in a transnational nature with little difficulty. Even increased homeland security enforcement measures due to the attacks of September 11, 2001, could not deter the flow of people from El Paso to Juárez and vice versa. Only the brutality of the drug cartel murders has managed to frighten El Pasoans from venturing south of the border on a regular basis. Only those with urgent business attempt the dangerous trek. One of my father's tías, the last to reside in Juárez, passed away in 2012 and wished to be interred in a Juárez cemetery. However, my youngest sister convinced him not to attend the services because of the random nature of the cartel violence. The twin cities of El Paso and Juárez, once one unified city, are taking two disparate paths into this new millennium. Juárez, though its murder rate is decreasing, may never recover from the recent spate of drug cartel murders and the unsolved femicides linked to the maquiladoras. El Paso, conversely, with its Chicanx majority population, is growing rapidly and is poised to become a major center of latinidad, along with San Antonio, as Texas's demographics continue to trend toward favoring the Latinx community. The desires and pleasures of Pérez's border queers, though, will not stay confined to one side of the border. Due to the revolutionary ethos of the region, border queers will continue to negotiate their identities, desires, and pleasures in a courageous manner. Thus, the heroic and transnational legacies of Pancho Villa, Carmelita Torres, and, of course, Wonder Woman will give strength to future generations of jotas locas. Border jotx, like Arlene Díaz, refuse to allow the attitudes of their disapproving families or the heteropatriarchal church, the senseless violence of the drug cartels, or the homophobia of either society to confine them to a life of static borders. ¡Que viva la jotería!

Note

1. Other cultural productions include the 2008 novel by Stella Pope Duarte, *If I Die in Juárez*; the reportage texts *The Daughters of Juárez: A True Story of Serial Murder South of the Border*, by Teresa Rodriguez, Diana Montané, and Lisa Pulitzer, and *The Killing Fields: Harvest of Women*, by Diana Washington Valdez; the academic anthologies *Making a Killing: Femicide, Free Trade and La Frontera*, edited by Alicia Gaspar de Alba with Georgina Guzman, and *Terrorizing Women: Feminicide in the Americas*, edited by Rosa-Linda Fregoso and Cynthia Bejarano; the long-running play at the Frida Kahlo Theater in Los Angeles *Las Mujeres de Juárez*; the 1999 Tori Amos song "Juárez"; the 2004 Roberto Bolaño tome, *2666*; and the 2009 film *Backyard: El Traspatio*.

References

Anzaldúa, Gloria. 1987. *Borderlands / La Frontera: The New Mestiza*. San Francisco: Aunt Lute Books.

Borunda, Daniel. 2010a. "El Paso Named Safest US City." *El Paso Times*, November 22. https://libproxy.csun.edu/login?url=https://www-proquest-com.libproxy.csun.edu/docview/898879917?accountid=7285.

———. 2010b. "In El Paso Hate Crimes Few, but Gays Are Majority of Victims." *El Paso Times*, December 27. https://libproxy.csun.edu/login?url=https://www-proquest-com.libproxy.csun.edu/docview/821188563?accountid=7285.

Dorado Romo, David. 2005. *Ringside Seat to a Revolution: An Underground Cultural History of El Paso and Juárez, 1893–1923*. El Paso: Cinco Puntos Press.

"Marcha Gay Ciudad Juarez." 2010. YouTube, uploaded by Milenio Hey, September 25. https://www.youtube.com/watch?v=lo5CuK8w324.

Moran, Lee. 2012. "Mexico's Ciudad Juarez Has 3-Year Streak as Most Murderous City Broken in Upset by San Pedro Sula in Honduras." *New York Daily News*, October 10. https://www.nydailynews.com/news/world/murderous-city-san-pedro-sula -honduras-article-1.1179656.

Paterson, Kent. 2012. "God, Gays, Ganja and Mexican Politics." *Frontera NorteSur*, New Mexico State University, May 20. https://fnsnews.nmsu.edu/god-gays-ganja-and-mexican-politics/.

Pérez, Emma. 2012. "Decolonial Border Queers: Case Studies of Chicana/o Lesbians, Gay Men, and Transgender Folks in El Paso/Juárez." In *Performing the U.S. Latina and Latino Borderlands*, edited by Arturo J. Aldama, Chela Sandoval, and Peter J. García, 193–211. Bloomington: Indiana University Press.

"Po'pay." Architect of the Capitol. https://www.aoc.gov/art/national-statuary-hall-collection/popay.

Rechy, John. 2006. "Adelante Gay Pride Gala." *John Rechy: Speaking Out*, June 24. http://www.johnrechy.com/so_adel.htm.

Rio Grande Adelante. http://riograndeadelanteinc.memberlodge.org.

Saldívar, Ramón. 2006. *The Borderlands of Culture: Américo Paredes and the Transnational Imaginary*. Durham NC: Duke University Press.

Schulze, Jeffrey M. 2012. "The Chamizal Blues: El Paso, the Wayward River, and the Peoples in Between." *Western Historical Quarterly* 43 (3): 301–22.

5

Vaqueeros

Muy machos, Wearing the Pants, and Living la vida loca

CARLOS-MANUEL

Sex is a subject most of us do not easily discuss with everyone. If you add the fact that I wanted to talk about sex with Mexican men, then the task becomes a tad more difficult. And if you include the fact that I wanted to engage in this conversation not only with Mexican men but with Mexican men who *engaged* in sexual activities with other men *and* did it in secret, well, you can imagine the obstacles I encountered with this project. Nonetheless, I was able to interview twenty-three men, and I wrote a play about them and our conversations.

The interview process and writing of the play took place between 2005 and 2007. And since then my curiosity with the subject matter of "Mexican men having sex with other men and keeping it secret" has not stopped. But before I go on, I believe it necessary to share some of the research findings that emerged from interviews.

There were twenty-three interviewees, and except for one, all are of Mexican descent or Mexican born. From the thirteen who are Mexican born, five are undocumented immigrants. Out of the twenty-three men, five of the interviewees are married men, two are divorced, two are separated, three are engaged, one is dating a woman, two are dating both a man and a woman, and six are single. Eleven out of the twenty-three men have children in or out of wedlock. The youngest person I interviewed was twenty-three, the oldest fifty-six. One of the interviewees did not finish elementary school, three have a bachelor's degree, two finished graduate school, one has a PhD, and the rest (sixteen) finished at least high

school. All interviewees have a steady job, ranging from the custo-
dial services to being employed by a major company or university.
Some are bilingual, while others only speak Spanish. Some go to
gay Latino clubs "de vez en cuando," while others "never go out to
gay clubs in town." Most of the interviewees have never cared about
getting tested, while at least two of them know they are HIV positive. Four have friends who know about their sexual encounters
with other men, while at least one has "never told a soul." Ten considered themselves straight, eight of them considered themselves
gay, three classified themselves as bisexual, one likes to wear wom-
en's clothing in secret "y dejémoslo así," and one said he considers
himself a "free-spirited person." The majority of the interviewees
considered themselves tops or givers in the sexual act, while only
three like to "give and receive," and just two of them admitted they
are the bottom. And lastly, the only interviewee who is not Mexican but Latino used to be in the army and was part of an "organized underground military sex network while serving the country."

When the interviewees were asked why they like to engage in a
sexual act with, be in a relationship with, or date another man but
still be "in the closet," their answers varied from "I wish I could
come out, but I can't and I won't" and "it's a difficult situation, one
you many never understand" to "it is my life and my choice" and "I
don't think there is a law or rule that says we need to be out or gay
in order to have sex with another man, is there?" When those interviewees who have children were asked if they would mind if one
of their children came out as gay, lesbian, or bisexual, the majority
said they would not care, some hesitated but leaned more toward
not caring, while one of them had a very strong opinion: "I care. I
don't want my son to be gay. I want him to be completely straight
and get married and have kids, and . . . you know . . . do what society expects of him. . . . It's depressing. Gay people don't have a very
happy life. So, no, I don't want my son to be gay. I want him to be
a very happy straight man."

When talking about sexual encounters and how they go about
finding them, the men gave these answers: "I meet them at straight
clubs, or fiestas. One I met at a bus stop." "It's hard. To find someone,

whether it's a man or a woman, it's hard." "I meet them online. I'm very discreet about it, and everything happens by my rules." "Anywhere—at the mall, at work, at clubs, even at my brother's games."

I learned many different and interesting stories while interviewing these twenty-three individuals. For example, there was the sexual relationship between two gay men who married each other's sisters in order to gain legal status in the country but without letting the sisters know the two men are a couple; and the story of the interviewee who is married but whose wife allows him to have sexual encounters with other men as long as he comes home every night and doesn't bring any of his tricks home *and* the encounter is not with a particular young man the interviewee had an affair with; and the story of the three compadres who belong to a club that organizes private BBQs where food is not the main reason to attend. Or the story about the straight guy who has sex with different "fags" because "they can't live without me, so they pay me to keep them happy." And there are more stories, but time does not allow me to reference them all.

As mentioned before, because of this project, a curiosity to comprehend the different views and philosophies on such practices grew within me. So I decided to do some research.

In our traditional mainstream society, humans are divided into two different genders: male and female. Nothing else. Males are supposed to be masculine, and females are supposed to be feminine. End of story. Within this classification, most members of society view males as the superordinate half while viewing women as the subordinate half, or, as I like to say, men make the decisions and give the orders, while women respect such resolutions and obey such commands.

According to Alfredo Mirandé, author of *Hombres y Machos: Masculinity and Latino Culture* and professor of sociology and ethnic studies at UC Riverside, this male/female classification gives way to viewing the masculine gender as "ambitious, assertive, rational, analytical, individualistic, competitive, dominant, and aggressive," while the feminine gender is seen as "warm, emotional, understanding, cooperative, compassionate, sympathetic, loyal, and affectionate" (1997, 9). These descriptions tend to line up with the general belief about how men and women are supposed to act and interact with each other, but such gender conceptions are, as Mirandé states, "inadequate explanations of Mexican/Latino masculinity" (1997, 9).

To understand these (mis)conceptions about Mexican/Latino masculinity, it is necessary to identify the origins of such beliefs. According to Mirandé (1997), there are three theories about masculinity: (1) masculinity is the direct result of the Spanish conquest, an event so disturbing that it created a sort of obsession with images and symbols of manhood among Indians and mestizo men; (2) masculinity is a characteristic of Spanish society that was imposed on the native population; and (3) masculinity behavior has pre-Columbian origins that predate the Spanish arrival. These theories are supported with extensive explanations, research, and documentation. However, what's important is that Mirandé discredits these theories while describing the concept of machismo from the point of view of the three different theories. He then describes the concept of machismo in different Mexican periods, starting with colonialism, going through the Mexican Revolution, and ending with the present (and by present, I mean 1997, when his book was written).

Although Mirandé offers a definition for each period, he generally defines machismo as "nothing more than a futile attempt to mask a profound sense of impotence, powerlessness, and ineptitude, an expression of exaggerated masculine characteristics, ranging from male genital prowess to towering pride and fearlessness, weakness, and inferiority where the macho is seeing as a mujeriego, who is also referred to as a conquistador for he is seen not only as seducing but also as symbolically 'conquering' women" (1997, 40). This agglomeration of definitions falls within the many different descriptions I found in other sources, such as *NTC's Dictionary of Mexican Cultural Code Words*, the *Encyclopedia Britannica*, *Merriam-Webster's Collegiate Dictionary*, the *Larousse diccionario usual*, and Guadalupe Loaeza's book, *El ABC de las y los mexicanos*.

With this in mind, and for the purpose of this discussion, I propose that a machista mentality is that of a man who not only exaggerates his masculinity, believes he is superior to the female gender, and can engage in a sexual relations with any woman he wants but also never allows anyone to question, deprecate, or attempt to thwart his manhood.

By using this definition, I can deduce why at least the twenty-three men I interviewed are able to have sex with other men, keep it in the closet, and still have heterosexual relationships in the open. Their actions, their reasoning, and their points of view regarding their behavior originate, in my mind, in a machista Mexican culture mentality where the embodiment of manhood is seen in revolutionary heroes such as Pancho Villa and Emiliano Zapata, as well as in today's public figures like Vicente Fernandez and Lupillo Rivera.

At the same time, I believe this "machismo mentality" is not the only factor that contributes to hidden male/male sexual practices. There is, it seems, also a cultural attribute. As one of the interviewees pointed out:

> In Western European cultures homosexuality is defined by choice. If you chose to be with a man, regardless of what you do, you are gay. If you're walking downtown holding hands with a man, you're gay. If you kiss a man, you're gay. If you have sex with another man, you're gay. But in Mexican culture and other Latino cultures, it is what you do in bed that determines your homosexuality. Having sex with a man doesn't make you a homosexual. What makes me a homosexual is whether I'm the one receiving the sex or not.

The interviewee's mentality resonates with Tomás Almaguer's understanding of Mexican and Chicano masculinity and sexuality in his 1993 "Chicano Men: A Cartography of Homosexual Identity and Behavior." My belief is that Mexican men who have sex with other men and keep it secret do so not only because of a macho attitude but also because of a cultural attribute. Specifically, these men can have sex with other men in private and feel okay about it as long as (1) they continue to be viewed as manly by those around them and (2) they are the "active partner" in the sexual act or perhaps can be the active/passive partner as long as no one else besides the ones involved know about it.

To prove this theory and to make sure that my interviews/research were not becoming outdated, in the summer of 2011 I decided to have a conversation with six Mexican men, all of whom are practicing sex with other men but keeping it secret. This meeting took place in Mexico City, and it was possible thanks to a close friend who, while living in California, was completely out of the closet, yet once he moved back to his hometown, he went back into the closet. My conversation with these six men touched on many subjects about gay life in Mexico City and the country but mainly on their points of view about living this hidden male/male sexual life.

The six men are educated professionals and somewhat affluent members of society. Some of them are university professors, others are renowned theater and/or film/T V artists, others work for international companies, and some even own their own business. Some are married, while others are single, yet they are all in the closet to their families and closest family friends. Their views did not vary from the views of the twenty-three men I had interviewed years before. In fact, the similarities, actions, and explanations are parallel.

Listening to their points of view did not surprise me in the least and reminded me of this double life juxtaposition I present in my one-man show *La Vida Loca*. During the play I share with the audience an experience where cousins and friends perform a hypermasculinity among themselves and in front of others and at some point making fun of, taunting, and physically abusing "effeminate males," yet in private more than one of them engaged in sex with such males, and as long as no one knew about it, it was acceptable to do so. This also reminds me of the gay parades in Mexico City where the young and proud gay members of the community march in the streets chanting, "Ese bigotón, también es maricón" (That guy with the mustache is also a faggot) or "Ese mexicano, le entra por el ano" (That Mexican man takes it / gives it through the anus) or "Tu, parado en la acera, no marchas porque eres bien culera" (You standing in the sidewalk, don't march because you're an asshole or because you "literately" like assholes). To the onlooker, these chants are funny, yet they carry a strong message against the double life of many Mexican men and against Mexican machismo attitudes. When I mentioned these observations to the six Mexican men, they chuckled and laughed. They told me they understood what I was saying, but they do not really pay attention to "them" because "ellos son una bola de loquitas" (they are a bunch of effeminate/delicate men), as if being out and/or effeminate was less valuable or less important.

This response brings me back to the time I told one of my brothers that I was gay. His answer: "It's okay, bro. Just don't be a fag." When further discussing this matter with my brother, I came to understand that he was okay with me being gay as long as I was not effeminate or decided to wear makeup, dresses, or things like that because, in his own words, he himself will beat me up. When comparing myself and my best friend in Mexico City to the ones that were marching, he was very offended and very direct to clarify that he and I were not like "them" because "we were gay-putos" but they, "they were putitos, loquitas." He then proceeded to confess that if I was "una de esas loquitas," he would not feel comfortable having me around his family. Luckily for me, I guess, I am perceived as a masculine man, so his family has no idea I am gay, and those who know (because there are relatives who know my friend and I am gay) don't ever make references or talk about it with us or anyone.

This negative attitude toward effeminate gay men and the overall hidden men/men sexual practice philosophy among the Mexican community in both countries bothers me, mainly because it perpetuates stereotypes and it delays the acceptance of LGBTQ+ people, as well as nonbinary, gender neutral, nongender, and third gender people, among others. The ideology that men, regardless of their sexual identity, must be masculine—and most of the time hypermasculine—is harmful, mentally, emotionally, psychologically, and physiologically. It also has political and cultural repercussions because, in my opinion, people who hold this ideology view femininity as weak and inferior.

Luckily, in the United States, this attitude is being challenged by writers like Tomás Almaguer, Daniel Enrique Perez, and Rita Urquijo-Ruiz and by artists like Cherríe Moraga, Dan Guerrero, and yours truly, among many others. In Mexico, it is being challenged by the many "loquitas" who dare to march on the streets and by gay and transwomen activists like Julia Antivilo, Tito Vasconcelos, Alexandra Rodriguez de Ruiz, and Mika Aslan and by writers like Luis Zapata, Carlos Monsiváis, and Elena Poniatowska, as well as by the many people who in 2018 contributed to Michael K. Schuessler and Miguel Capistrán's first ever and much-needed book, *México se escribe con J: Una historia de la cultura gay.*

In one of his chapters, Mirandé states that there was not much writing about gay Chicanos and masculinity. But he said it twenty-three years ago, and things have changed. I think. And this brings me back to the beginning. I stated that I had conducted interviews and written a play based on those interviews. The play is titled *Vaqueeros*, and it has had a couple of staged readings and three different rejections from Latino theater companies. As an artist, I expect my work to be accepted and rejected; it is a given. But when you find out that your work is rejected because producers are afraid of its content or because someone's religious beliefs do not agree with your artistic themes, it bothers me. I do not mention this as a complaint but as an example of how even today, artistic work that tries to bring to light what is going on within the Mexican community in relation to sexual practices among men still is taboo.

As of today, there are hundreds if not thousands of men having sex with other men who keep it a secret, and they all have reasons as to why they do so. I like to call these men "vaqueeros" because they may be "muy machos" and they may be wearing the pants, but in the end, in some dark corner of their own house, in the privacy of a hotel room, at the city's park, or at the most popular bathhouse, their pants are halfway down, if not totally off. At the end of the night, they are doing what "esos putitos y esas loquitas" are doing: having sex with other men. And whether they like it or not: "De noche o de día, andan en la jotería."

References

Almaguer, Tomás. 1993. "Chicano Men: A Cartography of Homosexual Identity and Behavior." In *The Gay & Lesbian Studies Reader*, edited by H. Abelove, M. A. Barale, and D. M. Halperin, 255–73. New York: Routledge.

Carlos-Manuel. 2013. *Vaqueeros*. In *Vaqueeros, Calacas, and Hollywood: Contemporary Chicano Plays*, edited by Carlos-Manuel, 167–217. Tempe AZ: Bilingual Review Press.

Loaeza, Guadalupe. 2007. *El ABC de las y los mexicanos*. Barcelona: Grijalbo.

Mirandé, Alfredo. 1997. *Hombres y Machos: Masculinity and Latino Culture*. New York: Routledge.

Schuessler, Michael K., and Miguel Capistrán. 2018. *México se escribe con J: Una historia de la cultura gay*. Mexico City: Debolsillo.

Home(bodies)

Transitory Belonging at LA's Oldest Latinx Drag Bar

KATHERINE STEELMAN

La Plaza nightclub was founded in 1975, making it the oldest operating Latina/o gay bar in Los Angeles. According to Leo, the general manager, not much has changed in the thirty-five years he has worked there. In fact, he said that nothing has changed, that La Plaza is like the Twilight Zone and that customers who come back after a long time away are surprised to see the same people working there. In his book *Cruising Utopia*, José Esteban Muñoz also comments on the time warp sensation that one feels at La Plaza: "The codes that organize time and space are disrupted in this performance space. The first time I visited the club I felt like I was in 1950s Guadalajara" (2009, 108). Time, according to Muñoz, is disrupted by the atmosphere of the bar, the type of music being played, and the costumes, while space is being disrupted because most of the songs performed are in Spanish, and the travesti performers are introduced according to their village or province in Mexico. Leo says that it is not only the performers who contribute to the transitory spatial phenomenon that occurs within the walls of La Plaza. The customers, he says, hail from all over Latin America—Honduras, El Salvador, Nicaragua, Costa Rica, and Venezuela. He says that on Thursday nights, when the club has male and female strippers, the MC will say, "Let's hear it from the people from México," and then continue to mention several countries. A group of people will cheer loudly for every country mentioned.

From reading Muñoz's work, as well as from my conversation with Leo, it is clear that La Plaza is in some ways a paradox, at once frozen in time but somehow embodying spatial transition. With this in mind, I interrogate the relationship between drag performance, transgender identity, and migration as it manifests itself in the physical location of La Plaza, drawing on the scholarly works of Muñoz, Nael Bhanji, Vek Lewis, and David Román, as well as interviews with people who inhabit the space of La Plaza. Through sites like La Plaza, LA can be theorized as a border space where contradictory notions of liberation and homophobia are at play.

One text that examines these contradictions is Vek Lewis's book chapter "Forging Moral Geographies." Lewis is looking at the cultural context behind a 2002 law passed in Tecate, Baja California, Mexico, that criminalized public nonnormative gender expression. Lewis asserts that the media attention given to the passage of this law essentialized the issue as being one related primarily to a macho, homophobic culture. While he argues against this notion, he is also looking at the ways in which legal discrimination against northern Mexico's trans population also challenges the contemporary theorization of border spaces as sites of liberation. He writes that trans people are often compared to transnational migrants, with a focus on the act of crossing, and that his research focuses not on border crossers but on border dwellers: "But what of those who have stayed put or grown up in these sites and are also trans? Such questions are very rarely raised in scholarship that goes under the name 'border studies' in the Anglo-American academy" (Lewis 2012, 34). Focusing on the anti-cross-dressing law in Tecate, Lewis explains that, counter to the idea that Mexico is a place of intolerance and homophobia, even the border dwellers, those who live in Tecate and face discrimination firsthand, do not see the city as particularly oppressive:

Hence Tecate was not seen—even by those who bore the brunt of the new anti-cross-dressing law—as being especially intolerant, something to which the gays and *travestis* I spoke to there testified. The well-known gay activist Max Mejia explained:

"These days they don't target the gays; years of gay male activism have secured a place in the discourse of human rights that would make reference to same-sex activity in a hypothetical prohibition impossible. Now, however, the most visible among the sexually diverse—the *travestis*—are targeted." (2012, 51)

Thus gay people in Tecate, through decades of activism, have won some rights and a place in society closer in from the margins, just as gay people in the United States have, and the trans community continues to be marginalized and targeted for violence, just as trans people in the United States continue to be.

Lewis's discussion of survival and passing in Latin America resonates with the story told to me by Adriana, a performer at the club whom I interviewed in March 2014. Adriana, who had migrated to LA from Guatemala six years before, told me that her migration to the United States was a necessary act of survival. She said that her home country is the most difficult country for transgender people, that there is machismo and homophobia, and that it is a corrupt country. She said that she would travel to the capital for (somewhat) safe spaces to be trans. Here, she said, there is more support for transgender people. Adriana said that she now works as a hairdresser during the week, that it is going very good for her here. She said that the two things that make her happy are working at La Plaza and that she recently became documented.

As evidenced in the experiences of patrons and performers alike, La Plaza is a place where people feel at home. In his book chapter "Trans/scriptions: Homing Desires, (Trans)sexual Citizenship and Racialized Bodies," Nael Bhanji asks just what home looks like for physical, national and sexual border dwellers. Arguing against an "'imagined community' of transsexual belonging" (2012, 174), Bhanji writes out of both skepticism of and respect for transgender theory, stating that there has been a trend toward theorists fetishizing and exoticizing transgender subjectivity. Bhanji writes that behind the stereotype of trans space as liberatory is the erasure of racial difference within the trans community. Bhanji poses the question, "To what 'home' does the trajectory of transition, the act of border-crossing, lead the already in-between diasporic, gender liminal subject?" (2012,160). This question can be explored in the context of

Los Angeles and La Plaza through the experiences of Betty, a performer at the bar, and Presley, a longtime patron. I interviewed them both in April 2014.

Presley, a trans man from Long Beach, says that his aunt and her girlfriend took him to La Plaza for the first time when he was a teenager. He says that he had been in a deep depression while coming to terms with his nonnormative gender and sexuality and that La Plaza was the first place he felt free to be who he was. Betty also speaks of the space of La Plaza as one of freedom. Tony, who has managed the performers for decades and whose partner designs all of the costumes, spoke to me about his first impression of Betty: "She started as a boy, she was so cute. I really thought she was a girl at first, she was so innocent, and look at her now! She's a full-fledged queen." She herself said that working at La Plaza helped her to become a more confident woman. In her day job as an assistant manager at Jack in the Box she is faced with transphobia on a daily basis, but her job at La Plaza offers some relief: "They criticize you, but once you are here, you're free. This is your place. It's such a nice experience to get so much attention. They make you feel good, to see their faces. It's just a blessing."

Even within the context of the performance, there are contradictions at play. The act of performing is at once freeing and, paradoxically, oppressive. The travesti performers at La Plaza are increasingly being viewed through the gaze of the outsider—of straight, upper-middle-class white people who have begun to frequent the bar in recent years. On the social media network Instagram on October 6, 2010, these new patrons posted photos of the performances with captions that reveal how they view the space and themselves in it. One user, thepianofixer, posted the caption, "Mexican drag bar=best bar ever. #plaza #dragqueens #weho #ghettofabulous." The user suzieblock commented, "Amaze-balls!!," and the poster responded, "Tucked balls." While audience members like those posting on Instagram may be engaging in gentrification, cultural appropriation, and even transphobia, the performers are still having an overwhelmingly positive experience. Both Betty and Adriana said that they feel tremendously happy when they are onstage.

It is possible that the love and gratitude emanating from the largely queer and migrant audience cannot be diminished by a few people who choose to inhabit the space to have some cheap drinks, laugh at what they see as a novelty, and leave after the first song.

The question of temporality is one that comes up both in Muñoz's discussion of La Plaza and in Bhanji's discussion of home. Queerness for Muñoz and home for Bhanji are in a constant state of becoming. As Muñoz writes in *Cruising Utopia*, "The present is not enough. It is impoverished and toxic for queers and other people who do not feel the privilege of majoritarian belonging, normative tastes, and 'rational' expectations. . . . [T]he present must be known in relation to the alternative temporal and spatial maps provided by a perception of past and future affective worlds" (2009, 27). Muñoz's book, besides being the sole academic source I could find that mentioned La Plaza specifically, is vital to the formation of my research question. Writing about Los Angeles, Muñoz notes that being involved in the LA scene through music as a teen in Miami allowed him to "imagine a self that was in process" (2009, 100). Specifically, he writes that the transitory nature of migration and of being transgender somehow come together and are embodied by the physical location of La Plaza: "I was able to imagine a time and place that was not yet there, a place where I tried to live. LA and its scene helped my proto-queer self, the queer child in me, imagine a stage, both temporal and physical, where I could be myself, or more nearly, imagine a self that was in process, a self that has always been in the process of becoming" (Muñoz 2009, 100).

Muñoz as a gay teen in Miami was able to imagine LA as his queer home even though he was physically removed from the place of LA by thousands of miles. Home for him was a place where he could be free and, paradoxically, that has to be somewhere far away from his "real" home. Bhanji explains this beautifully in his discussion of the contradictions inherent in the expression "home is where the heart is." He writes that for trans people and for people in diaspora, home is often not where the heart is but wherever you can survive. Unlike the expected migration narrative in which the migrant leaves "home" for a place that is not home, trans migrants are always already in exile. According to Bhanji, "Thus, in a note-worthy reversal of the diasporic trajectory, the transsexual migrant must leave the space of unhomeliness to arrive at 'home'" (2012, 165). Sometimes, like for the young Muñoz, that place of home is in the imagination. As Bhanji writes, "In other words, we must pay attention to the different ways in which people (re)imagine and (re)create the edifice of homely belonging; where one's 'real' home can only exist as a romanticized cathedral of constancy—like a strongbox of memory kept safe from the siren dance of moder-nity through spatial and temporal sleights-of-hand that effectively render it, as Canadian poet Dionne Brand would say, 'in another place, not here' (Brand 1996)" (2012, 161). In the space of La Plaza, one can observe firsthand this notion of the re-creation of home as a "romanticized cathedral of constancy." As Muñoz suggests, the bar brings the atmosphere of 1950s Guadalajara to modern-day Los Angeles, and as the manager states, this has not changed in thirty-five years. This illusory constancy adds to the paradox of La Plaza, creating a space that at once is home and is not home. The sensa-tion of being in a time warp when you enter the bar is an illusion—a performance. In fact, the space itself is in a constant state of trans-formation because of the realities of deportation, AIDS, incarcer-ation, and gentrification facing the communities who work at and patronize the bar.

In Bhanji's examination of the contradictions inherent in the con-cept of home for transgender migrants, he also makes the point that many gender-conforming people in the United States find home-like places and spaces at the expense of these migrants: "Of course, 'home' can easily be a space of exclusion, a space where the nostal-gic dream of communal belonging depends on the 'invisible labor of migrant border dwellers,' and a luxury that belies the realities of those who cannot afford to dream of home (Halberstam 1998: 171)" (2012, 164). It is precisely this luxury that the aforementioned Instagram posters are indulging in when they claim La Plaza as a homelike space.

The idea of outsiders to queer and trans communities claiming homes in LGBTQ spaces is by no means a recent phenomenon. Writing from 1990s Los Angeles, which was then in the throes of the AIDS epidemic, David Román discusses the ways in which Latino performance became a channel of expression for this crisis and offers an extensive discussion of camp and drag in his book chapter "It's My Party and I'll Die if I Want To." He argues that the nostalgia of camp for mainstream queer culture was no longer relevant in 1990s LA because it pointed to a time before AIDS. La Plaza, which is now and has been a palace of drag and camp, enters into this conversation by posing the question of why this type of performance has maintained a very real relevance for patrons of the club who lived through the AIDS epidemic. Román argues that camp was a survival tactic for gay men in the early and mid-twentieth-century United States and offered them a way to distance themselves from the humiliation they felt in their daily lives while allowing them to create an aesthetic they could control:

> Mainstream spectators, some with no sense of gay and lesbian history, may leave with impressions that see gay men *as* entertainment. The success of drag on Broadway in the 1980s, in such commercial hits as *Torch Song Trilogy, La Cage aux Folles*, and even *M. Butterfly*, demonstrated the demand by mainstream audiences for this type of gay performance to such an extent, as Mark Gevisser argues, that "gay culture is presented to mainstream heterosexual America as a drag show." The survivalist quality that so marks camp and drag for the gay spectator is reconfigured and depoliticized in the commodification process. (1998, 99–100)

This reconfiguration is exactly what is happening at La Plaza when members of mainstream society post photos of themselves on Instagram with the hashtags "#happyplace #heavenonearth #imhavingmybirthdaypartyhereforreal" (from Instagram user "gmenduni"). As with gentrification, people who are not part of the cultural history of the space are entering La Plaza and speaking of it as if they have "discovered" something wonderful and exotic.

In my conversation with Tony, I brought up a bartender whom Presley had mentioned to me. He had worked at the bar for many years and had come into his place of work seeking services for HIV.

Tony informed me that the bartender had passed, saying that AIDS hit La Plaza hard, that there were plenty of sad times, and then he smiled and said, "But there's mostly fun. And drama too, that's where I come in. I'm the bitch."

References

Bhanji, Nael. 2012. "Trans/scriptions: Homing Desires, (Trans)sexual Citizenship and Racialized Bodies." In *Transgender Migrations: The Bodies, Borders, and Politics of Transition*, edited by Trystan Cotten, 139–56. New York: Routledge.

Brand, Dionne. 1996. *In Another Place Not Here*. New York: Grove Press.

Halberstam, Jack. 1998. *Female Masculinity*. Durham NC: Duke University Press.

Lewis, Vek. 2012. "Forging Moral Geographies." In *Transgender Migrations: The Bodies, Borders, and Politics of Transition*, edited by Trystan Cotten, 32–56. New York: Routledge.

Muñoz, José Esteban. 2009. *Cruising Utopia: The Then and There of Queer Futurity*. New York: NYU Press.

Román, David. 1998. *Acts of Intervention: Performance, Gay Culture, and AIDS*. Bloomington: Indiana University Press.

Memory and Memoir

BETWEEN SUEÑOS Y PESADILLAS

7

Pesadilla convertida en sueño / A Nightmare Turned Into a Dream

El sueño nunca soñado / A Dream Never Dreamed

BAMBY SALCEDO

Reflexionando, aquí estoy en lo que fue el ayer, en mi niñez, pensando en lo que quería ser, cuando creciera, cuando grande yo fuera, cuando de mi yo me pudiera valer, y me preguntaba cómo era que yo iba a ser... Sueños tempranos, de inmadurez, sueños tempranos con una visión imposible de ver. Mi realidad era que yo no pensaba en que era lo que en mi futuro yo podía ser, por que en mi niñez mi prioridad era mi madre, ayudarla para que nos pudiera dar de comer, ponerme a trabajar en ese momento era lo que tenía que lograr, para poder dar, aportar, contribuir a poder subsistir para que en algún futuro dar valor a mi existir y poder resistir a esa vida que me causaba intriga...

Yo quería ir a la escuela, estudiar, con la esperanza de algún día poder superar, lograr, lograr, lo que nunca nadie en mi familia había podido lograr y poder avanzar, la escalera social escalar y aferrarme a escalar como un escalador se aferra hasta con sus uñas a esa pared que le ha de sostener, para al vacío no caer y con arduo trabajo una mejor calidad de vida poder obtener y poder, triunfar, destacar, luchar, la historia marcar, librar, superar, y poder demostrar que la pobreza se puede arrancar, esa pobreza que presionaba mi pecho bajo ese lecho al cual yo quería llamar hogar... Mi niñez fue desterrada, arrebatada, sexualizada, violada, traicionada, distorsionada, confundida, frustrada, aprovechada, apagada, borrada, olvidada y viví esclavizada, por un sistema donde la explotación laboral de un niño es legal para beneficiar a esos que tenían el poder de conmigo cualquier cosa hacer, y a mi mente traían trauma.

La carnicería que de mi casa estaba en la esquina, en la esquina de las intersecciones, que marcaban mi vida, que marcaban las intersecciones que yo vivía, cuando los dueños de la carnicería, los hombres que me situaron en la mesa de cortar carne cuando mi feminidad ellos veían y pensaban lo que sexualmente harían conmigo cuando en esa mesa de cortar carne mis ojos la sierra veía, y de arriba a abajo se movía lentamente, escuchando a esos hombres que me decían que si no hacía, complacía, favorecía sus satisfacciones sexuales en pedazos me cortarían. Y yo la sierra veía que de arriba a abajo se movía como una guía que marcaba, dictaba y decía que mi vida nada valía, y en esos momentos de mi niñez mi vida veía como yo desaparecía y me hundía como si me estuviera hundiendo en un pantano de arenas movedizas donde no tenía salida, donde nadie me escuchaba aunque imploraba, rogaba y lloraba con impotencia, mi alma ya sin fuerza, sin poder liberarme de esos hombres que me sujetaban con toda su fuerza al yo implorarles que no me hicieran daño, que yo haría lo que a ellos les favoreciera y sus fantasías sexuales complacería con la implorancia de que me dejaran aun con vida, aunque que yo ya había visto a través de la sierra que por dentro yo ya había muerto . . .

Hasta que por fin un día, el inhalar pegamento de mi realidad me sacaría, el amor que buscaba encontraría, no solamente por que me hacía olvidarme de todo, pero también esa sensación que por mi cuerpo corría, el inhalar pegamento me hacía sentir, en mi mente reír, mi cuerpo temblaba, se estremecía, el cuero en mi piel se enchinaba con cada inhalada. El pegamento de mi realidad me sacaba y yo pensaba que con cada inhalada el amor que buscaba, el pegamento divino me brindaba . . . Y así fui creciendo con cada olfateada, inhalada de pegamento o activador yo me daba valor, sentía que el pegamento otra vida me daba y me encerraba donde nadie podía ver lo que dentro de mi yo llevaba, por que al mundo otra realidad yo mostraba, una realidad falsa, confundida, perturbada, marginada que solo mentiras formaba por que el vivir mi verdad sería ser avergonzada, apagada, marginada, acabada, rechazada, torturada . . .

Mi adolescencia no fue comprendida, atendida, recibida, al contrario, por el sistema fue ultrajada, robada, martirizada, golpeada, abollada, amordazada, sin oportunidad, sin lugar a donde ir, con quien acudir para yo poder decir que necesitaba ayuda poder acudir, decir que necesitaba guía, que necesitaba amor, que necesitaba aprender a ser alguien que quiere ver, lo que la vida le puede tener, traer, merecer... con la esperanza de siempre poder ver, y de ser lo que se veía en el sueño en una atardecer, en mi niñez aunque empañado mi sueño, aun seguía ahí avivado, mi sueño de poder ser, un ser de bien, sin tener que cambiar mi manera de ser, viviendo mil vidas, mil identidades y a la vez ninguna... mi adolescencia estaba manchada, parchada, apachurrada, quebrantada, distorsionada... pero yo quería sonreír, compartir, en el lugar prometido quería vivir... llegar, alcanzar, descubrir, perseguir, subsistir... a ese lugar quería yo ir, a ese lugar del cual todos hablaban, donde se reía, donde se vivía, a ese lugar que yo desconocía, y lejos de mí existía... mientras yo muerta en vida seguía...

Viviendo mis mil identidades, escondiendo mis verdades, escondiendo mi vida haciendo maldades, esperando que el amor llegara a mis paladares, y poder probar, de una forma mi vida tocar, sujetar, agarrar, apretar... apretar con tanta fuerza hasta ya no aguantar, por que ese amor ya no quería añorar, y esperaba, añoraba, deseaba que ese amor llegara... pero mientras tanto yo seguí aguantando las injusticias que experimentaba por la sociedad en la cual me encontraba, aguantando violaciones sexuales de la policía y de los hombres los cuales tener sexo conmigo querían, a veces por dinero, a veces con engaños y promesas de falso amor, el cual me causaba furor, el amor que yo buscaba, ese amor que yo idolatraba, el amor que yo añoraba... y a cambio lo que yo recibía eran maltratos, encarcelamientos, ataques, achaques y también ultrajes... por ser yo, mal me miraban, me señalaban, de mi se burlaban, y muchas veces hasta me golpeaban, por que en sus ojos era yo una cosa rara, alguien despreciable, alguien miserable, alguien que con nadie quería ser comparable, por que mi vida era algo marcado por la suciedad de la sociedad en la cual mi adolescencia estaba forzada a vivir y yo para poder subsistir y resistir, dejaba de existir al hacer contacto con el pegamento que me libro de todo argumento que siempre existía en mi pensamiento y que siempre mantuvo mi Corazón contento...

Y así viví hasta que al fin pude huir, de la realidad, de mi verdad, de lo que yo quería ocultar por que me decían que yo era maldad, falsedad, terquedad, ansiedad, malestar, me decían que mi existencia les causaba pesar . . . hasta que yo al norte vine a dar, huyendo de mi verdad, con la esperanza de poder encontrar el amor que yo siempre buscaba, por que a mis diez y seis años no podía encontrar lo que en realidad que era el amor, por que mi cuerpo, mi mente y alma estaba perturbada, atormentada, traumada, ultrajada . . .

Es verdad que yo existía en cuerpo, pero todo de mi por dentro estaba muerto, y yo vivía con una esperanza, la esperanza de poder llegar a ver a el hombre que me dio ser, que aunque no me vio crecer pensé que talvez feliz con el podía ser, pero yo no sabía lo que para mi el futuro traería por que el nuevo país en el que viviría yo desconocía, otra lengua, otra gente, a otro estilo de vida me acostumbraría y escondiendo quien era yo seguía, porque el temor en mi existía, que el rechazo de mi padre tendría cuando el supiera que el amor que a mi me habían dado hasta entonces había sido a través de sexo por todo hombre que yo conocí, sexo, sexo que me mantenía como un anexo, que el amor que por el se me dio, heredo, paso, incrusto . . . Yo tuve que construir esa fuerza de sobrevivencia, de paciencia, de subsistencia, esa fuerza de ser, de permanecer, de mi espacio poder hacer, en el norte, la explotación laboral pude experimentar y maldiciones los gabachos tuve que escuchar, sin poder encontrar cómo contestar por que la lengua del güero no podía hablar . . .

A mis diez y siete años en la lucha, en la busca de amor, lo que yo encontré fue la coca y heroína por mis venas correr y muchas veces la combinación de ambas por que quería sentir ese amor que me motivara, que me estremeciera, el amor que mis penas me hiciera olvidar, que me hiciera olvidar mi manera de ser, mi manera de pensar, pero lo que yo en esos momentos veía que en realidad yo no podía ser quien yo estaba destinada a ser por que lo que existía en mi cabeza en mi mente, mi alma y corazón, era una desilusión que me decía que quien yo era no tenía razón. La desilusión me decía que si quería el amor de mi padre tenía que vivir sin compasión, sin compasión para mi o para otras personas que se parecían a mi . . . y yo actuaba, mostraba, acertaba, que era una persona sin escrúpulos, sin principios, con mucha vergüenza de ser quien yo estaba destinada a ser . . .

Cuando por fin pude descubrir, que no podía seguir viviendo esa mentira, la cual había vivido toda mi vida, la decisión tuve que tomar, de tener que aventurar, de ver lo que el destino podría tener en ese lugar donde alguien me iba a valorar, a querer y no maltratar, el poder llegar a ese lugar a donde el fin pudiera yo despegar, desterrar, arrancar, mi pasado, mi martirio, mi pesar . . .

Al llegar a Los Ángeles, encontré una traición, al descubrir que esa atracción tan publicada, para mi fue perdición, y seguí y seguí buscando amor en lo que yo ya sabía, lo que yo conocía en la época del SIDA mi vida en riesgo ponía, jeringas yo compartía y sexo sin protección yo tenía cuando yo misma en mi mente decía sexo, drogas, rock and roll, buscando ese falso amor por que para mi, mi vida no tenía valor.

Me quería morir, yo ya no existir, de este mundo huir, y no poder seguir con esa vida que me causaba la vergüenza que la sociedad me había dicho que yo era, y seguía existiendo, vendiendo e intercambiando mi cuerpo y algunas veces hasta regalando mi cuerpo para poder subsistir, en las esquinas de la calle, las doce, una, dos, tres, cuatro, cinco, seis, siete de la mañana, la gente pasaba, me señalaba, se burlaba, murmuraba, me maltrataba, atacaba . . . los niñ@s a la escuela en grupo marchaban, me veían, entre ellos burlas hacían, de mí se reían, sin darse cuenta que yo por dentro ya no existía . . . pero yo en esa esquina seguía con la esperanza de que alguien por mi vendría y se acercaría, me rescataría, de mi miseria me sacaría, darme de comer me daría una cama donde poder descansar me ofrecería y una ducha donde tomar me ofrecería por que yo sabía que la llegada de la noche nadie la podía parar y en esa misma esquina yo me volvería a encontrar para poder seguir buscando el amor deseado, el amor que yo tenía que esperar . . .

Así seguí, como un robot funcionaba, sin sentimientos, sin dolor, sin en mi cara color, en mi alma con mucho ardor, por que mi vida era puro furor al yo pensar que al huir y poder descubrir que yo al ser yo ya podría vivir sin importar lo que mi familia iba a decir y que no me importaba si me iban a condenar, culpar, juzgar, desheredar, maltratar, rechazar, pero la sorpresa fui a encontrar que a donde siempre fui a terminar, la gente en las calles me iba a atacar, rechazar, juzgar, marginalizar y hasta golpear por querer poder de alguna manera mi vida empezar ... sin tener que recordar que hasta ese entonces mi vida había sido puro pesar ... pero no había para donde correr, solo con la esperanza que el anochecer me daría lo que buscaba, la manera de coexistir, persistir, subsistir, resistir, para de alguna manera poder vivir, y así continúe mi vivir, fumando piedra, inyectándose heroína, cocaína, metanfetamina, sin importarme lo que el destino para mi tendría ...

El crack, cocaína, yo pensaba era mi heroína, heroína que entraba en mis venas, que quemaba pero me gustaba, que me hacía sentir lo que yo añoraba, y aunque mi mente estaba distorsionada, yo así funcionaba, y cantaba, reía, gritaba, bailaba, y muchas veces viéndome en el espejo me miraba, fumando esa pipa a la cual yo estaba condenada, y miraba a mis ojos en lo más profundo, y podía ver el vacío que tenia en mi ser y sentía, veía, sufría al ver como yo más me hundía, a mi dolor, a mi vicio a mi escape, a mi busca por ese imposible y falso amor ... y con ese dolor, condenada a seguir institucionalizada, como presa, como carnada, me encerraban, me esculcaban, me ultrajaban, me violaban, sexualmente y dentro en mi mente como una corriente esas imágenes continuamente se narraban y navegaban como un barco sin destino, como un blanco sin tino, como un pájaro sin un nido ... Yo esas imágenes borrar trataba, pero yo sabia que estaba condenada, no solo a estar encerrada, encerrada en esa prisión de barras de acero, en jaulas de asbestos y baños de acero que frio se sentía en mi cuero y en mi trasero, pero mi trasero se confortaba después de que fui violada por ese hombre que con una navaja en el cuello me murmuro un te quiero, y sin poner luchar cedí a que se comiera mi alma, como un lobo se come a un cordero y cada penetración de su verga sentía en mi trasero, con cada estrujo sentía como cada mordida que el lobo me daba y me dominaba y de mi se apoderaba, pero en el fondo con mi tercer ojo, veía y pedía, seguir viviendo yo quería y la navaja en mi cuello sentía y pensaba que en mi cuello esa navaja se enterraría pero me alentaba diciéndome que ya pronto al final del túnel llegaría y que al otro lado la luz encontraría, a mi misma me veía, y sonreía por que sabia que las heridas de las mordidas del lobo pronto pasarían . . .

Y así seguí, institucionalizada en la prisión por el estado fui ultrajada, violada, amordazada, golpeada por mi propia gente fui condenada y me preguntaba ¿donde ser yo podría? Si en mi familia no me querían, el Dios que yo conocía no existía, las drogas que me aliviaban ya no tenia llegaron al punto que ni en la prisión yo ya no cabía y me preguntaba entonces, ¿Qué quieren de mi, culeros? Si en la prisión todos son embusteros, dicen que me repugnan pero cuando apagan la luz me buscan, su pinga me enseñan, sexo me ofrecen como si yo por tener sexo estuviera deseosa, pero la verdad me hicieron sentir una Diosa, y pude sentir que era el momento de resistir, de decir basta de sus maltratos, de sus insultos de sus achaques . . . La venada salió a resaltar y cuando otro hombre de mi se quiso aprovechar tuve que saltar y las baterías en un calcetín tuve que emplazar para poder demostrar que ya no iba a tolerar lo que por mucho tiempo a mi me tuvo que pasar, la cabeza a ese hombre le fui a quebrar para poder demostrar que conmigo ya no iban a jugar, ni su burla iba a continuar sin yo saber que por defenderme por seis meses me iban a apartar, en una celda sola me iban a aislar, sin poder salir a comer, caminar, aire puro poder respirar por que mi audiencia con el comandante tenia que esperar, para que ellos pudieran determinar si era yo a la que tenían que culpar por la agresión que al hombre le causó malestar que segura estoy de que en su vida de mi se va a acordar y cuenta se va a dar y dos veces la va a tener que pensar cuando a alguien como yo trate de chingar, abusar, reprimir, maltratar, pero mientras, mi futuro tengo que esperar para que puedan determinar lo que conmigo va a pasar, lo que me queda por el momento poder pensar en que es lo que voy a hacer para que loca no me pueda volver, sin mucho que hacer la decisión tuve que tomar de un libro de ingles agarrar y ponerme a leer, sin poder entender y mi miedo vencer por que si no hago algo mi mente de mi toma poder, por que mi mente es un torbellino que trae con el esas imágenes que por mi mente no dejan de pasar con un dolor en mi pecho que no me deja respirar, esas imágenes de sangre que en el piso vi antes de que me llenaran los ojos de spray de chile que a ciegas me dejo, y el aire me corto, me sofocaba, me torturaba, lo único que escuchaba eran las sirenas de esa alarma que retumbaba los tímpanos de mis oídos . . . hasta que al fin termine en solitud, sola con mi soledad, con mi verdad, al escuchar cuando me decían los otros compañeros que hacerme su esposa querían y que como una reina me tratarían . . . y así seguía con mi nostalgia, con mi alegría perdida, asustada, traumada, intrigada sin saber lo que a mi me esperaba . . . hasta que al fin pude salir, de ese infierno huir, a la población general me dijeron después de seis meses de ese pesar, y como olvidar esos meses vacíos, en solitud, en esclavitud, esclavitud del estado . . . para tapar mi dolor en el juego de hándbol me refugie, tratando de esconder, para ya no yo poder saborear el dolor que marcaba mi pesar, me hice muy buena en la cancha de la pared tercera, y los hombres me odiaban y se decían a si mismos, "¿cómo es que este pinche puto me pueda ganar?" y así yo les demostraba que para jugar las bolas buena yo era . . . nueve meses ahí me quede . . .

Me transportaron a otra prisión, cuando ellos descubrieron la enfermedad maldecida que yo traía, que a otros reos yo contagiaría si en esa prisión me dejaran, que no había lugar para alguien como yo, que a una facilidad medica me llevarían porque tenia que ser separada, apartada, una vez más marginada . . . catorce horas de camino, inmenso, intenso fue el recorrido con esposas en mis piernas, en mis brazos, ese recorrido me hizo pedazos, ni los gritos de otros reos, atajantes, arrogantes me hacían olvidar, de que mi corazón cargaba mucho penar . . . A la prisión en el norte me trasladaron y el amor de mi vida fue capturado, Bobby me valoro, amor me dio, como nunca había sabido yo, su amor me entrego a mi todo me dio, a pesar de la discriminación que el recibía por otros reos, y la policía, sin importarle Bob su amor me daría . . .

Así seguí viviendo, de la prisión entrando y saliendo, doce años de mi vida consumiendo, dentro y fuera como un rehilete que da vueltas sin sentido, sin algún lugar dirigido, y seguí conociendo que la vida para mi era un cuento, un cuento de terror, con muchos encuentros de temor, temor a morir, temor a no poder descubrir lo que la vida en mi podía cubrir, navegando las calles, a lo que yo ya me había acostumbrado, porque hasta entonces en mi vida yo nada había logrado, en las calles vagaba como alguien que nos es nada más que un desgraciado.

Cocaína fumaba, eso el dolor me apagaba mientras yo vagaba, y me inyectaba heroína y cocaína y agua sucia en las calles del centro de los Ángeles yo recogía para inyectarme lo que en mis venas correría, por que nada me importaba, amigos no tenía, solo gente que sacar provecho de mi quería, lo que fuera, mi cuerpo, mi droga, mi esperanza, mi tormento . . . sobredosis de heroína, tirada en un callejón me fueron a encontrar, la ambulancia me fue a salvar y me hizo recordar que en si mi vida nada valía, pero en mi una chispa de luz me decía, que algo yo tendría que hacer con mi vida, por que aunque nadie mi vida a la gente pura madre les valía, un Ángel me estaba protegiendo . . .

Hasta que llegó ese día que mi Ángel de mi guarda se me aparecería, y me diría que en esta vida yo valía, que hiciera algo, ¿y yo preguntaba? ¿Que puedo hacer, si no se hacer nada más que sobrevivir en las calles, sobrevivir en la prisión, hacer drogas, vender mi cuerpo, hacer crimen? ¿Que puedo hacer si solo hasta sexto año de primaria he ido? Nadie me quiere, nadie me estima, ni mi familia, la sociedad me mira como si yo fuera una basura, como alguien que no tiene cordura, como un costal sin costura, como alguien que tiene que vivir con censura por que mi existir les causa agruras y me señalan, me golpean, me apalean . . .

Sin yo poder percibir que todo mi Ángel ya lo tenia planeado, como un arquitecto marca su plano, construyendo su plan bien destacado, y me deje llevar, a ese sueño el cual yo no sabia donde iba a terminar, y me deje llevar a donde tenía que llegar, a un centro de rehabilitación fui a parar, en donde mi vida iba a empezar, el principio de una vida la cual nunca me podía imaginar, al despertar de esa pesadilla que llenaba mi pesar, arduo trabajo y lágrimas tuve que derramar y formar un concepto de un poder superior determinar para yo poder comprender, entender, emprender el propósito en mi vida que mi Ángel tenía concebida . . . resistir mi existir tuve que inferir, transfobia en ese centro tuve que combatir para yo poder subsistir, en la escuela me enrole para yo poder entender que no sabía nada en la vida, que tenía que aprender otra manera de vida, la escuela, computación, desesperación, aferramiento, tristeza y depresión experimente con esas clases y en ese salón por que lo que aprendía no entendía, pero me aferre, a ese libro agarre y lo tuve que leer para poder aprender, tarea, lectura, escritura, mecanografía . . .

Sin ninguna experiencia, de justicia social una agencia, vio en mi clemencia y por medio de mi Ángel me mando otro Ángel con un nombre de santa, su nombre María, quien estaba llena de alegría, y esperanza me daría, al creer que yo algún día podría hacer lo que yo no creía, por mi ella abogaría para que el empleo que era para mi se me daría . . . pero en un día la historia de mi vida cambiaria por que un atroz y horroroso crimen ocurriría, la muerte de Gwen Araujo mi vida marcaria, por que el asesinato de Gwen Araujo el fondo me tocaría, me pude ver a mi misma, como yo había sido asesinada por la sociedad con anterioridad, pero Gwen su historia no podría contar . . . en cambio yo, estaba aun con vida, pensando, analizando, interpretando lo que había pasado y que podría hacer . . . empecé a organizar, con mis otras hermanas trans que cansadas estaban de ver como nos tratan, de ver como nos maltratan, de ver como nos matan, y empezamos a marchar, nuestras voces y gritos a alzar, para poder alcanzar la justicia social que como seres humanos habíamos haber recibido, pero todo era mentira, nadie escuchaba, todos nos ignoraban, no había plan, no teníamos educación, no teníamos salvación . . .

Con el apoyo de mis hermanas trans seguí con la lucha que parecía no avanzaba, parecía que estaba estancada, me daba cuenta que mis palabras se las llevaba el viento cuando después de aprender a hablar decía: "paren la injusticia" dejen de agredirnos, dejen de matarnos, dejen de encarcelarnos, pero mis gritos, palabras, halagos, eran ignorados por las personas que pueden hacer la diferencia en nuestra comunidad, toda su ignorancia era por que mis palabras no tenían peso de educación, que en esos momentos eran como una maldición, me oían pero no me escuchaban, al contrario me ignoraban . . . hasta que decidí que a la escuela tenía que ir para que al fin mi voz se pudiera oír, escuchar, por mi comunidad abogar, pero el reto fue que en esa organización la cual la oportunidad me dio, sus puertas me cerró al negarme la oportunidad de poder progresar, por lo tanto yo tuve que pensar, en que era lo que el futuro me iba a esperar si yo dejaba ese trabajo al cual yo le tenía mucho amor, agradecimiento y compasión por que por primera vez en mi vida mis hermanas trans en esa agencia compartían conmigo sus experiencias de sobrevivencia y yo alzaba sus voces con la mía...

Mi Ángel nuevamente se vino a manifestar, cuando la oportunidad se vino a presentar y me anime a otra agencia aplicar, entrevistar y al final la decisión de huir de la agencia que me había dado la oportunidad, porque también me empezó a marginalizar, yo pude ver la verdad, cuando me di cuenta que todo era mentira y que yo simplemente era un parapeto para todos ellos quienes decían que la comunidad trans les importaba, que ellos cambios hacer querían pero de su boca salía pura porquería por que en realidad lo que querían era mantenernos en el margen de donde nunca ninguna de nosotras de ahí saldría... pero que se puede esperar, si trabajo para nosotras no hay, y si nos dan una oportunidad, no la podemos dejar por que nuestra única solución es volver a las calles, es por eso que para muchas de nosotras es preferible recibir maltratos de los que nos emplean que de la gente que nos encontramos en la calle, por lo menos algunos de nuestros patrones no nos golpean físicamente, pero si nos golpean en la mente, ni tampoco nuestros patrones nos matan físicamente, pero si nos matan el espíritu...

Un Nuevo Ángel a mi vida se vino a presentar con el nombre de Miguel quien en esta nueva agencia la oportunidad se me iba a dar, de poder demostrar de lo que yo podía lograr, y un programa pude realizar, para poder amplificar las vidas de la comunidad joven trans, que hasta entonces la gente no podía ver o valer como se lo han de merecer, para que estos jóvenes trans reconocidos pudieran ser, es así como surgió Angels of Change... Angels of Change fue una creación que fue creada no solo por necesidad, pero fue algo que nació de mi corazón, Angels of Change les daba la oportunidad a jóvenes trans de poder desenvolverse, desarrollarse, desempeñarse y poder realizarse. Angels of Change es un proyecto en el cual jóvenes trans muestran su amor por sí mismos, pero también muestran amor y compasión a su propia comunidad por que por su participación compensan a otras personas jóvenes que no pueden su salud valer por la falta de documentos, aseguranza como lo suelen poner . . . Angels of Change ha marcado la vida de muchas personas jóvenes trans, que en la historia han de quedar y hasta un documental se pudo crear, para poder alzar, las vidas y las experiencias de muchas personas jóvenes trans. Angels of Change fue uno de mis bebes, pero como todo bebe crece, llegó el momento en el que le tuve que dejar ir, con la esperanza que otras personas pudieran seguir levantando las vidas de personas jóvenes trans . . .

Ocho años pude desempeñar y poder realizar y levantar y a un nivel nacional poder llevar la clínica para la cual yo tuve el privilegio de poder dirigir y comandar . . . pero mi vida cambio, mi liderazgo, abogacía y hambre de crecer, de esa agencia tuve mi persona que remover por que había fuerzas que estaban en contra de mi, de mi crecer . . . Mi Ángel nuevamente se volvió a aparecer para que yo pudiera ver que el final en esa agencia había llegado a ser, otros senderos que me esperaban, como un barco espera en un crucero, esperando como la novia espera al cartero, sin yo darme cuenta que otro capitulo estaba destinado en mi vida . . . Sin darme cuenta, hice lo que mi Ángel me sugirió, tomar el riesgo de lanzarme al vuelo como un vaquero se avienta al ruedo sin importarme que lo que vendría primero por que mi fe era lo que me decía que todo iba a estar bien, que la estabilidad si se puede lograr, lo trabajoso es poder mantenerse, con en alto la frente, y no ser incoherente, porque el que se porta bien, bien le va, y hasta el momento yo ya pague todo lo que se pudo considerar fuera malo, mi sobrevivencia es mi única experiencia que tal vez nadie la puede entender, pero yo sí la entiendo y también la entienden esas personas que la siguen viviendo . . . Ahora me encuentro en este capítulo en mi vida, en el proceso de seguir destacando, de seguir creciendo, creando el Centro de Prevención para la Violencia y el Bienestar Transgenero.[1] Estoy formando este lugar, el cual en un futuro las personas trans van a poder llamar hogar, paraíso, ese lugar a donde todas las personas que sean trans o se identifiquen en el espectro, puedan decir que este es el lugar al cual esas personas pertenecen, por que la suciedad de la sociedad continúa achacándonos, condenándonos, matándonos . . . Este es el lugar el cual va a poder derribar esas estructuras que continúan infligiendo la violencia para con las personas trans, es en este centro en el cual las personas trans van a poder mirarse a los ojos y valorarse una a otra, sin temor, sin que a nadie le falte amor . . . este es el camino en el cual yo me encuentro hoy en día, el camino que mi Ángel ha creado para mi, solo para mi . . .

A través de los años me he desarrollado, he crecido, he triunfado, y he creado programas y organizaciones, en conferencias discursos he dado, talleres de capacitación he mostrado, mi historia en una película he narrado, de la universidad con una maestría me he graduado, me he destacado y he demostrado que una persona como yo si puede haberse despertado de esa pesadilla que en sueño se ha realizado.

The Dream Never Dreamed

Here I am, reflecting on what yesterday was my childhood. Thinking about what I wanted to be, when I grew up, when I was old enough, when I could depend on myself, and I asked myself, *How will I be?* Early dreams of immaturity, early dreams with an impossible vision. I could not see. The reality is that my future I could not see, who or what I could be. In my childhood, my priority was to help my mother feed us, help her provide for us. Finding work was what at that moment I had to achieve. I had to be able to give, to contribute, to be able to subsist so that in the near future my existence could have worth, to be able to resist that life that caused me intrigue.

Going to school to study, with the hope that someday I could overcome, achieve, achieve what no one in my family had ever been able to, to advance the social ladder, to climb, and hold on to that ladder and climb, as a climber who clings with his nails to that wall that gives him support so he would not fall into the abyss. I needed to obtain, with hard work, a better quality of life, to be triumphant, to fight, to mark history, to liberate, to surpass, and to demonstrate that poverty can be replaced, that pressure in my chest. I wanted to crawl under the bed. Call it home. My childhood was taken, stolen, sexualized, raped, betrayed, distorted, confused, frustrated, exploited, muted, erased, forgotten. I lived enslaved and exploited.

It was child labor for the benefit of those who had the power over me and who would do anything to me, bring trauma to my mind.

In a butcher shop, on the corner from my house, in the middle of the intersections, my life was marked. It marked the intersections that I was living. The owners of the butcher shop, those men who placed me on the butcher's table, saw my femininity, thought about how they could sexually take advantage of me. I was placed on that cutting table. I saw the blades of the meat cutter moving from top to bottom in slow motion as I heard the men who told me that if I would not give in to their sexual desires I would end up in pieces. And I saw the saw those blades moving from top to bottom as if it was a guide that marked, dictated, and said that my life was worth nothing, and in those very moments, I could see my life disappear, sink as if I were sinking in a swamp of quicksand with no way out, where nobody would have listened to me even though I begged, cried, cried with impotence. And my soul with no more strength, without being able to get rid of those men who held me with all their strength, I begged for them not to hurt me, that I would do what they wanted me to do to them and make their sexual fantasies a reality as I implored for them to spare my life and keep me alive. However, I had already seen through those cutting blades, that on the inside, I was already dead . . .

Until at last, one day, I learned that inhaling strong glue would make me forget my reality, that through it, I could find the love I was looking for, not only because it made me forget everything but also because it gave me that ecstatic feeling that would run through my body when I inhaled glue. My mind wandered, my body trembled, my skin filled with each inhale. The feeling set me free from my reality. I thought that with each inhale of this divine glue, I found the love that I was seeking. That is how I grew up, through my nostrils, every inhale of glue or activator solution gave me courage. I felt that the glue gave me another life and that I could hide what I had inside, that no one could see what I was carrying within me because to the world I showed another reality—a show, a false reality, confused, disturbed, marginalized, and all I had were lies, because to live my truth would mean to be shamed, doomed, marginalized, finished, rejected, and tortured.

My adolescence was misunderstood, unnurtured, and the system robbed me of my adolescence. It was stolen, martyred, beaten, gagged, with no opportunity, no place to go, no one to go to when I needed help, when I needed to scream, to scream and say, *I do need love.* I needed to be a person with clarity. I needed to exist and have hope. I needed to see what I saw in that dream, a dream I had on that late afternoon in my childhood. Even though it is a blurry dream, my dream would continue to be there—alive—my dream was of being a good person who didn't have to change who I truly was. I was living a thousand lives, a thousand lies, a thousand identities but at the same time not even one . . . My adolescent life was tainted, blotched, crushed, broken, distorted, but I wanted to laugh. I wanted to share, and in the promised land, I wanted to live . . . to get there, to reach, to discover, to pursue, subsist . . . I wanted to go to that place where everyone lived, where everyone spoke, where everyone laughed . . . It was that place that I did not know, that I didn't know existed, while I was living life with a dead soul . . .

Living my thousand identities, hiding my truths, hiding my life, doing evil things, hoping that love would reach my palate, taste it. I wanted to be touched, to be held, squeezed . . . to be squeezed with so much strength until I could no longer endure, because I no longer wanted to miss that love. I hoped, missed, wished for that love to come . . . But in the meantime, I continued to endure the injustices that I experienced from society, putting up with and surviving sexual violence from the police and men who wanted to have sex with me, sometimes for money, sometimes with deceptions and promises of false love.

This caused me rage for the love I sought, that love that I idolized, the love that I longed for . . . and what I received and expected was mistreatment, imprisonment, attacks, ailments but also outrages . . . Because of who I was they looked at me, they pointed at me, they mocked me and sometimes even beat me. In their eyes I was a rare thing, I was someone despicable. I was someone miserable, someone nobody wanted to be compared to, because my life was marked by the filth of society in which I was forced to live during my adolescence. In order to subsist and resist, I ceased to exist. Inhaling glue would get me away from any argument that existed in my thinking. And so I lived like this until finally I could flee from my reality, from my truth, from what I wanted to hide because they told me that I was evil, false, stubborn, anxiety, malaise. They told me that my existence caused them regret until I ended up north, fleeing from my truth, with the hope of finding love, the love that I was always looking for, because at seventeen years of age I was not able to find what love really was. Because of that my body, my mind and soul were disturbed, tormented, traumatized, outraged ...

It is true that I existed in the body, but inside I was dead. But I lived with hope, the hope of being able to see my father, the man who gave me life. Although he did not see me grow up, I thought that maybe I could be happy near him. But I did not know what my future would bring. The new country in which I lived was a country I did not know, another language, other people, another way of life. I would have to acclimate and continue to hide who I really was. I was scared of my father's rejection when he learned that the love I had received up until that point had been through sex. With every man I got to know, sex, sex was what kept me attached. *That* was the love that I was given, it was the love that I inherited, it was the kind of love that was passed on to me. I had to build a way for me to survive, through patience, a place of subsistence. I had to stay, had to make my own way despite experiencing labor exploitation in the North, in el norte, and curses from the gabachos. I had to listen without being able to respond because the language of the gueros I could not speak.

Still a teen and in the fight, in the search for love, what I found was cocaine and heroin. Many times, it was the combination of both substances, because I wanted to feel that love that motivated me, the love that made me forget my sorrows, that made me forget my way of being, the way I would think, but what in those moments I saw was that in reality I could not be who I was destined to be, because what existed in my head, in my mind, in my soul, and in my heart was disillusionment that would tell me that who I was was not right. If I wanted the love of my father, I had to live without compassion for myself and for others who looked like me. So I behaved like an unscrupulous person, without principles, with much shame about who I was destined to be.

When I finally found out that I could not live out that lie, the one I had lived all my life, I had to decide. I had to venture, to see what fate might have in place for me, a place to love me and not to mistreat me, for me to be able to get to that place where I could begin brand new, where everything would vanish, to forget my past, my martyrdom, my sorrow . . .

When I arrived in Los Angeles, I found betrayal. I discovered an attraction that became my perdition. I continued on and on looking for love in what I already knew. It was the AIDS era, and I put my life at risk with syringes and unprotected sex when my mind would tell me "sex, drugs, rock and roll" as I looked for that false love because my life had no value.

I wanted to die, no longer exist, and flee from this world. I could not continue with a life that caused me the shame that society had placed on me. I kept on existing, selling and exchanging my body, sometimes even giving my body away to survive. I was on street corners at twelve, one, two, three, four, five, six, and seven in the morning. People would pass by. They pointed, mocked, murmured, mistreated me. They attacked me. Groups of children marching on their way to school would see, make fun of me among them, laugh at me. They didn't realize that inside I was no longer existing . . .

I continued to stay on that corner because I had the hope that someone would get close, that someone would come for me, that someone would save me, rescue me from my misery, that someone would feed me some food and provide a place to rest my head on a real bed, that someone would offer me where to clean up, because I knew that on night's arrival, no one would stop, and on that same corner I would find myself again continuing to search for love, the love that I had been longing for . . .

So I continued. I functioned as a robot, without feelings, without pain, without color in my face, in my soul, so much pain, because my life was nothing but rage. I continued to think that if I ran away, I could live my life no matter what my family would say. I did not care if they would condemn, blame, judge, disinherit, mistreat, reject me. But to my surprise, I was to find that anywhere and everywhere I went people in the streets would attack me, reject me, judge me, marginalize me, and even beat me for wanting my life, wanting to start over, and I couldn't forget that at that point my life had been nothing but regret . . . I wanted to start all over, but there was nowhere to run. The only hope that I had was that night was near, and it would give me what I was looking for, a way of coexisting, persisting, resisting, a way to somehow be able to live. And I continued to live that way, smoking crack, injecting heroin, cocaine, meth, not even caring for what fate would have for me . . .

Crack cocaine was my heroin, heroin that would penetrate my veins. It burned, but I loved it. It made me feel what I was longing for, and although my mind was distorted, that's the way I would function. I would sing. I would shout. I would dance, and many times I would see myself in the mirror, smoking that pipe that had doomed me. I would look into my eyes, deep into my eyes, and I could see the emptiness I had in my being, and I felt, I saw myself sinking more and more into my pain and into my addiction. In my search for that false and impossible love I found an escape. In pain, condemned to remain institutionalized, as prey, as bait, I was locked up, I was scoured, insulted, raped. In my mind, like a stream, these images were continually narrated, and I navigate them like a ship without destiny, as a target without a bull's-eye, like a bird without a nest I tried to erase those images, but I knew that I was condemned to be locked up in that prison of steel bars, in cells that were concrete cages and bathrooms of stainless steel, cold against my skin and on my ass. I was sexually assaulted by a man who softly whispered I love you in my ear while he held a razor blade. Without a fight, I let him eat my soul, like a wolf eats a lamb. Every penetration of his hard dick, felt on my back, with each stroke, I felt every bite of the wolf. He had dominated me. I was seized. Deep down with my third eye, I could see, and I asked him to allow me to live. I felt the razor blade on my neck, knowing it might soon be buried inside, but I would encourage myself by saying that really soon, at the end of the tunnel, I would see the light. I would find the light. I would see myself, and I would smile, because I knew that the wounds of wolf's bites would soon pass.

And so I continued, institutionalized. In the state prison, I was robbed, raped, gagged, beaten. I was condemned by my own people, and I wondered and asked myself, *Where can I be myself?* If my family did not love me, the God that I knew did not exist. I did not have the drugs that relieved me, and it got to the point that I did not even fit in in prison. I would ask myself, *What the fuck do you assholes want?* because they were all fucking liars in there. They said that they hated me, but when they turned off the lights, they sought me, they wanted me, they showed me their dicks, offered me sex as if I was desperate to have it. But the truth is that they also made me feel as if I was a goddess, and I felt that it was the moment to resist, to say enough of their mistreatment, of their insults, of the injustice. The swift deer inside me jumped out one day when another man wanted to take advantage of my body. I hit him with two large batteries I placed inside a pair of socks. I showed them that I would not tolerate what had been happening to me for a long time. I had to crack open his head to be able to prove that they no longer were going to play with me and be ridiculed. Little did I know that because I defended myself I was placed in a cell for six months, away from everyone else. I was deemed a troublemaker and thrown in a single cell. I was isolated and unable to go out to eat, walk, or breathe fresh air. In the meantime, I had to wait for my hearing and for a decision about whether I was the one to be blamed for the assault that I was forced to enact on that man who wanted to hurt me. I know I caused him pain, and I am sure he is going to remember me for life. I know he must think twice now about messing with someone like me. While I waited to see what my future would bring, I just had to wait it out. I had to wait while they determined what would happen to me. I thought, *What I have to do now is to think about what I'm going to do so that I don't go crazy.* Without much of a choice I grabbed a book in English and forced myself to read. I was unable to understand what it said, but if I did not do something, I would for sure lose my mind. I lay on the bed with pain in my chest, a pain that did not let me breathe. My mind was a whirlwind that brought back images of blood on the floor, right before the guards filled my eyes with pepper spray and left me momentarily blind. These images running through my mind did not stop. The air that I breathed, congested with hate, filled my lungs, suffocating me. It tortured me. At that moment, during the fight that had led me to solitary confinement, the only thing I heard were the sirens of an alarm that echoed in my eardrums until I passed out and ended up in isolation. I was alone in my loneliness, sat with my truth, listening to all the inmates saying that they would make me their wife, that they would treat me right as the queen that I am. And so I continued with my nostalgia, my joy lost, scared, traumatized, intrigued, not knowing what I was waiting for . . . Finally, at last I was able to leave that hell. After six months in solitude they said I would be transferred to the general population, six months of that regret, six empty months. How to forget solitude and enslavement by the state . . . To cover my pain, I took refuge in the game of handball. I was trying to hide so that I could no longer taste the pain that marked my regret. I became really good on the court of three walls, but men hated me. They would say to themselves, "How is it that this fucking faggot can beat me?" To me that was the way that I would show all of these "men" that I knew how to play ball well. Nine months I stayed in that place . . .

I was then transported to another prison when they discovered the cursed disease I had. They said that there was no place for someone like me there and that I would infect other inmates if I stayed. I was taken to a medical facility because I need to be separated and secluded once more. Marginalized again. Fourteen hours on the road, the route intense. My legs, my arms were shackled. That journey cut me to shreds. The cries or the insults of the other inmates weren't enough to make me forget that my heart was heavy with much pain . . .

I was transferred to a prison in the northern part of the state. There, the love of my life was captured. Bobby valued me, gave me love as never before I had known. He gave me everything, even though he was also discriminated against and harassed by his homeboys and by the guards. Without caring what anything anyone had to say, Bob gave me his love . . .

Thus, I continued to live, in and out of prison, fourteen years of my life consumed, inside and outside like a pinwheel that turns without meaning, without direction. I continued to live, life for me was a story, a horror story, with many incidents of fear, fear of dying, fear of not being able to know what life had in store for me. I navigated the streets, something that I already had become accustomed to, because up until then I had achieved nothing, my life had no meaning . . . On the streets I wandered like someone who is nothing, like someone who is a nobody.

Smoking cocaine helped me lower the pain I was living with. I smoked as I wandered the streets, injected heroin and cocaine fixed with dirty water that I found on the streets of downtown LA, because I did not care. I did not have friends. People only wanted to take advantage of me, of my body, my drugs, my hope, my torment . . . Heroin overdose. I found myself lying in an alley. The ambulance came, saved me, and reminded me that my life was worth nothing. But a spark of light inside me told me something. That I had to do something with my life, because although I felt like my life meant nothing to anyone, an angel was close to me, an angel was protecting me.

Until that day that my guardian angel would appear to me and tell me that my life had worth, that I needed to do something, and I asked, What can I do? I don't know how to do anything but survive on the streets, survive in prison, do drugs, sell my body, do crime . . . What can I do if I only finished up to sixth grade? What can I do if nobody loves me, nobody likes me, not even my family? If society looks at me as if I am trash, like someone who has no sanity, like a seamless sack, like someone who has to live in censorship because my existence causes them headaches, and they point me out, they beat me, they hit me. What can I do?

Without me perceiving that my angel had it all planned out already, like an architect that makes his sketch, building his plan well highlighted and detailed, I let myself go to that dream despite not knowing where I was going to end up. I let myself go until I ended up at a rehabilitation center. I ended up where my life was to begin, the beginning of a life that I would have never imagined. Waking up from that nightmare that filled my heart, I had to let go of the tears and form a concept of a higher power for me to learn, to understand, to undertake the purpose my angel had designed for me. I had to resist. I had to fight transphobia in that center so that I could survive. I signed up for school so I could understand that I did not know anything in life, that I had to learn another way of life— school and computers. I experienced desperation, clinging, sadness, and depression in those classrooms because I did not understand what I was learning. But I held on, gave that book a good grip, and read so I could learn, do homework. Reading, writing, typing...

Without any experience in social justice, an agency saw something in me and through my angel sent me another angel with the name of a saint. María is her name. Full of joy, she gave me hope and believed that someday I could do something. Even though I did not know it then, she advocated for me so that I could get the job that was destined for me. One day the story of my life changed when a horrible crime happened. The death of Gwen Araujo marked my life. The death of Gwen Araujo touched me deep in my soul. I could see myself how *I* had been murdered by society before, but Gwen could not tell *her* story. I was still alive, thinking, analyzing, trying to understand what happened and what I could do. I began to organize with my other trans sisters who were tired of seeing how they treat us, how they mistreat us, how they kill us, and we started to march, our voices with chants we raised, to try to achieve the social justice that as human beings we were supposed to receive. But everything was a lie. Nobody listened. Everyone ignored us. There was no plan. We had no education. We had no salvation.

With the support of my trans sisters I continued the fight that seemed not to advance. It seemed as if it was stagnant, it did not seem to go anywhere, I realized that my words were gone with the wind, even after learning to speak I would say: "Stop the injustice. Stop attacking us. Stop killing us, stop putting us in jail." But my words, my begging and screaming were ignored by the very people who can make a difference in our community. All of their ignorance was because my words did not have the weight of education. In those very moments my words were like a curse. They would hear me, but they did not listen to me. On the contrary, they ignored me. I decided that I had to go school so that at the very least my voice could be listened to. I had to plea for my community, but unfortunately, the very same organization that gave me the opportunity closed its doors on me. They denied me the opportunity to progress, so I had to think about what was in store for me in my future. I had much love, gratitude, and compassion for that job because it was the very first time in my life that my trans sisters in that agency shared with me their experiences of survival, and I would uplift their voices with mine.

My angel came and whispered again. When an opportunity came about, I was encouraged to apply to another agency. I had an interview and finally made the decision to leave from the agency that had given me the opportunity, yes, but it also was a place where my trans sisters and I were marginalized. I could see the truth now. When I realized that everything was a lie and that I was simply a barrier for all of them who said that they cared for the trans community, that they wanted to make changes, but what came out of their mouth was sheer crap. The reality was that they only wanted to keep us on the margins where none of us would ever get out. But what can we expect when work is scarce for us? If they give us a chance, we cannot leave it, because our only solution to our exploitation is to return to the streets. That is why for many of us it is preferable to receive mistreatment from those who employ us than from the people we meet on the streets. At least some of our employers do not beat us physically, we think. However, they do beat us mentally. Our bosses do not kill us physically, but they do kill our spirit.

A new angel came to my life and presented himself with the name of Miguel. In this new agency I was given the opportunity to demonstrate what I could achieve. I designed a program that would amplify the lives of young trans people. Until then, people could not see how these beautiful trans youth deserved to be recognized. This is how Angels of Change came to be. Angels of Change was created because of a need, but it came from the heart. Angels of Change is a project in which young trans people show their love for themselves but also for others. This program gave young trans people the opportunity to develop as human beings, show love and compassion to their own community, and through their participation compensate for other young people who cannot and who do not have the access to health care due to lack of documentation or insurance. Angels of Change has boosted the lives and experiences of many young trans people. A documentary was created in order to make sure it is part of the trans historical record. Angels of Change was one of my babies, but as every baby grows, the time came when I had to let it go, hoping that other people could continue to uplift the lives of young trans people.

I was there for eight years and was able to perform, to create, to transform. A good program was brought to a national platform, a program that I was in charge of. But my life changed, my leadership, my advocacy and hunger to grow. I had to leave that agency because there were forces that were against me, against seeing me grow. My angel again appeared. The angel appeared so that I could see that the end had arrived for me at that agency. Other paths awaited me, like a sailor waits for his ship. I waited, like a bride awaiting the postman to deliver a love letter. I waited, without me realizing that another chapter was written in my life. Without realizing it, I did what my angel suggested for me to do, to take a risk, like when I throw myself in a skydive, like a cowboy that challenges the bull in the arena. To take a risk without caring or thinking of what would come first, because my faith would tell me that everything was going to be okay, that stability can be achieved. The hard part is keeping up, with my head held high, and not being incoherent. Good comes to those who do well. I know that as of now, I have already paid for the wrong I did. My survival is my only experience. That, maybe no one can understand, but I do understand it. I also understand those people who continue to exist, to live, to breathe in a world that continues to kill us. And now here I am, in this new chapter of my life, continuing the process of bringing awareness. I continue to grow as I create the Center for Violence Prevention and Transgender Wellness.[2] I continue as I build this place, a future go-to for trans people, a place that trans people will be able to call a home, a paradise. This will be a place where all trans people or those who identify on the spectrum can say that that is the place where they can belong. Because this dirty society continues to belittle us, condemn us and kill us, this is the place that can bring down those structures that continue to inflict violence on trans people. In this center, trans people will be able to look into each other's eyes and value one another without fear, with no one missing out on love. This is where I am today, on the path my angel has created for me, just for me.

Over the years, I have developed. I have grown. I have succeeded. I have created programs and organizations, spoken at conferences, rallies, and colleges, facilitated trainings and workshops. My story has been told in a film. I graduated from college with a master's degree and excelled, and I showed that a person like me could be awakened from a nightmare that turned into a dream.

Notes

1. Center for Violence Prevention and Transgender Wellness es un centro que actualmente provee una multitud de programas de apoyo a la comunidad transgenero en Los Ángeles.

2. The Center for Violence Prevention and Transgender Wellness is a center that currently has a multitude of programs that support the transgender community in Los Angeles.

8

"¿Qué harás si algo me pasa?"

An ofrenda

NICHOLAS DURON

Sitting alone at a Japanese diner near Washington Square Park, mi amante sends me a Snap on my phone: "Queriéndote me ayuda quererme." I read it silently to myself, whisper it out loud. I take a picture of it before it disappears. I need time to understand the message, to translate and to process it, and I believe if I don't save it immediately, store it someplace safe where I can retrieve it later, I'll lose it forever and never discover its intended meaning. It's summer, about mid-June, and as I wait for my order of burger and fries I begin reading Benjamin Alire Sáenz's Aristotle and Dante Discover the Secrets of the Universe, *a book that mi amante once recommended to me and that he wanted to teach in his summer courses on queer Latina/o literature. This summer his class didn't meet the minimum student enrollment requirements, and so he's working at an ice cream shop near his apartment. He asks why I'm reading it, and even in a text message I can detect that he's slightly overwhelmed when I tell him that he'd mentioned it and that he liked it and that those reasons were enough. He texts me that he can't believe his feelings would matter to anyone, and, reading this, it breaks my heart.*

He and I met a few months earlier in April at a conference in New York for LGBTQ scholars of color. When I applied to the conference the winter before, I was inundated with uncertainties. I had just moved from San Antonio, Texas, to enroll in a graduate program in New York, where I was the only queer person of color in my cohort and, as far as I knew, the only Latinx student in the program. My entry into the program coincided with the department's first hires of scholars specializing in Latinx studies and Latinx literatures. This coincidence certainly came with doubts. While the pedigrees of my colleagues ranged from Cambridge to Columbia, I wondered if I really deserved to be in this space where I only dared to dream I could be. At department events I'd get asked embarrassing questions like, "What exactly *is* a Chih-caah-no? What do they write?," as though our history, our identity, or our art could be so easily consumed and digested during small talk along with the catering of wine and cheese platters that attended these occasions. I'd sit through courses in which I was among the few who would vocalize my agitation at dismissive statements made by white students about writers of color like, "I think Audre Lorde sounds naive here." I witnessed disheartening neoliberal nods as I explained to my colleagues who Cherríe Moraga and Emma Pérez were, how their works challenge our readings and class discussions, only to find that few, if any, of these quiet assenters would later cite or even read their works. In a word, I felt lost, and without the usual markers like family, longtime friends, food, familiar places where I had a history or about which I had a story I could tell, I moved through the city, inhabiting disorientation. I seemed nobody; nowhere resided in my chest.

What I desired at that conference more than anything was a community, to feel at home in a space created without thought of someone like me. By the time of the conference, this place-making enterprise had already been under way, though I was already at my lowest point. Rather than spend time on my coursework, reading and producing scholarship, or exploring and experiencing New York City's vast archive of art, culture, and activism, I spent most of my time partying at the gay bars of Brooklyn with my partner, whom I found to be struggling with addiction, in a peculiar effort to try to repair our deteriorating marriage. It was in these spaces that I made many deep and lasting friendships with some of the most ingenious and passionate minds of queer nightlife. I was privileged to observe some of the most creative productions and performances that I had only read about in queer literature. I saw my first drag shows and "boylesque" numbers, stripped almost naked at genderqueer and sex-positive parties, and listened to some of the most intellectually stimulating and nuanced discussions of pop culture while in between karaoke numbers or during the commercial breaks at viewing parties of our campy television favorites. These countless experiences later inspired me in my academic writing. But as the planning of my days and nights came to be organized around managing my time around drugs and alcohol, I lost my sense of time. I wasn't able to spend the hours per day required of a young scholar toward reading and writing. Instead I spent my days sleeping in or, when at class, quietly working through the evening's fights with my husband, some lasting until past dawn, or otherwise strategizing how I was to negotiate these unfamiliar cityscapes.

In December, as I was struggling to write my seminar papers, I reconnected with a friend and mentor I had made while a master's degree student in San Antonio, Norma Elia Cantú. I had written to Norma about some of my struggles, my recent commitment to the literatures and scholarship of Chicanx writers and the accompanying feelings of isolation and uncertainty. She was kind, offering me her advice and reassurance, which she continues to do for me today. One thing that struck me from our conversation was her reminding me that as she was doing her doctoral work there were no more than five or six scholars doing work in English literary studies on what we now call "Chicanx literature." I began to imagine what it must have been like to create a place for oneself when such a place must have seemed only imaginable. Whatever we mean when we talk about Chicanx literature, however complex its content and its contours, I know that it is, that it has a life and a history, and that there exists a community, however far away it seemed to me, who believes the lives of the people whom that literature is about have meaning and depth, and no justification is needed for why they deserve our attention. I felt hope that in my lostness this community was out searching to find me, to welcome me back home. I felt grateful to Norma and the others who came before me, for, as Gloria Anzaldúa once phrased it, doing the work that matters ("vale la pena"). I felt honored to be part of the generation of activists and scholars who continue their work today.

Norma further directed me to some of her friends and colleagues for whom the literatures of people of color were important, including telling me about La Casa Azul, a small but lively bookstore in East Harlem specializing in books by Latinx writers. I learned that its founder, Aurora Anaya-Cerda, began La Casa Azul as an online store in 2008 but that after a successful crowdfunding campaign, she opened a retail space a few years later in 2012. As Aurora loved to share in each event I attended, the store was more than just a retail space. By the time I learned about it, the store had already put on hundreds of events, from painting and poetry classes, to book readings and film screenings, to children's educational programs. The first event I attended was a reading called "Queer LA/NYC," featuring writings and performances by queer Latino artists from both the West and East Coasts. As I listened to poetry and watched the performances of these queer Chicanos and Latinos, I was reminded of Anzaldúa's *Borderlands / La Frontera*, in which she writes, "Yet leaving home I did not lose touch with my origins because *lo mexicano* is my system. I am turtle, where I go I carry 'home' on my back" (1987, 21). This being the first time I truly lived away from home, I began to perceive these words in a way I never understood before. Sure, even living away from the place of our origin, our experiences and memories of home live within us. We wear them in our very flesh. What was new to me was the embodied experience that carrying home on our back is not necessarily a comforting feeling, not only because for some home can be a site of trauma or loss or shame. To carry home on one's back is to place the familiar and the indeterminate in intimate contact with each other. In order to survive, to dwell within these opposing spaces, one is solicited to put home to work, to use one's own personal sense of place to transform the space around them. But to do so also entails an unsettling transformation of one's sense of home; it involves risk and uncertainty and, at least for me but I think also for others, a profound sense of feeling lost while still allowing that feeling to guide you toward some undetermined somewhere and potentially produce something meaningful. I returned to La Casa Azul again and again until its closure in 2016, and the memories and the people I came to know there I still carry with me on my back like home.

In order to alleviate the stress of schoolwork and the anxiety I felt because of my failing marriage, I took several steps that shifted the trajectory I thought life had determined for me. My first decision was to invite Norma to my school to read from her soon-to-be rerelease of her classic book, *Canícula: Snapshots of a Girlhood in La Frontera*. Having had a semester getting to know my department, I was able to get a sense of the kinds of resources available to students not only for travel but also for other related academic and social events, including hosting guest speakers. Within just a few short weeks I was able to secure funds to sponsor the event, to find a space for it, to design and print posters to advertise the event around campus, to create online event pages to advertise on social media, to arrange for catering, to book her hotel, and finally to set up and clean up the night of her reading. No one explains to you all the minutiae that go into planning an event and the time and energy you expend coordinating the many different and disconnected parties involved. Coupled with the support from faculty and administrators in my department, I was able to manage. Although only one English faculty member was in attendance—one of our new Latinx literature hires—I felt encouraged to see several English graduate students attend and to have staged what for many was their first encounter with Chicana literature. I felt empowered not only by the sheer sense of accomplishment for organizing the reading but also by being able to make a space for brown voices in what at the time felt like a univocal din of whiteness.

Hosting Norma became for me a way of identification, a way to make myself recognizable and relate to a larger Latinx community that I've always identified with but that was not always willing to identify with me. I remember one particular moment as a junior in high school as I was immersing myself in what I considered my father's language. A small group of boys who were migrants themselves or whose parents were migrants from México called me a faggot, a maricón, in Spanish to my face and accused me of not being *really* Mexican. This accusation was in part, I learned, because I do not speak even the somewhat broken Spanish of my father. Having a monolingual white mother, I only heard Spanish spoken by my father, his parents, and some older relatives on his side of the family. Most often Spanish was used by them to show affection, such as my paternal grandmother, who would always greet me with "¡Ay que chulo míjo!," or to keep secrets from my sisters and me. I tried teaching myself Spanish when I was ten by listening to music, specifically the tejana artist Selena's crossover album. In the morning when my dad drove my sisters and me to school, my dad would put on the local radio station, and we'd listen to Mexican conjuntos playing norteño music. It drove my sisters and me crazy, but every so often the station would play Selena, whose voice and rhythms, coupled with my emergent queer identification with her, were more near to the pop music I was accustomed to but also had a catchy and distinctly tejano sound. I must have asked him who she was, and he then lent me her album, *Dreaming of You*, though it's possible and perhaps more likely that I took it from his truck without asking.

The album's booklet contained lyrics to her songs in Spanish but also their English translations, displayed side by side. I would spend many of my evenings listening to that album and reading the English alongside the Spanish, memorizing every line to learn what each word meant. The first song I learned in its entirety was "Como la flor." I practiced it for a few weeks, and when I thought I had perfected it, I called my grandmother one evening to sing it to her over the phone. I used to love singing to my family and even to strangers, mostly gospel music. I remember when my tía Lydia, one of my grandmother's sisters, would come over to my grandparents' for family occasions, we'd sneak off to the room of one of my uncles, and she'd teach me some of her and her other sisters' favorite gospel music. ("De colores" continues to be a family favorite.) All of which to say that it was not unusual for me to call over the phone at night and sing to some of the older women in my family. After I finished singing, my grandmother was in tears. What I thought were tears of pride turned out to be something very different. You see, my grandmother was very religious, being raised Pentecostal and, I learned later, reluctantly converting to Catholicism for my grandfather. She grew up believing that dancing and singing anything but religious music were sins. Choking through her tears, she asked me never to sing that kind of music to her again, that I should only sing for the Lord. She even suggested to me that perhaps God allowed Selena to die because she did not sing for him. I hung up the phone, dejected, and I ceased my efforts to learn Spanish for a number of years. It was not until high school, when I gave up Catholicism, that I took up learning Spanish again, but by that point whatever possibility I had to develop what some call "native fluency" had long passed. As I tried to learn Spanish then and use what I learned to reach out in kinship to other fluent Spanish-speaking Mexicans and Latina/os, I was and am often still met with ridicule and shame.

I am a third-generation Mexican American, and by the time I was in high school, I came from a securely middle-class household. Although I know the Durons migrated from Aguas Calientes, México, I know relatively little about my family history, especially on my paternal grandmother's side. My grandmother and some of her sisters are now passed, and even in their later years most suffered from severe Alzheimer's; much of that history I fear will remain lost. Being born in Waco, Texas, a five-hour car ride north of the imaginary border, I grew up feeling very cut off from my historical ties with México. I also didn't grow up with those common cultural markers that so often help other Chicanas and Chicanos recognize one another as kin: I've never played lotería; my grandmother rarely cooked Mexican cuisine and never passed on any recipes; I never learned to fear el cucuy; I also had no idea that la chancla was so imbued with such frighteningly effective disciplinary power. None of these, of course, are essential components to Mexican or Chicana/o identity, but from what I've observed, they do seem to make communal recognition and identification easier. I've learned about many of these markers over the last several years online through social media and popular Latinx publications, though they rarely activate any embodied or affective memories for me. When I evoke them, it often feels uncomfortably performative.

Yet I *always* knew I was Mexican. I never once passed as or identified with being white. I feel certain that some of this identification is partly due to my inscription by whites in the Southwest. Despite my own illegibility as Mexican to many migrant or first-generation

Mexican Americans, to most whites in Texas I am distinctly and visibly brown. It wasn't until I moved to New York that I felt like I was routinely mistaken for being of white European descent. In New York, although I'm never mistaken for being Anglo, I often hear that I look French or perhaps some Italian mix. In Texas both my white friends and white strangers never mistook me for being white. Anytime the topic of race was raised, I was Mexican. Maybe mixed, but definitively Mexican. Although I don't recall facing many overt forms of racism, I was often solicited to act as some kind of race-relations mediator. For some whites, I often functioned as a kind of native informant: I was an authority on race, would be asked questions about what Mexicans really thought about some subject or another, or would be asked about why some Mexicans do this or believe this and that. For some whites, I suppose because I am mixed and college-educated and therefore more "reasonable" I was often solicited to confirm their sometimes racist or otherwise vexed opinions about race relations, such as the so-called lawlessness of the "illegals" crossing the border into the United States or the "detriment" of bilingual education for the children of migrants who aspire to rise to the middle class. My other "half white, half Mexican" friends from Texas shared these same experiences with me, and though I find those experiences to be problematic now, it is strange how much I find myself missing them at times. In New York my legibility as Mexican by either whites or other Latinxs is almost nonexistent except in a bureaucratic sense to fulfill some kind of institutional mandate for multiculturalism. The diversity of Latinxs in New York from such varied national backgrounds and layers of migrations positions someone like myself outside the racial logics of this region, though perhaps too, as a graduate student living in Brooklyn and socializing in queer nightlife, I simply occupy social spaces that are different from the ones I occupied in Texas, which hails different kinds of racial performances from me.

Of course, I did not experience my mexicanidad only in the negative sense, as nonwhite. Every other morning before work and at noon during lunch in his work's break room, my dad would put on the most current telenovela, which I would listen to even if I could not understand what they were saying. I learned to dance cumbia before I can remember, and I shared with other tejanos a perfectly timed and exuberant anticipation of the fast-paced chorus in Fandango U.S.A.'s "La Charanga." I recognize A. B. Quintanilla and the Kumbia King's "Azúcar" and "Boom Boom" within just a few bars. Additionally, I was a chambelán in three or four quinceañeras, including my two sisters', and danced in many others. My cousins and I always had piñatas at our birthday parties until our parents thought we were too old for them, even though you're never too old for a piñata at a party. My grandmother maybe never made mole, but she had a delicious Mexican rice dish that she knew by heart and that our other relatives could never perfectly imitate. I knew our last name was originally spelled Durán and not Duron, a change that occurred when my family migrated north of the border. While these experiences were deeply personal, I knew too that I shared them with many other tejanos, which helped me develop a sense of my own brownness and my identification as Mexican.

Still, many times my own *self*-identification was not enough to make me legible to others who shared that relation. Hosting Norma at my university was a somewhat uneasy way for me to verify that I was part of the community. I remember when I learned of that queer event at La Casa Azul where I first met many other Chicana/os whom I now consider my dear friends. It was like I had a script for my self-introduction: "Hello, my name is Nicholas Duron. I'm a Chicano graduate student here in New York focusing on Chicana/o literature. Oh, do you know Norma? She is my mentor from when I lived in San Antonio." I always felt uncomfortable in these performances as well, and, in retrospect, perhaps they weren't strictly necessary. Over the past few years I began to truly believe that there are multiple ways to be Chicanx, multiple stories that can be told, that need to be told. And as I met more people and connected at events and through social media, such uneasy verifications no longer seemed necessary.

It was within this context that I attended the LGBTQ scholars of color conference, where I met mi amante. We were at the postconference dance on a Saturday when a friend of mine told me that he knew someone else who was also Chicano and a graduate student in Chicanx studies, and I asked him to introduce us. I had my script ready, but when I approached him to deliver the lines, I had barely gotten out that I was Chicano when he grabbed me to go dance with him to some slow love song. I remember feeling shy, and even though I kept looking away, down or to the side, somewhat afraid of the intimacy, each time he would lightly press the underside of my face with the edges of his fingers, bringing my gaze up to meet his, greeting me with a sly, inebriated smile. By the time we met, the dance was nearly over. He was only in town for a few days; he wanted me to come back to his place with him after, but I knew I couldn't. We exchanged numbers and texted the next morning. He remembered relatively little from the night before, but we set up a date to meet again a few days later at a coffee bar. He talked about migrating from México to the Midwest. I talked about migrating from Texas to the Northeast. He talked about his dissertation on queer Chicano art and utopia. I talked about a seminar paper I was writing about Cherríe Moraga and *This Bridge Called My Back*. He told me later he wasn't paying too much attention to my work, though I was hanging on every word he spoke about his own. He ordered a beer, and I ordered a cider. We held hands as we drank, and we kissed and more. After closing time he walked me to my train and promised to keep in touch. He flew home the following afternoon. He sent me songs I'd never heard of by artists I'd never heard of, "Mi eterno amor secreto" by Patricia Navidad and "Nunca voy a olvidarte" by Cristian Castro. I sent him two poems by Lorna Dee Cervantes, "Before You Go" and "Como lo siento." We talked and texted every day until we couldn't any longer.

When he had texted me that June, "Queriendote me ayuda quererme," that loving you helps me to love myself, I don't think he knew then that he was speaking for us both. I think both of us suffered from an inability to see ourselves as beautiful, to see ourselves as desirable. I can't speak for him here, but for myself, I had always located my undesirability as inherent within my body. My first introduction to queer desire as a teenager was online through the white publication *XY Magazine*, a magazine intended for gay male teens, which ran from 1996 to 2007. If you do an online image search of *XY* now you'll notice immediately that the majority of the models are white, seemingly tall, with body types ranging from twink-skinny to jock-fit. Although I never desired to be white, as a small-framed, fourteen-year-old teen at five feet, two inches and 110 pounds, I looked at these images and became eager for another growth spurt with increased muscle mass, hoping that a jolt of testosterone would reshape my bone structure and maybe straighten my nose, hoping at least that I could obtain a more masculine frame to hide my perceived femininity. I want to be a macho, but, having listened to my dad teasing me for being what he called a "sissy Sara" (with the trilled *r* sound) from the time that I was little, I felt I could never be that. A friend of mine, short and small-framed like me, was proscribed testosterone injections to help trigger another growth spurt. I asked my mother, a nurse, to take me to an endocrinologist to see if they could help me. I remember crying in the backseat of the car coming home from the hospital after hearing the endocrinologist tell my parents that I would never grow taller; I recall later crying in the dressing rooms with stacks of ill-fitting clothes that evidently were never intended for me. Over the course of my adolescence I came to perceive my body as constituted by lack. This embodied negativity ultimately left me ambivalent toward it. I desired for it to be seen but also feared its visibility lest its inadequacy be all the more apparent. I adopted rituals of disappearance: wearing baggy clothes, losing as much weight as I could bear, hiding in my room, absenting myself from social functions to stand outside alone, and many others. Yet these rituals were always accompanied by the fantasy that somehow my absence would be noticed, that I would be missed, and that someone would come looking for me, lost but not forgotten, more present in my complete absence.

As I got older I became resigned to my small stature, though after hearing mi amante tell me how he loved that I was such a shorty, I've begun to see my body as beautiful. Indeed, there was something about a queer, brown-on-brown desire that I can only gesture toward now but that fundamentally altered the way I perceived myself. Although mi amante was different from me, someone with his own unique experiences and history, in queerly desiring and loving another brown Chicano, I was able to see in him a trace of myself. Not complete or full, but never empty. It was akin to looking into a black mirror, like holding a darkened screen so closely that you can just make out the shaded outlines of your figure on the glass. To love him was also to love myself. It was a nurturing desire.

As an effect of our relationship my body became more ghostly present, seemed to queerly occupy space in a way different from white or even brown heteronormative masculinity. I began to make my presence felt even if on the margins of perception, just outside of transparent visibility. I would speak in asides, loudly enough to be heard but quietly enough so as to not be clearly understood, requiring that the listener ask me to speak again. If people bumped into me due to their apparent failure to notice me, I would stumble or fall quite dramatically to elicit their apology but disappear before they could offer it. I would smile at the wrong time, show looks of deep concern while being told a funny story, or erase emotion from my face altogether. In other words, I summoned a different repertoire of being in the world that didn't require an assertive masculine dominance or normative legibility. I wouldn't say that, therefore, I became any less ambivalent about my body, that my relation to it was in any way repaired or healed, that my body felt complete or whole. Rather, I was able to take its disassembled parts and put them to work.

The desire mi amante and I shared was also facilitated by a radical openness toward each other. Because we didn't want to erase the many moments of tension and uncertainty—we both had our own traumas we carried with us—I don't think it would be overly romantic to say that we fostered a time and space that enabled us to express our thoughts and feelings, to be vulnerable before one another and still be scared of getting hurt, to be ignorant and experimental, to be proud and ashamed. Such a location as the one we created was not without *risk*—no place really is—but such risks no longer had to be taken entirely alone. Some of our most dangerous and most mundane conversations would occur through Snapchat, allowing us to text, to share videos and photos, although the site purportedly deletes them after being viewed, though, technologically speaking, of course, they're never entirely deleted. Still, the app allowed the performance of speaking out loud without being restrictively bounded by what was said. I mourn all those lost conversations, which I carry with me now only in my memories, but their absence enabled a kind of openness that wouldn't have been possible otherwise.

For our most personal conversations we usually wrote in Spanish. He told me once how "English is about feeling sorry for someone, but Spanish is all about empathy." I'm not sure this is entirely true, but at least in practice this has turned out to be the case. Writing to each other in Spanish did evoke the atmosphere of secrecy and affection that surrounded its use in my childhood memories. There was also something romantic about it as well. Even now I'm not a fluent Spanish speaker. I would have to consult my electronic Spanish dictionary on my phone or search online to learn how to say certain words or phrases to express my feelings. These acts for me literalized learning the language of love. Although most of our conversations are now lost, some small fragments I can still recall:

"I'm busy Sunday. We'll have to wait to meet on Monday."
"Malo."

"I could love you."
"You could?"

"Somos amantes?"
"Sí, claro."

"I love how protective you are of me!"
"Fuck you."

"No me olvides, amante."
"Nunca."

"Oye, un día quieres ser mi novio!"
"¿*"
"Sí, claro."

"Te quiero."
"Y yo te quiero."

Since he's a fluent Spanish speaker, I would always feel embarrassed to use Spanish in front of him. When I went to visit him at his home in Minneapolis at the end of July he was kind and encouraged me to try. He held my hand as we went to a taquería and I nervously mumbled my fussy order for "tres tacos de bistec, solamente con carne y queso . . . no salsa, no lechuga . . . nada." He wrote to me later, "i love the fact you don't speak Spanish perfectly. It makes you more Chicano!" While I visited he drove me around the city with a car he borrowed from a friend, showing me where he grew up and telling me stories about his childhood. He pointed out which neighborhoods were historically Black or Latino and which ones had been gentrified. He regretted the fact that he as a college graduate may himself be a participant in the gentrification process, and we discussed strategies on how we can support local residents and prevent them from having to abandon their homes. He showed me historically Latinx neighborhoods that had been predominantly Mexican but were seeing an influx of Salvadoran migrants. He taught me how to discern which Mexican restaurants were owned by actual Mexicans and which ones were owned by non-Mexican whites. I've come to think that loving while brown involves a deep appreciation and archaeology of one another's history. It was too much to take it all in during a single trip, but I followed what I could. He played a local nineties R&B and hip-hop station, and we held hands as he drove, sometimes speaking, sometimes not. Most of our time on this trip was spent at his apartment learning about one another's lives and childhoods, telling one another our stories. These were lessons in loving.

I returned home to New York from Minneapolis. When I learned the following weekend he'd passed away, everything looked pale to me. I think his loss was the first time I had ever experienced true mourning. Filled with longing and regret, I replayed and rescripted conversations that would have been more perfect, that might have better eased his pain. I thought back to one of our final days together in which he couldn't bring himself to say "I love you." "I l . . . ike you. I almost said I love you," but he couldn't; it was too soon, we'd spent so little of our time together. I quietly, though maybe not completely, agreed. Why hadn't I said "I love you"? Hadn't we said it? "Te quiero . . . Y yo te quiero." I wasn't sure, my Spanish too imperfect to know for certain. I searched online, asked friends to find the exact meaning of the phrase to see if I knew what he'd meant, if maybe he knew what I meant. Maybe "te amo" would have been better, more clear; maybe if I'd just said it that day.

I spent days in bed unable to imagine a future. At first, I tried reading literature and poetry, but the emotions they stirred were too much for me to bear. Falling into the habits of a student, I attempted to research grief, to try to understand it as I would a cultural practice. Perhaps it's common knowledge that the most persistent motif in the discourse of grief is that of *time*—given time, wounds will heal. But how could that be true of a feeling that existed in a different temporality, something that did not unfold linearly, something that emerged elsewhere other than in the bottomless and unaffected space of a voided and consumptive time? The only amelioration came from connecting with strangers who knew him and with whom I could share my loss. In a way I suppose I found a community I was so desperately seeking, lost together in our grief. I gathered strength by sharing the stories I have of mi amante and me and by listening to their stories.

After enough of these strengthening exercises, I turned to another practice. I began to build an archive. Much of this archive is material: a notebook he lent me, a spare copy of Carla Trujillo's *What Night Brings*, which I read alone in his apartment when he went out to do chores and which he gave me; his copy of Sáenz's novel, which his friend Alex sent me; a small bottle of contact solution that I bought while on my trip to see him and that I left in his car while he was out doing chores but he drove back to give to me, calling me a menso; a rose from the last picture I had taken and sent him, now wilted and covered in mold; the cell phone that I used to take the picture and that I'd brought with me to my trip to his home. I've added a few new objects that I didn't have while he was alive but that remind me of him. I added an abanico a friend bought me from Mexico, the country of his birth. I added a black-and-white Puerto Rican flag symbolizing the country's mourning of its occupation by the

United States, a topic that was important to him. I've arranged these objects into an altar, trying my best to imitate the one I'd seen on a chest of drawers in his bedroom that he'd created for his mother. I keep a yellow votive candle on the altar, his favorite color. Most of this archive, though, is made up of memories made material by speaking and writing about him and everything he meant to me.

I've forgotten many things now, so many precious moments I ought to have written down or documented somewhere. Fragments come up from time to time without order or context. Certain sensations, smells, the taste of salt still linger. A few pictures and a few texts remain.

The Thursday before he died, he asked me, "¿Qué harás si algo me pasa?" What will you do if something happens to me? I didn't have a response at the time except to say that I didn't know what I'd do. How could I know? Now I feel as though my whole life after his death will be an answer to his question. Here I offer some of the things I've done since then:

I lay in bed for days shedding tears of remembrance for you

I went to Europe and took pictures and became bored and angry at not being able to share them with you

I finished What Night Brings *and* Under the Feet of Jesus *and your favorite stories from* The Faith Healer of Olive Avenue *and I cried when I finished them*

I left my husband a month after you passed

I moved into an apartment with a cat also named Nick and three women who seemed very kind

I put together some furniture by myself without anyone's help

I stopped biting my nails for a little while, but I started again

I stopped falling asleep at night imagining I was someone else

I took part in my first protest, marching with ACT-UP NYC *to protest the closing of a clinic in Chelsea*

I joined a student labor union and was an active member and was elected to a seat on the Joint Council

I started a reading group in my department dedicated to the writings of feminist women of color, and we had our first meeting a month after you passed

I went on a few dates, and though I mostly thought about you, I still had a pretty good time

I wrote poetry for you, and though I know you wouldn't think it any good, I also know you'd love how hard I tried

References

Alire Sáenz, Benjamin. 2014. *Aristotle and Dante Discover the Secrets of the Universe*. New York: Simon and Schuster.

Anzaldúa, Gloria. 1987. *Borderlands / La Frontera: The New Mestiza*. San Francisco: Aunt Lute Books.

Cantú, Norma Elia. 2015. *Canícula: Snapshots of a Girlhood en La Frontera*. Albuquerque: University of New Mexico Press.

Moraga, Cherríe, and Gloria E. Anzaldúa. 1981. *This Bridge Called My Back: Writings by Radical Women of Color*. London: Persephone Press.

Muñoz, Manuel. 2007. *The Faith Healer of Olive Avenue*. Chapel Hill NC: Algonquin Books.

Trujillo, Carla. 2003. *What Night Brings*. Willimantic CT: Curbstone Books.

Viramontes, Helena María. 1996. *Under the Feet of Jesus*. New York: Penguin Books.

From the Urban Landscape to Sites of Incarceration

9

Queering el barrio

Latina Immigrant Street Vendors in Los Angeles

LORENA MUÑOZ

Clara and Elena work as street vendors in a Latino immigrant neighborhood in South Central Los Angeles. They sell on a noisy intersection filled with cars, buses, and people. Elena and Clara wear long skirts and floral print shirts; they stand on a street corner, selling home-cooked tamales, steamed corn, and fresh champurrado from their red grocery carts. Elena and Clara are street vendors from Mexico: Elena is from Tijuana, and Clara is from Mexico City. Elena and Clara arrived in Los Angeles at different times during the 1990s. During the day they both sell on a popular street south of the garment district and at night outside one of the Latino immigrant gay bars.

Elena and Clara are partners. Clara worked as a domestic before she met Elena. They live in a studio apartment close to where they work. Elena has worked as a street vendor since her arrival in LA. Once together, they decided to partner up in Clara's street vending business. Clara states that it has been a good business decision, since Elena has a border crossing card that allows her to visit Tijuana at least once a month to see her family and bring groceries and other household necessities while Clara stays in Los Angeles tending to the vending carts. Clara stays back in LA not only because of her "undocumented status" but also because Elena's parents think Clara is only her business partner and roommate. Similarly, in Los Angeles, Clara and Elena negotiate their "partnerships" differently depending on whether they are selling during the day or outside Latino gay bars selling at night. They are both life and business partners, constantly negotiating their gendered and "queer" identities in the many spaces they inhabit.[1]

Like thousands of Latino street vendors, Elena and Clara re-create vending practices on a daily basis. Their style—including their dress, behavior, and language, as well as what they sell and how they sell it—transforms the space they occupy. Their embodied practices, as well as the physical transformation of space, are place-making strategies used by immigrants to carve out their "place" in the urban landscape. In this sense, place is enacted through social and cultural displays, as well as through interactions informed by collective nostalgic imaginaries tied to "back home." These place-making strategies are vital to the process of landscape creation. Latina immigrants re-create cultural landscapes while constantly reinventing and reconfiguring vending practices and simultaneously performing and negotiating gendered and queer identities on the street. These gendered and queer identities are informed by heteronormative narratives and are articulated in space. That is, the vendors and customers organize the street to sell and consume a particular nostalgic narrative of vending landscapes that is rooted in their country of origin. Vending landscapes are presumed to be heteronormative, yet I argue that in Los Angeles they are in fact "pseudoheteronormative" spaces.[2] Elena and Clara negotiate and perform their queer and gendered identities differently across spaces in the city, creating a different place within each space.

This chapter examines how queer Latina immigrant women in my study who work as street vendors perform and negotiate their gendered and queer identities differently across multiple spaces in which they live, work, and love. Latina/o vendors transform and organize vending spaces and are complicit in the production of vending landscapes in Los Angeles that resemble vending landscapes from back home. These embodied geographies of "home" reify migration narratives that inform how Latina immigrants perform and negotiate their queer and gendered identities. Their identities are negotiated differently at home while they are street vending and in queer spaces in Latino immigrant neighborhoods. Thus, I argue that Latina immigrant vendors' spatial performance (Datta

2008a) helps us understand Latino immigrant street vending practices and the production of immigrant vending spaces as not only gendered but also queer.

Following Eithne Luibhéid and Lionel Cantú (2005), Kath Browne (2007), Martin Manalansan (2006), and others, I define "queer" as a highly contested term that deals with the intersectionality of identities. The term (re)defines nonnormative categories of multiple sexual, gender, and other marginalized identities as fluid. These identities are reproduced and embodied in space where normalization is contested as an ontological practice. In other words, the term challenges the heteronormativity that informs our way of seeing and systematically categorizing life processes (Rodríguez 2003).[3]

Performing "Queer" Geographies of "Home"

Queer geography emerged in the 1990s informed by queer theory. It focused on the production of space as it relates to nonnormative everyday social relations and the hybrid and fluid nature of embodied queer performances (Brown 2007). Current queer geographies have contributed significantly to the reconceptualization of queer geographical imaginations across disciplines (for discussion, see Knopp 2007). Queer geographers have struggled with the tensions that arise when grappling with materializing and spatializing queer embodiments, practices, and social relations while engaging with the hybrid and fluid nature of sexual subjectivities. Queer geographers have focused beyond celebrating "gay spaces" toward understanding these spaces as fluid, elusive, ongoing, and always changing, often with emotional and sentimental meaning and significance to the people who use and create "place" in space (Muñoz 2010).

Queer space can be understood as destabilizing the production of heteronormative space and heteronormative spatial practices. Currently, there is a growing number of studies that highlight complex queer identity formations in space (politics, bodies, performance, narratives, reproductions, etc.), deconstruct a multitude of normative categories, and reconceptualize the lens through which we view and contest these normative categories (Binnie 1997; Brown 2007; Browne 2004, 2006, 2008; Valentine and Skelton 2003).

The production of queer space can be analyzed as not only inform-
ing the performance of queer and sexualized identities but also determining how queer and sexualized identities inform the production
of queer space as a mutually constituted dialectical process. In other
words, space fluidly informs the process of identity production much
the same way that identities inform and produce space. Thus, sexualized and gendered identities are grounded in materiality that is
inscribed and embodied by the use, creation, and performance of
identities in space.

I build on this critique by suggesting that gender performance and
queer performance are constructed, created, and lived differently
while navigating different spaces, such as where and when performance takes place. In this sense, performances that are negotiated by
gender and queer identity are informed by heteronormative migration discourses that are fictional regulatory representations of Lati-
na/o vending spaces. In Los Angeles, Clara and Elena heighten their
gendered spatial performance by dressing up in skirts, selling "typical" prepared food, and often bringing their sons to work, where
their queer identities are invisible or hidden. As street vendors they
blend into the landscape, one that is recognizable across borders.

Heteronormative Spatial Imaginaries

Contemporary works on immigration and transnational migration
anchor heteronormativity as a central discourse where immigrants'
spatial, racial, gender, and sexual identities are highlighted within
this framework. Luibhéid and Cantú (2005) state that migration
scholars have defined migration in heteronormative contexts. It is
precisely these heteronormative narratives that define gender and
family structure in Mexican families (Rodríguez 2003; Hondagneu-
Sotelo 1994, 2001). Yet the everyday lives of Mexican immigrants in
Los Angeles break down such gendered expectations, which are often
more romanticized than real. That is, stories of men migrating alone
or with their families dominate, despite the fact that single women
who have not necessarily left a child or a husband behind have continually crossed the U.S.-Mexican border in search of work. These
dominant narratives construct transnational migratory identities

that often contradict Latina migration experiences (Hondagneu-Sotelo 1994; Hamilton and Chinchilla 2001). Mexican women have also migrated to the north of Mexico to work in maquilas without a male counterpart (Bank-Muñoz 2008), and there are a number of Mexican immigrant women living in Los Angeles who are queer, lesbian, out, activist, closeted, living dual lives, and so on and whose gender processes shape the everyday reality of immigrant women.

Current literature that focuses on gender and immigration such as transnational motherhood, domestic workers, and home-care workers reifies a model of transnational labor immigration that is centered on heterosexual marriage, heterosexual parenthood, and the nuclear family (Manalansan 2006). This literature neglects and makes invisible the experiences of immigrants whose identities are noncategorizable and rather fluid across nonnormative categories. The invisibility of queer migrants is also evident in contemporary studies of street vending in which transborder street vending landscapes are often constructed as reified heteronormative spaces (Hamilton and Chinchilla 2001; López-Garza and Diaz 2001; Spalter-Roth 1988; Zlolniski 2006). According to Martha Chen (2001, 2005, 2006a), women workers around the globe are concentrated in the most precarious forms of the informal economy, street vending being one of these occupations. From a global perspective, informal work is recognized as a heteronormative gendered occupation. Current research on the informal economy from a global perspective is centered on heteronormative social institutions that highlight inequities among gender within family structures and that promote economic vulnerability, particularly for women and children (Chen 2001).

Globally, street vending landscapes are read as heteronormative spaces. It is no surprise that Latino immigrant street vending landscapes in Los Angeles are constructed, supported, maintained, and (re-)created by "heteronormative" street vending practices from "home." Latino vendors re-create vending practices from imagined representations of nostalgic street vending practices from zocalos or plazas. Vendors in my study constantly referred to their vending strategies as the way street vending "is." As Clara stated, "This is the way you sell here and the way we sell back home." The way vending "just is" is the process of re-calling street vending through collective nostalgia and memory.

For street vendors, nostalgic representations of home shape in scope what the vendors sell, how they sell it, and to whom they sell it. Home is informed by both collective memory and individual memory of street vending landscapes across time and space. Embodied nostalgic representations of home are created and (re-) created through heteronormative migration discourses that shape and inform Latino immigrants' identities in space. That is, vending landscapes are informed and shaped by the nexus of multiple histories of colonialism and neocolonialism in relation to the past and present of the multiple and complex experiences and identities of Latin American immigrants. As stated earlier, street vendors actively reconstruct vending landscapes that resemble romanticized vending practices in zocalos, plazas, and parks. Thus, nostalgia aids in the construction of heteronormative vending landscapes where the queer and gendered identities of the vendors are negotiated through larger migration narratives.

It is not only economic spaces in Los Angeles that are constructed through Mexican romanticized narratives. From the 1970s to the 1990s in Mexico City, the "Marías," who were ambulant vendors, echoed this narrative. The Marías were women (and some men) who sold food and other items on the streets dressed in typical indigenous gear like huipiles, reconstructing indigenous informal economies of the romanticized past. Many of the Marías who sold in Mexico City were part of the rural-to-urban migration waves as a consequence of the economic destabilization of the nation's agricultural industry. These new urban vendors wore traditional garb as part of their selling strategy. By wearing traditional garb, these ambulant vendors claimed their "authenticity," especially with regard to domestic and international tourists in the historic center of Mexico City. This authenticity was enhanced by the presence of children. José Luis Lezama's (1993) study of Marías selling in Mexico City's historic center suggests that children provided additional labor. Children as young as six, provided childcare to infants and toddlers. In addition, Lezama suggests the women garnered more sympathy when they were seen as mothers, caretakers, and heads of households. However, these "sympathetic mothers" were also labeled "deviants" because of their perceived uncontrolled sexual reproduction practices as a source of additional labor. Currently, vendors in the historic center in Mexico City have been part of the city's plan to institutionalize street vending and reconfigure the center as a safe space for tourist consumption (Baroni 2009).

These complex and conflicting practices of deviance and entrepreneurship inform the narratives of informal economic spaces that permeate migration discourses. As Luibhéid suggests, "Heteronormativity animates both anti- and pro-immigrant imagery and discourses in ways that reiterate, yet continually recode, sexual, gender, racial and class distinctions and inequalities in relation to constructs of the nation-state, nationalisms, and the citizenry" (2008, 175). In Los Angeles, Latina street vendors are seen as entrepreneurial, hardworking, unskilled low-wage labor. Yet vendors are also criminalized, labeled "illegal" in the sense of having a perceived undocumented status but also as "illegal" in the sense that they are unlicensed, and therefore by selling on the streets they are breaking the law. However, most informal vending in Mexico City and Los Angeles is unregulated and unlicensed. These complicated and messy nostalgic vending narratives reify larger migration discourses, providing a context in which vendors organize their economic practices. That context in turn shapes the vendors' gender performance in vending landscapes.

Queering el Barrio: "Flexing" Heteronormative Space

Clara and Elena live and sell in a barrio in South Central Los Angeles.[4] It is primarily an immigrant community that, since the early 1960s, has been a place where Mexican immigrants have established social networks. Much like Boyle Heights in East Los Angeles, this community at the time of World War II was a mixed neighborhood comprised of Japanese, Jewish, Black, white, and Mexican residents. It was not until the late 1970s that this neighborhood became a primarily Mexican immigrant community. Unlike mainstream representations of *what* and *where* Mexican neighborhoods are in Los

Angeles (e.g., East LA, Boyle Heights), this particular neighborhood's current and past representations are rooted to Crenshaw Avenue, the 1992 riots, low riders, and African Americans. Yet the barrio is more representative of what South Central has become over the past twenty years: an area of Los Angeles where Latinos represent the majority of its residents. Latinos in this particular neighborhood comprise approximately 85.3 percent of the residents; 53.9 percent are foreign born, and 80.8 percent of the population speaks a language other than English at home (United States Census Bureau 2000). Thus, the commercial landscape in the area caters to the Latino residents. The residential streets often share land use with small commercial locales, which is allowable in mixed-use zoning; essentially, light industrial businesses are allowed to exist alongside residential and commercial buildings. Amid single and multifamily housing, businesses, construction for a new high school, swap meets and garment factories, Latino residents carve out vending spaces and reconfigure the urban cultural landscape of this neighborhood. On a daily basis, Mexican and Central American street vendors sell on sidewalks, out of the trunks of cars, in parking lots, from grocery carts, and from fruit and taco trucks. Even without a formal business license, these informal businesses are part of the thriving economic activities of this neighborhood. They exist despite ongoing police raids, protests by local business owners, and gang members collecting rent. In this neighborhood setting, vendors who are not unlike Clara and Elena sell their products, customers consume them, and pseudoheteronormative vending landscapes get created, enacted, and performed daily in public space.

Public spaces in general are built around heteronormative constructs of family, community, work, and understandings of public/private space (Frisch 2002). These spatial constructs permeate migration discourses that in turn inform the way Latina immigrants "do" street vending. Clara and Elena perform and negotiate their gender and queer identities differently depending on where they are selling. During the day, while working, they are seen as "Mexican women," mothers and good cooks who provide childcare on the street, but they are also seen as illegal and unlicensed and as unfit mothers. As

Elena states, "When I started selling in this block, I would bring my youngest son with me, he was just a little baby, while Rafaelito was in school. The police catched me, I don't remember how many times, but they would insult me, saying how I was a criminal breaking the law, that I was a bad mother. . . . They don't understand. . . . I do this because I am a good mother." Elena performs "street childcare" out of both necessity and convenience. The lack of traditional childcare access forces Elena to take her children to work, yet spending time with her children while she is at work is a perk. However, taking her children to work heightens her gender normative performance, which allows her to "pass" (as straight) and blend into the visible gendered landscape. Latina immigrant vendors engender vending landscapes by taking care of their children on the street. Often the streets in Latino neighborhoods are perceived as dangerous, unfriendly, and illicit. However, the presence of children in the landscape can transform that perception. These spaces become gendered and family-friendly and are perceived as unthreatening spaces during certain times of the day (Muñoz 2010).

In addition to street childcare, Latina immigrant street vendors in Los Angeles engender the sidewalks by their entrepreneurial strategies. The business-savvy strategies range from changing vending strategies when sales go down, identifying and stocking products that people demand the most, making traditional tamales in addition to their branded tamales (with "secret" ingredients), and placing their carts in strategic locations to make it easier for people in cars to "drive through" on their way to work. Additionally, vendors increase their productivity by selling seasonal products during holidays such as Christmas, Halloween, Valentine's Day, Mother's Day, Catholic religious holidays, and Mexican and Central American national holidays. During Christmas, vendors often sell homemade products such as Christmas stockings, floral arrangements with poinsettias, displays made out of pine cones, and religious artifacts with baby Jesus and Reyes Magos (the Three Kings). Also, vendors sell manufactured products typically found in dollar stores, such as Christmas lights, plastic Christmas trees, and toys for presents. Mother's Day, specifically the days prior to May 10 (the official Mother's Day in Mexico and some Latin American countries), is also a busy holiday for vendors. Mother's Day in Mexico, unlike in the United States, is not always on a Sunday; instead, it is always on May 10. Vendors sell floral arrangements, as well as anything that can honor the concept of motherhood, including la Virgen de Guadalupe products. Products range from plastic boxes for jewelry that display the word *madre* on the exterior, to plastic and natural flowers that display a banner with words honoring the concept of motherhood. Since there are two official holidays to celebrate Mother's Day, vendors usually sell their products during the official Mexican and U.S. Mother's Day celebrations. Latina vendors embody geographies of home by selling products that celebrate and commemorate Latina/o national, religious, and cultural holidays while navigating the complex and organized systems of street vending.

Ladies' Night and Night Vending in the Bar Queer

Queer identities are not always visible in Latina/o immigrant street vending landscapes. However, when queer Latina immigrant women vendors sell outside gay Latino immigrant bars, their queer identity is apparent for those who also create, consume, and inhabit the landscape. The queer vendors in my study build community through their friends and networks who frequent these bars. Not only do they sell outside the bars, they are also patrons of these bars during ladies' nights. For Elena and Clara, by frequenting these particular bars on ladies' nights, they build a queer community outside their private space. The dependence of social networks is not uncommon among lesbian communities due to their invisibility. Recent studies on lesbian communities in the United States and Canada describe networks of lesbians as a social process and not a spatial (physical) process, which reifies lesbian invisibilities (Valentine 1993). While lesbian or "women" queer spaces in Los Angeles (like West Hollywood, a "gay city") are visible, these are spaces of class and white privilege. Thus, Latina immigrant low-wage workers are invisible in these spaces as consumers but are often present as laborers such as janitors, flower vendors, or bathroom attendants, regardless of their sexual identity. Although queer Latina immigrants are not visible in privileged queer spaces, they are in immigrant queer public spaces. I say this hesitantly, since queer Latino immigrant spaces are often invisible to those who are not queer, including straight Latino immigrants. Queer Latina invisibility is informed by conflicting and complex narratives regarding homosexuality (since queer is not precisely a translatable term) from Mexico and other Latin American countries. On the one hand, representations of the puto and maricón (the effeminate male character) plague the Mexican social constructions of homosexuality. Yet female homosexuality is still invisible and, in some cases, considered socially immoral, punished by social marginalization and relegated to exist mostly in private spaces. Lesbians in some cases are rejected, as they are considered malinchistas, or traitors to the culturally assigned gender roles of mother and wife (Anzaldúa 1999). On the other hand, contemporary scholarship has focused on how global gay and lesbian tourism, particularly in Mexico and Cuba, is currently reconceptualizing, transforming, and making GLBT communities more visible (Luibhéid and Cantú 2005).

In Los Angeles, Latino immigrant queer "male" visibility runs the gamut from invisibility to out and everything in between. I would argue, however, that queer Latina immigrants, not unlike other racialized lesbians, are and continue to be for the most part largely invisible in public space. Certainly, queer spaces as spaces occupied by other than gay white males are understudied. Even studies on the invisibility of lesbian spaces often conflate "lesbian" as devoid of race and/or ethnicity (Podmore 2006). Other economic spaces that are considered part of the service informal economy where Latino immigrants, in particular women, constitute the majority of the labor force, such as domestic work, are also understudied in relation to Latina immigrant queer identities. Before working as a street vendor, Clara worked as a domestic in West Los Angeles, a primarily economically privileged area of the city.

"Home" Spaces, Queer Spaces

Private space is also negotiated differently from work and public space. At "home," Elena and Clara are partners and lovers who coparent their children while having a supportive community comprised of both gay and straight friends. Clara stated, "My closest friends are the ones I met at the bars when I first came here. Some of them live in my same building." I met Clara and Elena through Herminia, another queer street vendor in my study. She was the first one to disclose to me that she was not straight. Herminia lives in the same apartment building as Clara and Elena, and they are good friends. They support each other with childcare but also are part of a larger queer community of friends.

Clara and Elena negotiate and perform their queer and gender identities very differently at home than while street vending. Clara's attire can be interpreted as gender nonconforming, such as men's pants and a white tank top. Clara is very aware of her embodiment of a gender-nonconforming butch performance. She would constantly refer to her "real" self by making fun of what she wears to "work." With a "chilanga" accent (a regional accent from Mexico City), she stated, "No mames, si aquí en mi casa yo soy el rey como la canción, en la calle Elena me trae por los huevos" (Shit, here in my house I am the king, like the song, but in the street, Elena has me by the balls). Elena responded, "No seas payasa, deja de lucirte" (Don't be a clown, stop showing off). As Jack Halberstam suggests, "Often the Latina butch provides an interesting example of the double stereotype . . . along racial as well as gender lines" (1998, 181). These stereotypes often are performed and embodied by Latina butches. Thus, understanding how gender and queer identity performances operate within these different spaces calls for multiple, fluid, and complex gender and queer subject constructions in relation to both the resistance and embracing of larger economical, social, political, cultural, and immigration systems that define, restrain, and inform identities in space. In other words, Latina immigrants' queer identities are informed by homophobic and misogynist heteronormative social constructions of gender not only from back home but also from their new home, where gender and queer identities are renegotiated through structural raced and classed systems of oppression (Espín 1997, 1999).

"Home" for vendors like Elena extends south of the U.S. border. Elena's family depends on her mobility across the Tijuana–

San Diego border for economic sustainability. However, at home in Tijuana, Elena's queer sexuality is invisible. Elena negotiates her identity through complex processes and meanings that are informed not only by Mexican social norms but also by her family's dependence on her income. Elena provides for her mother and younger siblings, who do not share her border-crossing mobility. Elena talked about her life in Tijuana as not being too different from her life in Los Angeles: "Ahora que me haces pensar, creo que mi vida no es muy diferente en la casa de mi mama que la de aquí. Pues uno vive en las sombras" (Now that you make me think, I don't believe my life is very different in my mom's house [in Tijuana] than the one here. One lives in the shadows). Elena described her "not straight" experiences at home in Tijuana and home in Los Angeles as different but both in the shadows.

Katie Acosta (2008) explores how Latina lesbians in the United States create "in-between" spaces by distancing themselves from their families and constructing a borderland space in which to express their sexuality. She adds that outside of this borderland space, these migrants hide their lesbian existence out of fear that their families will discover them and consequently that their "self" will be unaccepted. Latina immigrant lesbians build borderland spaces by interweaving new families, queer networks, and lives apart and within their families across borders.

Elena's story contrasts liberationist narratives about queer migrants' journeys from repression to freedom, as the pioneer research about queer migration indicates (Luibhéid and Cantú 2005). Elena's queer and gendered identity negotiations in Tijuana and in Los Angeles while street vending and at home are different but not "liberated." However, these spaces create choice and economic freedoms that are created and lived by queer Latina immigrant street vendors.

This chapter sought to explore how queer Latina immigrants who are street vendors negotiate their queer and gendered identities differently as they navigate different vending spaces in immigrant neighborhoods. Thus, in Latino perceived heteronormative immigrant communities in Los Angeles, queer women are present, but their public embodiment of their queerness is invisible. Private and queer spaces, however, are constantly (re)negotiated and (re) constructed to embody the multiple fluid identities of Latina immigrants. Vendors like Clara and Elena take part in the reproduction of socially constructed heteronormativity in the ways they live and perform in both their home and work space across borders.

Notes

1. I collected the data that inform this article from 2002 to 2008. I formally and informally collected data in various Latino immigrant neighborhoods in Los Angeles. Through qualitative methodologies, I conducted "field" ethnographies using oral histories, participatory observation, interviews, photodocumentation, and photoelicitation. This chapter, however, engages with data collected in the last two years, when through my own self-disclosure as queer, vendors like Clara, Elena, and others also self-disclosed as "not straight."

2. Contemporary studies that have a global focus on street vending demonstrate that street vending is a gendered occupation (see Chen 2001). Yet street vending has not been understood as queer.

3. While trying to understand "queer" Latino immigrant identities in space, it is also necessary to grapple with the notion that "queer" is not a translatable term in Spanish (Rodríguez 2003). As María Amelia Viteri (2008) suggests, Latinos in the United States with transnational border-crossing identities oftentimes understand queer to be associated with white and therefore in conflict with their own Latino identities. The street vendors in my study that self-disclosed as not straight did not know or understand the meaning of queer, and since I could not translate the term, it became my own lens of understanding their way of flexing heteronormative space. Although Clara, Elena, and other vendors will not call their practices queer, they do consider themselves not straight, as one vendor describes herself "being" in nonnormative space by affirming, "No soy derecha" (I am not straight). It is important to note that the vendors who labeled themselves not straight did not call themselves lesbians. Thus, understanding the limitations and possible dangers of queering the vendors' practices, I acknowledge that the queer gaze is my own and not the vendors'.

4. Garment Town is the fictional name I utilize when discussing my research site.

References

Acosta, Katie L. 2008. "Lesbianas in the Borderlands: Shifting Identities and Imagined Communities." *Gender & Society* 22 (5): 639–59.

Anzaldúa, Gloria. 1999. *Borderlands / La Frontera: The New Mestiza*. 2nd ed. San Francisco: Aunt Lute.

Bank-Muñoz, Carolina. 2008. *Transnational Tortillas: Race, Gender, and Shop-Floor Politics in Mexico and the United States*. Ithaca NY: Cornell University Press.

Baroni, Patricia. 2009. "El centro histórico: Singularidad y recuperación." *Nuevo Mundo Mundos Nuevos*, January 20. http://journals.openedition.org/nuevomundo/48472.

Binnie, Jon. 1997. "Coming Out of Geography: Towards a Queer Epistemology?" *Environment and Planning D: Society and Space* 15 (2): 223–37.

Brown, Gavin. 2007. "Mutinous Eruptions: Autonomous Spaces of Radical Queer Activism." *Environment and Planning A: Economy and Space* 39 (11): 2685–98.

Browne, Kath. 2004. "Genderism and the Bathroom Problem: (Re)materialising Sexed Sites, (Re)creating Sexed Bodies." *Gender, Place and Culture* 11 (3): 331–46.

———. 2006. "Challenging Queer Geographies." *Antipode* 38 (5): 885–93.

———. 2007. "A Party with Politics? (Re)making L G B T Q Pride Spaces in Dublin and Brighton." *Social & Cultural Geography* 8 (1): 63–87.

———. 2008. "Selling My Queer Soul or Queerying Quantitative Research?" *Sociological Research Online* 13 (1): 200–214.

Chen, Martha A. 2001. "Women in the Informal Sector: A Global Picture, the Global Movement." *S A I S Review* 21 (1): 71–82.

———. 2005. *Towards Economic Freedom: The Impact of S E W A*. Self-Employed Women's Association. https://www.wiego.org/publications/towards-economic-freedom-impact-sewa.

———. 2006a. "Rethinking the Informal Economy: Linkages with the Formal Economy and the Formal Regulatory Environment." In *Unlocking Human Potential: Concepts and Policies for Linking the Informal and Formal Sectors*, edited by Basudeb Guha-Khasnobis, Ravi Kanbur, and Elinor Ostrom, 75–92. Oxford: Oxford University Press.

———. 2006b. *Self-Employed Women: A Profile of S E W A's Membership*. Self-Employed Women's Association. http://www.wiego.org/sites/default/files/publications/files/Chen-SEWA-Membership-2006.pdf.

Datta, Ayona. 2008a. "Architecture of Low-Income Widow Housing: 'Spatial Opportunities' in Madipur, West Delhi." *Cultural Geographies* 15 (3): 231–53.

———. 2008b. "Building Differences: Material Geographies of Home(s) among Polish Builders in London." *Transactions of the Institute of British Geographers* 33, no. 4:518–31.

———. 2008c. "Spatialising Performance: Masculinities and Femininities in a Fragmented Field." *Gender, Place, and Culture* 15 (2): 191–207.

Espín, Oliva M. 1997. "The Role of Gender and Emotion in Women's Experience of Migration." *Innovation: The European Journal of Social Sciences* 10 (4): 445–55.

———. 1999. *Women Crossing Boundaries: A Psychology of Immigration and Transformations of Sexuality*. New York: Routledge.

Frisch, Michael. 2002. "Planning as a Heterosexist Project." *Journal of Planning Education and Research* 21 (3): 254–66.

Halberstam, Jack. 1998. *Female Masculinity*. 1st ed. Durham N C: Duke University Press.

Hamilton, N., and Norma Chinchilla. 2001. *Seeking Community in a Global City: Guatemalans and Salvadorans in Los Angeles*. Philadelphia: Temple University Press.

Hondagneu-Sotelo, Pierrette. 1994. *Gendered Transitions: Mexican Experiences of Immigration*. Berkeley: University of California Press.

———. 2001. *Doméstica: Immigrant Workers Cleaning and Caring in the Shadows of Affluence*. Berkeley: University of California Press.

Knopp, Larry. 2007. "On the Relationship between Queer and Feminist Geographies." *Professional Geographer* 59 (1): 47–55.

Lezama, José Luis. 1993. *Teoría social, espacio y ciudad*. Mexico City: Colegio de México.

López-Garza, Marta Cristina, and David Diaz, eds. 2001. *Asian and Latino Immigrants in a Restructuring Economy: The Metamorphosis of Los Angeles*. Stanford CA: Stanford University Press.

Luibhéid, Eithne. 2008. "Queer/Migration an Unruly Body of Scholarship." *GLQ: A Journal of Lesbian and Gay Studies* 14 (2–3): 169–90.

Luibhéid, Eithne, and Lionel Cantú, eds. 2005. *Queer Migrations: Sexuality, U.S. Citizenship, and Border Crossings*. Minneapolis: University of Minnesota Press.

Manalansan, Martin F. 2006. "Queer Intersections: Sexuality and Gender in Migration Studies." *International Migration Review* 40 (1): 224–49.

Muñoz, Lorena. 2010. "Brown, Queer and Gendered: Queering the Latina/o 'Street-Scapes' in Los Angeles." In *Queer Methods and Methodologies*, edited by Kath Browne and Catherine J. Nash, 55–68. Farnham: Ashgate Press.

Podmore, Julie A. 2006. "Gone 'Underground'? Lesbian Visibility and the Consolidation of Queer Space in Montréal." *Social & Cultural Geography* 7 (4): 595–625.

Rodríguez, Juana María. 2003. *Queer Latinidad: Identity Practices, Discursive Spaces*. New York: New York University Press.

Spalter-Roth, Roberta M. 1988. "Vending on the Streets: City Policy, Gentrification, and Public Patriarchy." In *Women and the Politics of Empowerment*, edited by Ann Bookman and Sandra Morgen, 272–94. Philadelphia: Temple University Press.

United States Census Bureau. 2000. census.gov. https://www.census.gov/prod/2001pubs/c2kbr01-3.pdf.

Valentine, G. 1993. "(Hetero)Sexing Space: Lesbian Perceptions and Experiences of Everyday Spaces." *Environment and Planning D: Society and Space* 11 (4): 395–413.

Valentine, Gill, and Tracey Skelton. 2003. "Finding Oneself, Losing Oneself: The Lesbian and Gay 'Scene' as a Paradoxical Space." *International Journal of Urban and Regional Research* 27 (4): 849–66.

Viteri, María Amelia. 2008. "'Latino' and 'Queer' as Sites of Translation: Intersections of 'Race,' Ethnicity and Sexuality." *Graduate Journal of Social Science* 5 (2): 63–87.

Zlolniski, Christian. 2006. *Janitors, Street Vendors, and Activists: The Lives of Mexican Immigrants in Silicon Valley*. Berkeley: University of California Press.

10

The Privatized Deportation Center
Complex y la trans mujer

VERÓNICA MANDUJANO

The prison-industrial complex (PIC), a term first coined by Angela Davis in 1998 to address the organizational and industrialized structure of privatized prisons, should be expanded to consider privatized detention holding cells and profitable modes of deportation processing as a part of its structure. The massive incarcerated population of the United States is the foundation of a multi-million-dollar industry. Under this industry model, human bodies are commodified by means of contracts to beds, secured occupancy, and a legal system structured to maintain the growth of the private prison system. This multi-million-dollar industry, recognized as the PIC, has received national and global attention due to the fact that it contains the largest prison population in world history (Prison Policy Initiative 2018). Despite political debate over the necessity of such a large boom in the prison population, its growth does not align with statistical proof that violence and crime rates have dropped or remained stagnant in past years or that other methods to address crime rates utilized by other developed nations have proven more successful. The privatized prison industry is largely dominated by a few large corporations that successfully buy out smaller prisons and gain government contracts to build larger facilities. These same corporations are also the leaders of the rapidly growing privatized immigrant detention center industry.

My research focuses on the nature of privatized immigrant detention centers and what led to the growth of an industry entirely reliant on the migration and detention of large populations of people who are by definition refugees of a humanitarian crisis. Immigrants from Central America are fleeing their homelands due to deteriorating living conditions that are the aftermath of years of U.S. intervention in the region (*New York Times* 2019; *Vice* 2017; *The Guardian* 2018). Unacknowledged as such, the underlying mechanisms that have created the refugee crisis in Central America have yet to be entirely uncovered and presented. Although there is plenty of community and academic work alike being done, this work has only really just began. The magnitude of the aftermath of Central America's complex and interwoven history with U.S. intervention, the concealed motives of global capital, and corporate extraction of labor and land will require continuous work to unearth. Central American scholars who focus on the generational impacts of U.S. intervention and global capital and their devastating effects in the region provide a necessary and critical contribution through their subjectivity, their communities, and their insight. For this reason, in addition to a legacy of anti-immigrant sentiment toward immigrants arriving at the U.S. southern border, refugees and asylum seekers from Central America are not often contextualized as such by the mainstream media. They are not simply entering the United States for economic opportunities or the "American dream"; instead, their needs are constituted by a regional and historical phenomenon.

The United Nations 1951 Convention and 1967 Protocol define a refugee person as someone who is unable or unwilling to return to their home country and cannot obtain protection in that home country due to persecution or a well-founded fear of being persecuted in the future on account of "race, religion, nationality, membership in a particular social group or political opinion" (American Immigration Council n.d.). The unacknowledged refugee status of many Central American migrants draws in my other focus: gender and sexuality within privatized deportation centers remain fixated in the gender binary, which excludes trans and gender nonbinary people and exposes them to heightened levels of violence and abuse. The organizing structure, lack of humanitarian protocol, and corporately owned nature of deportation facilities have proven to expose trans women to high levels of sexual assault and gendered violence.

How has the configuration of the privatized deportation industry met with heightened levels of trans and gender nonbinary people seeking asylum, and to what degree has transphobia affected their migratory experience, especially through Mexico? I aim to contextualize the realities of trans women who flee heightened gender and sexual violence from Latin America and seek to make the claim that their gender and sexual identities qualify them for a type of refugee status that often goes unrecognized. In many cases, these women who risk their lives to escape the gender violence they faced in their home country find themselves caught in privatized detention processing or holdings in which they experience the same transphobia they sought to escape. I aim to demonstrate that the institutionalization and naturalization of the imposed gender binary system, which relegates trans women and gender-nonconforming people to a third "other," is the driving societal model sustaining negligence and state-sanctioned violence toward all people who do not neatly fit within its confines. The many factors that contribute to this human rights issue call for future scholarship and an intentional response by the U.S. government to end the suffering of the thousands of detained immigrants its facilities are responsible for each day.

The Industry Model Transfer

A specific focus on the unspoken and concealed violence of immigrant detention centers is necessary whether we conceptualize them as a part of the PIC or not. In order to deconstruct the validity of all industries that are reliant on incarceration, a focus on the incarceration of individuals of migratory status allows us to engage in radically rethinking why any human (or nonhuman) being should have a market value when in holding (or captivity). I believe that outlining how these institutions came to be is necessary to attest to their insidious and profit-focused motives. The PIC and the growing privatized deportation center industry emerge from different sectors of society but together encompass similar motives and business models. As the Americas undergo a refugee crisis that is not credited as such by the mainstream media, headline stories about increased migration from Central America continue to be contextualized through anti-immigrant rhetoric framed as an issue of border security. Marked by tens of thousands of increased asylum seekers in 2014, this refugee crisis emerging from Central America has yet to dwindle in numbers or garner an appropriate humanitarian response. U.S. political dialogue is full of debate about securing the border from immigrants who enter the country without documentation but without emphasizing that they have every reason to do so. Immigrants arriving at our southern border are fleeing some of the most dangerous countries in the world not currently engaged in war (Migration Policy Institute 2015). Refugees fleeing Latin American conditions primarily in El Salvador, Guatemala, Nicaragua, and Mexico have been arriving with an increasing influx after decades of violent U.S. infiltration and neoliberal trade agreements that devastated the area economically. Incarcerated trans women migrants who seek asylum find themselves in large-scale privatized facilities, detained alongside men or in newly developed "Trans Pods." They are the victims of capitalism's far-stretched reach to commodify the desperation that drives thousands of people to flee persecution in Central America and Mexico each year. My research intervenes in mainstream American immigration debates that emphasize border security to center the government's participation in the exploitation of the forced migration of thousands. To make this claim, I emphasize that by relegating trans women asylum seekers to a profit of $122 a day within corporate prison contracts (Leyro, Brotherton, and Stageman 2013), the U.S. government has now developed a system by which to commodify and profit off of the detention of victims of a humanitarian crisis born of U.S. interventionist strategy.

This chapter briefly focuses on the growth of the privatized deportation center industry while outlining corporate influence in legislature and policy making that has allowed for corporate government contracts and huge annual profits. I focus on the U.S. government's commitment to profit off of asylum seekers as another example of the settler-colonial state, which values profit over life, particularly over the lives of colonial and racialized subjects. As a Chicana, I utilize the field of Chicana/o/x studies as a philosophical domain from which I consider the reality of immigrants fleeing Central America and passing through Mexico and as a complex issue deserving of interdisciplinary and nondisciplined questions alike to uncover a multilayered truth that subjectivities made of border politics, borderlands, and nepantlera consciousness/experiences warrant of us. In her foundational text *Borderlands / La Frontera: The New Mestiza*, Gloria Anzaldúa describes "the U.S. and Mexico border [as] una herrida where the Third World grates against the first and bleeds." Although Central Americans and Chicana/o/x people have histories and identities that are unique, our experiences as racialized others and often immigrants within the context of the United States intersect frequently. Therefore, I believe that Chicana/o/x studies as a discipline is uniquely situated to interrogate the insidious nature of the settler-colonial empire known as the United States and forge scholarship that can aide resistance and reenvisioning efforts that call into question the hegemonic power of neoliberal colonialism. My hope is that this brief meditation is oriented toward the need to envision a new world in which the commodification of bodies in detention and violence toward people who challenge settler-colonial gender logics is no longer a naturalized process. This chapter intends to explicitly demonstrate that the privatized immigrant detention center industry is not the appropriate response to the refugee crisis of the Americas and that an adequate response would need to entail resources for particularly vulnerable trans women and gender-nonconforming people.

My methods to extract necessary information included reviewing and analyzing a wide array of government organization reports, activist network websites, national statistics, documentary interviews, and government census data. I felt that in order to fully analyze the privatized detention center industry as a whole, it would be necessary to consider all resources as insight into what is already a difficult industry to conceptualize due to its privatized nature. Currently, there is a plethora of information pertaining to the origins of the industry, its recorded profits, and what policy makers have done. I therefore utilized this information to formulate a concise explanation of the time frame in which the privatized immigrant detention center industry began and a depiction of the many influences that allowed it to grow into a multi-million-dollar industry in relatively little time. However, my intention is not to solely analyze the emergence and functioning of the privatized deportation center industry. I also intend to emphasize the specific experience of trans women within the U.S. hegemonic gender binary, that is, the heteronormative structure that denies the gender identity of people who do not conform to imposed gender norms. This binary gender system therefore exposes trans women to continual sexual and gendered violence while they are under government custody within privatized deportation center facilities.

To contextualize the state of the privatized deportation center industry today, I began by looking into the particular history that allowed the PIC to emerge and what kinds of policies and rationale were behind it. This analysis made it very clear that the PIC was widely supported and reinforced by local and federal policies, the War on Drugs, and corporate influence to continue its growth. Hence, I have outlined how the growth of the PIC sparked the incentive to create a privatized deportation center industry by the same model standards. Within this industry, however, there is a component of its inmates that makes it distinct from the PIC, and that of course is the immigrant and undocumented status of its detainees. The experiences of trans women require scholars critically engaged with the PIC and detention center industry to also consider the needs of the trans community as detainees, immigrants, and asylum seekers. I reiterate that privatized detention centers have no intention to protect and support members of the trans community because the nature of the industry is predicated on cutting costs and generating profits. Thus, this chapter centers the experiences of trans women within this system to fully convey and expose the outright negligence and heinous human rights abuses committed under U.S. government contracts with U.S. taxpayer dollars.

The state of the current privatized immigrant detention center industry could not have emerged without the presence of the PIC in the United States, which currently is the largest among all industrialized nations and has grown from a phenomenon of obscene racial policing and unjust incarcerating practices (Alexander 2010). In her national best seller, *The New Jim Crow*, Michelle Alexander unveils the insidious nature of the prison system's origins and functions. Ultimately, the rapid growth of the PIC is undeniable; the prison population in the United States has grown from three hundred thousand to two million in the past thirty years while incarcerating a largely Black and Brown population (Alexander 2010; Prison Policy Initiative 2018). Such growth owes itself to certain social and legal conditions that have restructured the flow of inmates to allow for a huge increase despite statistical proof that crime and violence rates actually dropped in the same period (Alexander 2010). Mainly, the War on Drugs, once a metaphorical term turned financed and armed effort, is responsible for the unprecedented growth of the United States' prison population. Launched by Ronald Reagan in 1982, the War on Drugs was a crackdown on drug activity; however, its methods involved heavy policing of poor Black and Brown communities and resulted in an overly militarized police force. It is also crucial to note that at the time of Reagan's announcement, less than 2 percent of the American public viewed drugs as a major concern (Alexander 2010). This, however, did not matter, since the war was not nearly as drug related as it was related to race. By waging a war on drug dealers and users, Reagan systematically cracked down on the racially defined "others" and criminalized the continual struggle of Black and Brown people within American capitalism. The war's efforts were no small feat; practically overnight federal law enforcement agencies' spending soared. From 1980 to 1984 FBI antidrug funding increased from $8 million to $95 million (Lartey 2015). Additionally, since 1971 the War on Drugs has cost the United States an estimated $1 trillion (Pearl 2018). However, in a supposed effort to eradicate drug use and behavior, the Reagan administration greatly reduced spending for drug treatment, prevention, and education by cutting the budget for the National Institute on Drug Abuse from $274 million to $57 million in just a three-year span. Without adequate government resources to educate and prevent low-income communities from resorting to drugs for either psychological or economic support or the confluence of an organized effort to incarcerate vulnerable communities, the

United States took a strong stance in its efforts to address drug use. It is critical to contextualize the approach the U.S. government took and its contribution to the largest spike in prison population the world has ever seen. In comparison, Alexander noted that Portugal responded to persistent problems of drug abuse by decriminalizing the possession of all drugs and redirecting money that would have been spent putting drug users in cages into drug treatment programs. Ten years later Portugal reported that the rate of drug use and addiction had plummeted, as well as drug-related crime. This comparison between nation-states is necessary in order to fully contextualize the strong hold corporate interests have in the approach the United States took in addressing the same issue. Why has the United States chosen to focus on punishing drug consumption and distribution rather than alleviate societal ills that drive its usage? Why has the United States instead allowed for the massive incarceration of the poor and most vulnerable? What purpose does a large prison population serve other than as an opportunity for corporate investment and profit? While Michelle Alexander did an exceptional job in answering these questions and outlining the origins and growth of the privatized prison system, she explicitly notes in her introduction that her focus is on the Black community; therefore, she leaves work to identify the effects of the privatization of prisons on other communities to scholars and researchers with a different lens. I took this call to action and internalized it within my own research to find that the ideology behind the PIC has not stopped at the limitations we may imagine but has grown into a neoliberal response to America's current refugee crisis.

The School of the Americas and Its Lasting Impact

The United States has experienced a drastic influx in immigration patterns in the past few years, a phenomenon that owes its origins to a deep history between the United States and countries experiencing an influx in immigrants fleeing dangerous conditions, mainly Mexico, Nicaragua, El Salvador, and Guatemala. Each country has its own specific history and relation to the United States, as well as reasons for why people risk their lives to immigrate thousands of miles toward our southern border. Migration patterns have largely been driven by economic hardship and instability since the 1980s; however, the sudden influx is undeniably significant of an ongoing crisis in the specific regions. The rapid increase of the Central American population in the United States began with violent civil wars in the region, and thousands of Salvadorans, Guatemalans, and Hondurans from rural areas fled north in response to the repression. The United States' influence within these conflicts is contestable and hard to pinpoint directly; however, the influence of the School of the Americas (SOA) as a combat training facility for the American-backed Contras in Panama is a huge contributor to the violence and repression that forced thousands to flee. Former Panamanian president Jorge Illueca stated that the School of the Americas was the "biggest base for destabilization in Latin America" (González and Shahshahani 2019). According to SOA Watch (2020), since 1946 the SOA has trained over sixty-four thousand Latin American soldiers in counterinsurgency techniques, sniper training, commando and psychological warfare, military intelligence, and interrogation tactics. These graduates have consistently used their skills to wage a war against their own people. Among those targeted by SOA graduates are educators, union organizers, religious workers, student leaders, and others who work for the rights of the poor. Hundreds of thousands of Latin Americans have been tortured, raped, assassinated, "disappeared," massacred, and forced to seek refuge by those trained at the SOA (SOA Watch 2020).

Violence has crippled the region for many years and continues to take on new forms. A report by the Council on Foreign Relations (CFR) in 2012 reported that organized crime is a clear legacy of the region's decades of war: "Organized crime grew following these civil wars, particularly in El Salvador, where war produced a 'large pool of demobilized and unemployed men with easy access to weapons'" (Renwick 2015). This has grown to include transnational criminal organizations, many of which are associated with Mexican drug-trafficking groups, as well as transnational gangs also known as maras, such as Mara Salvatrucha (MS-13) and M-18, or pandillas, which are the result of the lack of state capacity to protect citizens and disable violent actors. These organizations may be involved in the transnational drug trade or are now involved in kidnapping for ransom, human trafficking, and smuggling. Of the largest groups, the MS-13 and M-18 are now believed to have as many as eighty-five thousand members combined. Originating from the Los Angeles area, they established a presence in Latin America after the large-scale deportations of the 1990s. Their alliances and organized crime efforts are now outside the capacity of the governments of El Salvador, Guatemala, and Honduras to control, resulting in conditions that have forced the migration of thousands. This history should not be separate in understanding the growing migration patterns we are witnessing today, and although the School of the Americas was expelled from Panama in 1984, the lasting impact from imported guns and a legacy of organized crime has developed into a complex and violent situation widely spanning Central America.

Movimientos

While immigration patterns from Central America to the United States did decline somewhat in the 1990s, this period of stable immigration lasted until 2000, when numbers grew 56 percent until 2013, with 90 percent of the immigrants originating from the regions of El Salvador, Nicaragua, and Honduras (Migration Policy Institute 2015). From 2009 to 2013 the United States registered a sevenfold increase in asylum seekers at its southern border, 70 percent of whom came from the same three countries. These figures have increased as Mexico reported detaining 190,366 migrants last year, which is still another 50 percent increase from fiscal year 2014 (Stillman 2016). Migrants from the region cite violence, forced gang recruitment, extortion, poverty, and lack of opportunity as reasons for leaving (Amnesty International USA 2019). As a result, Mexico has developed a southern border plan that increases detention and deportation, while failing to safeguard immigrant rights. This has also forced people to take desolate routes to avoid deportation, resulting in traveling through rainforests with little to no protection.

In an article published by Public Radio International, Perrine Leclerc, the head of the United Nations High Commissioner for

Refugees Field Office in Tapachula, Mexico, regarded Mexico as "a real challenge for LGBT asylum seekers," noting that "there are few organizations that work with them, or can accommodate them, leaving them more open to abuse" (Stillman 2016). According to Leclerc, the office in Tapachula reported a sixfold increase in LGBT cases as of 2014, amounting to sixty-two cases. Meanwhile, Mexico still has little to offer trans women Immigrants whose identity is cited by local human rights activist groups as making them more vulnerable and open to physical and sexual assault. According to Diego Lorente, director of the Fray Matías de Córdova Human Rights Center in Tapachula, many of the trans and LGBTQ Immigrants arriving in Tapachula and other regions of Mexico are simply seeking short-term humanitarian visas so that they may continue their journey north rather than face the risks of traveling through Mexico without documentation. Yet their experience migrating through Mexico is anything but easy. In the same article, Dayanara Lisbet and Rubi Bracho, two trans women from Central America, shared their story of being kidnapped by two men in Mexican migration officials' uniforms and ski masks, who drove them to a remote location where they were beaten and raped. Public Radio International also reported that Mexico's National Institute of Migration refused to comment because the alleged incident happened outside of its facilities (Stillman 2016).

Emerging from rising migration statistics is a developing awareness of the experience of trans women as they migrate through Mexico, especially after the constitution was changed to support same-sex marriages in June 2011. While same-sex marriage recognition is obviously a step in the right direction, it does little to offer any protection for trans women, as Mexico continues to have the second highest index of crimes motivated by transphobia in Latin America, making Mexico a very dangerous yet unavoidable route for Central American trans women who are looking to eventually seek asylum in the United States (*transgender Respect* 2020). It is imperative that the recognition of same sex marriage is not conflated as guaranteeing the protection of trans women, as all members of the LGBTQ community are not equally situated nor affected when it comes to homophobic and transphobic violence. In the case of Mexico, for trans women migrating from Central America, they are essentially entering a country that has incredibly high levels of reported violence and homicides committed against them each year. In fact, the year after the approval of same sex marriage laws, there were more hate crimes reported against trans women than any year in recent history (*transgender Respect* 2020). Essentially, as the numbers of migrants fleeing Central America are increasing, trans women and gender-nonconforming people are entering Mexico not only at a time in which Mexico has initiated a southern border plan that has made it harder and more dangerous for migrants seeking asylum in the United States to make it to their destination, but also at a time in which their gender and sexual identities make them extra vulnerable to physical and sexual assault.

Mexico is not a challenge for trans women simply because of an unwarranted backlash of transphobic violence. It is also becoming increasingly apparent that Mexican police play an active role in the repression and abuses these women face. According to a report published in May 2011 by the transgender Law Center, police officers and the military subject trans women to arrest, extortion, and physical and sexual violence(García and Gómez 2011). Not every case is actually reported, and it is not exactly clear how easy it is for trans women to report sexual and physical abuses by police, especially if they are in the country without documentation. Yet according to Victor Clark-Alfaro (2011), professor at San Diego State University and the director of the Binational Center for Human Rights in Tijuana, Mexico, the police are the "primary predators" targeting trans women. According to the report, police arrest trans women arbitrarily for reasons such as "disturbing the peace" because they were wearing female clothing, for being perceived to be sex workers even if they are not, for failing to carry a valid health card, for allegedly selling drugs, and for being said to be gay (REDLACTRANS 2012). Therefore, as trans women from Central America migrate through Mexico, they receive virtually no protection from police, as it has been reported that police often extort them for sex or money for not arresting them (Bastida Aguilar 2014). Even within nongovernmental organizations and agencies geared toward assisting migrants passing through Mexico, a trans woman's identity has left her excluded from receiving assistance and support.

The Commodification of Refugee Migration

In response to the peaks of migration at the United States' southern border in 2014 and 2015, the Obama administration requested $1 billion from Congress for fiscal year 2016 to support its U.S. Strategy for Engagement in Central America. The plan includes a significant increase in annual spending in the region and focuses on security, governance, and economic development (Council on Foreign Relations 2012). The strategy was developed to prove that the increases in migration in most recent years are not separate from U.S. engagement of the past and still require a restructuring of power, economics, and accountability between all nations.

As the former Obama administration made plans to address heightened immigration, Border Patrol sectors were begging for help to grapple with numbers beyond their capacity. In 2005 the Del Rio sector of the Border Patrol apprehended fifteen thousand non-Mexican immigrants, five thousand more than the previous year. At the time, civil detention facilities were at capacity due to years of increasing numbers, and voluntary return to Mexico was only available to Mexican citizens. This overflow marked a turn of events within the legal system that gave leeway to immense corporate profits. According to the report published by Grassroots Leadership, "Operation Streamline: Costs and Consequences" (Robertson et al. 2012), Border Patrol decided to circumvent the civil immigration system by turning non-Mexican migrants over for criminal prosecution, a practice until then relegated almost exclusively to cases of violent criminal history or numerous reentries. Starting in December 2005, Operation Streamline required all undocumented border crossers in the Eagle Pass area of the Del Rio Border Patrol sector to be funneled into the criminal justice system and charged with unlawful entry or reentry. By 2010 every U.S.-Mexico border sector except California had implemented a "zero-tolerance" program of some sort. These zero-tolerance policies include a sentence of usually up to 180 days for improper entry, and a judge could impose a sentence of over ten years, depending on criminal history (Robertson et al. 2012). What resulted from this drastic shift in processing was an immediate overflow in detained Immigrant population, which has led the Bureau of Prisons in the Department of Justice to depend on private prison companies to aid in the rapid growth. Corrections Corporation of America (CCA) and GEO Group mainly accounted for the contracts, which amounted to hundreds of millions of dollars in federal revenues since 2005 (GEO Group 2005). While private prison corporations greatly benefited from the restructuring of immigrant detention and prosecution at the emergence of a refugee crisis, the federal dollars behind immigrant incarceration come at a huge cost to taxpayers, who in 2011 contributed $1.2 billion, which before the announcement of Operation Streamline in 2005 was about 58 percent of that total (GEO Group 2005). Grassroots Leadership determined that the government commits over $1.02 billion per year toward the criminal incarceration of undocumented immigrants, an amount that is nearly $430 million more than when Operation Streamline was first announced.

La Trampa de Trump

Up until the 2016 U.S. election, the privatized deportation center industry was sustained and supported by then president Barack Obama. Donald Trump's winning campaign for presidency in 2016 and his presidency were heavily reliant on anti-immigrant sentiment and the scapegoating of undocumented people for unemployment rates, crime, and internal funding issues (Meng 2017). Throughout Trump's presidency and onwards there is plenty of reason to be wary of the future expansion of the privatized deportation center industry, and the lack of protections available to the undocumented community. President Trump's executive order on immigration enforcement released on January 27, 2017, made the process of seeking asylum extremely difficult if not impossible for many. The ban allowed for migrants apprehended at the border to be detained as soon as they cross and to be deported to Mexico. Many of the migrants who are seeking asylum are not only from

Central America but also a part of the largest human rights crisis in the Americas (White House 2017). However, both President Trump and then president of Mexico Enrique Peña Nieto denied the refugee crisis and claimed the wave was comprised of mainly economic migrants, people who chose to leave their home country in search of a better life. The proposed system of President Trump's immigration ban violates the fundamental human right to not be deported to a country where a person would be at risk of suffering serious human rights violations and even death, which many of the migrants originating from Central America are forced to return to. Despite the efforts of federal judges to temporarily stop Trump's executive order, the fine print on border security and immigration enforcement, which pertains to Mexicans and Central Americans apprehended at the southern border, still remains.

To further exacerbate concerns of investments and growth in the privatized deportation center industry, Trump's deportation plan and his guidelines contrasted to the Obama administration (which already allowed for such rapid growth of the privatized deportation center industry) really demonstrates how much corporations and the government have joined efforts to ensure that as much profit is generated from the detainment and deportation of thousands as possible. For starters, Trump's plan called for the deportation of all undocumented immigrants, which even just the seven million reported out of the estimated twelve million total, would reduce the GDP by 2.6 percent over the period of a decade, according to research published by Ryan Edwards and Frances Ortega (2016) at the Center for American Progress. This decrease in the economy would be comparable to the job losses experienced during the recent recession. The cost of housing and deporting all undocumented immigrants would send spending on deportation to numbers simply unfeasible within Congress's budget; the mandatory detention of all immigrants would cost $902 million a year and $9 billion over a decade. On top of this figure, ICE would need to hire and train new officers. In total, Trump's deportation strategy to apprehend, detain, process, and transport every undocumented immigrant would cost the United States between $400 and $600 billion.

The continual growth of the deportation industry is a major concern for many different reasons, yet it is imperative that at the center of those concerns are the people that the industry has commodified. Special attention is needed for the most vulnerable, who are being exposed to a distinct level of negligence and violence. Trans women within the housing cells of the privatized deportation industry are experiencing unprecedented levels of sexual assault, which in some cases began in their home country and continued throughout their journey to their time in detention during deportation processing, as many trans women continue to be housed in male facilities. Deportation centers were operating at full capacity in the fiscal year 2016, at about thirty-one to thirty-four thousand detainees each day. According to Trump's published guidelines in memos to the Department of Homeland Security, he called on ICE to raise that number to eighty thousand people, an unprecedented number that almost ensures the heavy involvement of private prison corporations to aid in the drastic growth (Department of Homeland Security 2017; Pauly 2017). As of November 2016, approximately 65 percent of ICE detainees were housed in private facilities, and since Trump's election, private prison stocks have soared. Private prison corporations justify their role in federal detention holding by marketing their services on a platform to reduce government costs; however, the validity of this claim has yet to be proven. In a recent investor presentation, CCA stated that it had cut government costs by 12 percent; disclosed in the same presentation was the company's own footnote acknowledging that the data were drawn from the Temple University Center for Competitive Government, which "received funding by the private correctional industry." Therefore, full transparency whether the claims of cost effectiveness are accurate remains uncertain, and currently there have been no efforts made by the government or public institutions to conduct internal research to prove so. What is clear is that in many cases the manner in which private prison companies "cut government costs" is by augmenting the price of housing immigrants by relegating detainees to internal camp labor to maintain facilities. Workers are paid one dollar a day, and this form of cheap labor cuts the costs of hiring staff, who would have to be paid a minimum hourly rate (Kunichoff 2012). The expansion of the deportation industry is sure to have a human cost, as Margo Schlanger, a former Obama administration official who served as Homeland Security's top authority on civil rights, notes: "There are a number of bad things that happen if the number of beds is ramped up fast. . . . [T]he potential overuse of solitary confinement and inadequate safety measures . . . means [that] detainees could die" (Pauly 2017).

Gender and Sexual Identity in the Asylum-Seeking Process

Trans women have had a significantly challenging time receiving acknowledgment and support from institutions that are fixated within the male and female gender binary, making it much harder if not impossible for them to receive the same humanitarian aid as cisgender-identified people. For the purpose of the transparent usage of identity terminology, the following terms are given context in accordance with the report *transvisible: transgender Latina Immigrants in U.S. Society* (2013), published by the national nonprofit organization TransLatin@ Coalition. The term *cisgender* is used to describe people who conform to the dominant gender behavior by living in the sex category that was assigned to them at birth. The term *gender identity* is used to describe a deeply felt internal and individual experience of gender that may or may not correspond to the gender a person is assigned at birth and may include, if freely chosen, the modification of physical appearance by either surgical, medical, or other means, including dress and mannerisms. *Gender self-determination* is the autonomous right to choose one's gender identity and presentation with the unwavering demand to be treated with respect and dignity. *Sexual preference* indicates a person's romantic and/or erotic attraction to a particular group (or to particular groups) of people based on sex. Sexual preference and gender identity are different, such that a female-identified person who is attracted to males is heterosexual. Many transwomen do identify as heterosexual if they are attracted to males, or they may identify as lesbian if they are attracted to other women. *Structural violence* is defined by anthropologist Paul

Farmer as the embodiment of macroforces that result in distinct patterns of social suffering. These terms, provided by the TransLatin@ report, are necessary to understand in order to fully depict the experience of trans women within privatized detention centers and the systems that enable their suffering due to ignorance and negligence. Cis-identified people must work to deconstruct their own gender biases and ignorance for the trans community, because at this point in time that ignorance is materializing into very dangerous conditions for trans people as it creates a culture of fear and hatred, especially for trans immigrants. Ignorance of the experiences and challenges trans people face also stimulates a sense of superiority and entitlement to a quality of life that is not allotted to the trans community, even if they do have citizenship status.

The history of trans women seeking asylum in the U.S. court system and the process of actually receiving that on the basis of a clear recognition of their identities and lived experiences as trans women is relatively recent. According to the transgender Law Center's report (Garcia and Gomez 2011), an immigrant is eligible for asylum in the U.S. if they have a well-founded fear of persecution based on their "race, religion, nationality, membership in a particular social group, or political opinion."[1] In 2000 the Ninth Circuit Court of Appeals decided *Hernandez-Montiel v. Immigration and Naturalization Service*, finding that a transgender person from Mexico qualified for asylum as a member of a "particular group" (Hazeldean 2012). However, the court's decision did not refer to the asylum seeker as transgender; and instead called Hernandez-Montiel a "gay man with a female sexual identity" (Hazeldean 2012). Hernandez-Montiel had been living as a woman since the age of twelve. She had undergone hormone therapy, and she identified as "transsexual," yet the first immigration judge who tried her case denied her asylum on account of an "immutable" characteristic. Essentially, the judge found that she could have simply decided not to dress as a woman. However, on appeal, the Ninth Circuit found that Hernandez-Montiel's identity was an "innate characteristic, or so fundamental to her identity that she should not be required to change it" (Fernandez 2016, 5). She was therefore granted asylum on the basis of her membership in a particular social group.

Although Hernandez-Montiel's granted asylum is a step in the right direction, the error of the court's conflation of her gender and sexual identity does have harmful consequences, and in 2015 the Ninth Circuit Court of Appeals recognized that error in the *Avenando-Hernandez v. Lynch* case. Initially, Avenando-Hernandez was denied asylum based on the passage of same-sex marriage laws and protections in Mexico City. In overturning the decision, the Ninth Circuit Court of Appeals declared the relationship between gender identity and sexual orientation to be distinctly different though overlapping and criticized the previous court's analysis as "fundamentally flawed because it mistakenly assumed that laws protecting the gay and lesbian community would also protect Avenando-Hernandez" (Fernandez 2016, 6), who in fact faces unique challenges as a transgender woman.[2] Therefore, as recently as 2015 a U.S. court of appeals was finally able to justify and approve an asylum claim for a trans woman's unique experiences facing sexual and gendered violence even after the passage of same-sex marriage laws in Mexico. This decision has broken a ceiling that was once unforeseeable for many trans asylum seekers. However, the process of seeking asylum is still very difficult for trans women fleeing sexual persecution, as they are typically the only witnesses of their assault, and they need to prove there is at least a 10 percent chance of persecution should they return that cannot be avoided by relocating to another region of the country. They also need to apply within one year of entering the United States. Other stipulations apply, too many to be considered here. Many trans women are detained in centers in desolate regions that make seeking legal aid extremely difficult as they await their trial. Also, with Trump's recent immigration ban, migrants are being turned away at the border before receiving any access to legal assistance. According to Nicole Ramos, an American human rights attorney working in Tijuana who has accompanied nearly seventy asylum seekers to the American border over the past year, U.S. Customs officers and the Border Patrol refuse to process many of them (Schatz 2017). Despite Trump's immigration ban, under U.S. and international law, border agents must admit asylum seekers to review their cases and begin the evaluation process for "credible fear," but for immigrants who speak little to no English and have no understanding of the American legal system, emboldened Trump-supporting agents often succeed in turning them away.

"¿Que no vez que estamos sufriendo?":
Trans Women's Conditions in Detention

Although human rights abuses and sexual violence shouldn't be the only motivating factors to ensure adequate asylum accommodations for trans women migrants fleeing their homelands, the fact that they occur at such alarming rates is a strong-enough indicator that the U.S. government and its privately contracted companies are complacent in the suffering that these women undergo for months or even years at a time. The privatized immigrant detention center industry is profiting hugely from a refugee crisis that is unavoidable to the subjects it has commodified, and still, there is little being done to actually ensure the survival of the thousands of people within its custody every year. According to a report published by Human Rights Watch, Immigration and Customs Enforcement (ICE), the federal agency that is responsible for overseeing immigrant detention, self-reported in 2016 that it is unsure of how many transgender women are in its custody each night, let alone where and in what condition they are being housed (Frankel 2017). However, at the time of ICE's self-reporting, the maximum capacity of migrants and asylum seekers was around thirty thousand, and ICE estimated approximately sixty-five transgender women were in its custody each day among the nationally detained population. This figure is relative to the size of the immigrant population, and with Trump's plans to drastically increase detention processing, the number of trans women in detention is also set to increase. ICE's routine protocol had previously always placed trans women in male facilities, making sexual violence and harassment by male guards and detainees a common factor in their overall experiences within privatized facilities. Recently, however, trans women have begun to be housed in separate facilities from men and even in newly established separate Trans Pods, yet this has not solved the issue of the conditions they are faced with.

Beginning in 2011, ICE began transferring some trans women from detention facilities all over the nation to a separate facility in Santa Ana, California, in a city jail that exclusively houses trans women in the nation's first Trans Pod. However, this is not a definite change to ICE policy, which still allows immigration officials to elect to house trans women in male facilities. It was not until June 2013, June 2014, and again in June 2015 that ICE trained its jail staff on LGBT matters. In a statement given to *Rewire*, ICE officials claimed the trainings consisted of "ICE policy and procedure addressing sexual assault prevention and response; searches; medical care; privacy; LGBT sensitivity and transgender detainee care; and specific instructions on the provisions of the transgender care memorandum" (Vasquez 2016). This memorandum was released in June 2015 as a set of guidelines for the care of trans detainees. According to the report by Human Rights Watch, despite ICE's public release of its intentions to adequately process and house trans detainees, several trans women detained in the Santa Ana facility reported that they were regularly subjected to humiliating and abusive strip searches by male guards; that they had not been able to access medical services, including hormone replacement therapy; and that they were forced to endure unreasonable use of solitary confinement (Frankel 2017, 20n32). In another report by *Fusion*, its investigators found that approximately one out of five hundred detainees in immigrant detention is transgender, yet of every five victims of sexual abuse, one person is transgender (Costantini, Rivas, and Rios 2017). Therefore, we know that ICE detention is a very dangerous place for trans women, and many of them have fled the same type of sexual violence they experience while in ICE custody. The use of solitary confinement is so pervasive that it is not only used as a response to a lack of accommodation and support for trans women, but also leveraged as an incentive to speed up deportation, as trans women tend to ask to be deported after a substantial period in solitary confinement. Clement Lee from Immigration Equality reports, "I have clients that talk about being beaten and raped in their home country, but the most distressing part for them is detention here in the United States" (Constanti, Rivas, and Rios 2017). Solitary confinement is a harsh and cruel punishment for asylum seekers who have not committed any crimes but crossing a border in the hopes of a life free from persecution. The fact that most privatized detention centers are not equipped to provide separate and, most importantly, safe housing for trans women has evolved into the excessive use of solitary confinement to remove them from the male and female binary system altogether. This is not a solution to the sexual violence they experience from male guards and detainees in other daily tasks such as searches and showers. The United Nations expert on torture, Juan E. Méndez (UN News 2011), believes that indefinite and prolonged solitary confinement in excess of fifteen days should be banned, as scientific studies prove that lasting brain damage occurs within just a few days of isolation.

The purpose of this chapter is not to assume that the privatized immigrant detention center industry will correct itself and somehow restructure the functioning of its facilities to provide appropriate and humane care for asylum seekers. That is not the nature of the industry, which is predicated on cutting costs and maintaining a maximum level of detainees at all times. Therefore, any reliance on ICE or the corporations that have been privately contracted would simply be a compromise within the hegemonic and heteronormative structure under which the United States currently operates. I have laid out what has been confirmed of the experiences of trans women as they migrate through Mexico on their journeys to the United States and the conditions they face within a privatized industry that insistently silences and oppresses them in an effort to deconstruct the argument that supports the government's response to the refugee crisis of the Americas. Centering in on the trans woman's experience and emphasizing the immense vulnerability and injustices she is confronted with on her journey north is one step in the process of fully asserting autonomy and justice for trans and gender-nonconforming people, whether they are citizens or refugees seeking asylum. For the final portion of this chapter I will provide some contrast by highlighting the efforts of the trans activist community's response along with many other entities that are predicated on restructuring and reimagining the experience of trans women migrants not only in deportation centers but as they embark on the asylum-seeking process.

Three undocumented queer and trans activists, Deyaneira García, Jennicet Gutiérrez, and Jorge Gutierrez, launched a hunger strike, demanding that ICE end its detainment of transgender Immigrants. In an interview, Gutierrez stated, "Detention has to end because trans women, globally, are in a crisis. We are being targeted, we are being murdered, we are being discriminated against and denied basic access and rights. Putting us in detention isn't the solution to that" (Frankel 2017, 20n33). In response to Santa Ana's Trans Pod, the activists launched their hunger strike in an effort to "shut the model practice of incarcerating queer and trans people down" (Vasquez 2016) and to bring an end to the solidified detainment of trans people. In regard to the contrast between ICE's establishment of Trans Pods and the queer and trans community's response, it's important to contextualize why the city of Santa Ana was willing to accept the expansion of the facility in the first place. At the core is a contract and the possibility of debt alleviation for Santa Ana City Jail. An estimated debt of $27 million through 2024 makes the jail's expansion and its probable $2.2 million annual profit a worthy venture, on top of the $7 million annually already made off the incarceration of queer and trans Immigrants. The organizing strategy of these three brave activists was intended to send a strong message to ICE that it could not assume it knew what was best for the trans community and that violence inside detention is a symptom of transphobia, which will not be fully eliminated as long as transphobic guards and detainees are present; therefore, the best option for trans women would be to be housed with their communities. Nell Gaither, the founder of the Dallas-based trans Pride Initiative, has suggested solutions such as alternative-to-detention programs that would include telephone monitoring and self-recognition software (trans Pride Initiative 2018). This would allow for housing accommodations that can ensure trans women's safety and could potentially speed up the asylum-seeking process by allowing them more access to legal aid and support. This option, however, does exclude private prison corporations from the opportunity to profit from the women's detention.

The future of trans women migrating or fleeing dangerous locations and seeking asylum is not something that can be ignored simply because the privatized detention center industry refuses to validate and protect them based on their gender and sexual identities. Rather, trans Immigration must always be present within discussions of border politics, asylum seeking, and deportation, and it should be centered within entities and organizations that intend to advocate for Immigrants. The TransLatin@ report emphasizes the importance of community-based participatory research "as an alternative research paradigm . . . [that] integrates education and social action to improve health and reduce health disparities" (Rewire News Group 2016). The report, which was produced by trans Latinas, also emphasizes the importance of organizations and institutions of higher learning to provide continual research and support so that service providers and policy makers have access to information necessary for a better understanding of the needs of the trans community. This aspect is crucial for advocates and allies of the trans community who have membership in institutions of higher learning that can produce knowledge to deconstruct and reimagine the aspects of society that do not protect and validate trans people. People whose gender and sexual identities benefit from the heteronormative gender binary should realize that the privilege of gender self-determination and the instant acknowledgment of an individual's identities within society's institutions are not yet the lived reality of trans and gender-nonconforming people. The United States is a settler colonial society and operates under a social structure that was intended to create a hierarchy for colonial control of its oppressed groups. The praxis of decolonization, a tenet that is integral to merging the field of Chicana/o/x studies to the community from which it was born, requires not only analyzing and critiquing the hegemonic systems of power but also asserting protection for and honoring the sovereignty of all bodies, regardless of gender assignments at birth or citizenship. Similarly, reconstituting and reenvisioning relationships to gender and sexuality while challenging imposed colonial norms is a quality of a Chicana feminist scholarship that must attend to transphobia. Therefore, support for the trans community, especially trans Immigrants, is a pivotal aspect of decolonizing gender and sexuality and cannot be excluded from projects that consider themselves decolonial or liberatory. There is plenty of work to be done, and it is the duty of those with the capacity to contribute to such projects to produce work and spaces that will raise the consciousness of future generations so that they may live autonomous and free lives regardless of their gender identities, sexualities, or place of birth.

Notes

1. Hernandez Montiel v. Immigration and Naturalization Services, 8 U.S.C. § 101(a) (42)(A).

2. The U.S. Citizenship and Immigration Services and the Executive Office for Immigration Review keep records of how many people apply for asylum based on membership in a particular social group but not for which particular social group, so there is no way to know how many sought asylum based on particular social group. For example, these agencies do not distinguish between "homosexual," "gay," and "transgender."

References

Alexander, Michelle. 2010. *The New Jim Crow*. New York: New Press.

American Immigration Council. n.d. "Asylum in the United States Fact Sheet." https://www.americanimmigrationcouncil.org/research/asylum-united-states.

Amnesty International USA. 2019. "Fleeing for Our Lives: Central American Migrant Crisis." July 29. www.amnestyusa.org/fleeing-for-our-lives-central-american-migrant-crisis/.

Anzaldúa, Gloria. 1987. *Borderlands / La Frontera: The New Mestiza*. San Francisco: Spinsters / Aunt Lute.

Bastida Aguilar, Leonardo. 2014. "Acción urgente en defensa de los derechos de trabajadoras sexuales transgender de Chihuahua" [Urgent action in defense of transgender sex workers' rights in Chihuahua]. *LETRA S*, March 13.

Clark-Alfaro, Victor. 2011. "Transgéneros: Derechos negados, derechos violados" [Transgender: Denied rights, rights violated]. Centro Binacional de Derechos Humanos [Binational Center for Human Rights], no. 3.

Costantini, Cristina, Jorge Rivas, and Kristofer Rios. 2014. "'Why Are Transgender Women Locked Up with Men in the Immigration System?': Trans Asylum Seekers Face Appalling Treatment in Immigration Detention." *Fusion*, November 17. http://interactive.fusion.net/trans/.

Council on Foreign Relations. 2012. "Central America's Turbulent Northern Triangle." https://www.cfr.org/backgrounder/central-americas-turbulent-northern-triangle.

Department of Homeland Security. 2017. "Executive Orders on Protecting the Homeland." March. https://www.whitehouse.gov/presidential-actions/memorandum-secretary-state-attorney-general-secretary-homeland-security/.

Edwards, Ryan, and Frances Ortega. 2016. "The Economic Impacts of Removing Unauthorized Immigrant Workers." Center for American Progress, September 21. https://www.americanprogress.org/issues/immigration/reports/2016/09/21/144363/the-economic-impacts-of-removing-unauthorized-immigrant-workers/.

Fernandez, Johanna Theresa. 2016. "Report on Human Rights Conditions of Transgender Women in Mexico." transgenderlawcenter.org, May. https://transgenderlawcenter.org/wp-content/uploads/2016/05/CountryConditionsReport-FINAL.pdf.

Frankel, Adam. 2017. "Do You See How Much I'm Suffering Here?" Human Rights Watch, June 6. https://www.hrw.org/report/2016/03/23/do-you-see-how-much-im-suffering-here/abuse-against-transgender-women-us.

Garcia, Frida, and Oralia Gomez. 2011. "Mujeres trans: Discriminación y lucha por derechos." *Referencias: Revista de derechos humanos*, no. 11. http://www.corteidh.or.cr/tablas/r27476.pdf.

GEO Group. 2005. "2005 Annual Report." http://www.annualreports.com/Company/the-geo-group.

González, Devóra, and Azadeh Shahshahani. 2019. "Shut Down the School of the Americas." *Jacobin*. www.jacobinmag.com/2019/11/shut-down-school-of-the-americas-whinsec-ice-border-patrol.

The Guardian. 2018. "Fleeing a Hell the US Helped Create." June. https://www.theguardian.com/us-news/2018/dec/19/central-america-migrants-us-foreign-policy.

Hazeldean, Susan. 2012. "Confounding Identities: The Paradox of LGBT Youth under Asylum Law." *University of California, Davis Law Review* 45:373–443.

Kunichoff, Yana. 2012. "'Voluntary' Work Program Run in Private Detention Centers Pays Detained Immigrants $1 a Day." *Truthout*, July 27. https://truthout.org/articles/voluntary-work-program-run-in-private-detention-centers-pays-detained-immigrants-1-a-day/.

Lartey, Jamiles. 2015. "By the Numbers: US Police Kill More in Days Than Other Countries Do in Years." *The Guardian*, June 9. http://www.theguardian.com/us-news/2015/jun/09/the-counted-police-killings-us-vs-other-countries.

Leyro, Shirley, David Brotherton, and Daniel Stageman. 2013. *Outside Justice: Immigration and the Criminalizing Impact of Changing Policy and Practice*. New York: Springer.

Meng, Grace. 2017. "Trump's Dangerous Scapegoating of Immigrants." Human Rights Watch. https://www.hrw.org/news/2017/07/27/trumps-dangerous-scapegoating-immigrants#.

Migration Policy Institute. 2015. "Central American Immigrants in the United States." August 31. www.migrationpolicy.org.

New York Times. 2019. "Echoes of Central America's Proxy Wars." https://www.nytimes .com/2019/02/27/lens/finding-echoes-of-todays-headlines-in-central-americas-proxy -wars-in-the-1980s.html.

Pauly, Madison. 2017. "The Private Prison Industry Is Licking Its Chops over Trump's Deportation Plans." *Mother Jones,* February 21. https://www.motherjones.com/politics /2017/02/trumps-immigration-detention-center-expansion/.

Pearl, Betsy. 2018. "Ending the War on Drugs by the Numbers." Center for American Progress. https://www.americanprogress.org/issues/criminal-justice/reports/2018 /06/27/452819/ending-war-drugs-numbers/.

Prison Policy Initiative. 2018. "States of Incarceration: The Global Context." https://www .prisonpolicy.org/global/2018.html.

REDLACTRANS. 2012. "The Night Is Another Country: Impunity and Violence against Transgender Women Human Rights Defenders in Latin America." Report no. 38. http://redlactrans.org.ar/site/wp-content/uploads/2013/05/Violencia-e-impunidad -English1.pdf.

Renwick, Danielle. 2015. "Central America's Violent Northern Triangle." Council on Foreign Relations. https://www.files.ethz.ch/isn/195071/Violence%20and%20Gangs %20in%20Central%20America's . . . pdf.

Robertson, Alistair Graham, Rachel Beaty, Jane Atkinson, and Bob Libal. 2012. "Operation Streamline: Costs and Consequences." Grassroots Leadership, September. http://grassrootsleadership.org/sites/default/files/uploads/GRL_Sept2012_Report %20final.pdf.

Salcedo, Bamby, and Karla M. Padrón. 2013. "TransVisible: Transgender Latina Immigrants in U.S. Society." Trans Latin@ Coalition.

Schatz, Bryan. 2017. "200 Refugees Are Crossing Mexico to Escape Violence—and to Confront Trump." *Mother Jones,* May 1. http://www.motherjones.com/politics /2017/04/asylum-seekers-caravan-mexico-american-border.

Sentencing Project. November, 28, 2020 "The Facts: Criminal Justice Facts." https://www .sentencingproject.org/criminal-justice-facts/.

SOA Watch. https://soaw.org/home/.

Stillman, Amy. 2016. "Migrating to the US Is Already Risky. Try Being a Transgender Migrant." Public Radio International, February 17. https://www.pri.org/stories/2016 -02-17/migrating-us-already-risky-try-being-transgender-migrant.

"Transgender Europe: Transgender Murder Monitoring: March 2013." 2015. *Transgender Respect versus Transphobia Worldwide,* May 5. https://transrespect.org/en/map /trans-murder-monitoring/.

UN News. 2011. "Solitary Confinement Should Be Banned in Most Cases." https://news .un.org/en/story/2011/10/392012-solitary-confinement-should-be-banned-most -cases-un-expert-says.

Vasquez, Tina. 2016. "Hunger Strikers to ICE: End Transgender Immigrant Detention." *Rewire,* May 17. https://rewire.news/article/2016/05/17/hunger-strikers-ice -transgender-immigrant/.

Vice. 2017. "The Violence Central Americans Are Fleeing Was Stoked by the US."
    June. https://www.vice.com/en/article/qvnyzq/central-america-atrocities-caused
    -immigration-crisis.
White House. 2017. "Executive Order: Border Security and Immigration Enforcement
    Improvements." January 25. https://www.whitehouse.gov/presidential-actions
    /executive-order-border-security-immigration-enforcement-improvements/.

In Our Own Words

An Afterword

ELLIE D. HERNÁNDEZ, EDDY FRANCISCO ALVAREZ JR., AND MAGDA GARCÍA

Ellie D. Hernández

Some five years ago, I had an idea for a book project that would encompass *trans* as act and concept within both queer and migration. All along I hoped the idea of transmovimientos from the intersections of *trans* in transnational and the *trans* in transgender would become salient. Both suggest a movement from a place of geography, as in to radically transform one's location, to a movement within, as in to change one's gender identity. I saw it as a transmovimiento. Something happens within consciousness that changes everything within the spaces of trans or being in the movimientos de ser trans. There is an urgency. A need to move or change either place and beingness. No hay mas; there is no other way. Migration, relocation, and movement all characterize the epochal time of global and transnational culture. There was a feeling that things were moving in a way that benefited people. My original formulation for this book had been geared toward rethinking transmovimientos as a natural effect of people and a thriving societal moment. Barack Obama was still in office, so there was still a buzz from the audacity-of-hope administration. There was also reason for this feeling of exuberance. Those of us in the queer community felt optimistic about the trend toward same-sex marriage being fought in the Supreme Court: *Obergefell v. Hodges*, June 26, 2015. Now since passed and with an abundance of criticism about its significance to the marginalized queer communities, the case is nevertheless a triumph of major seismic proportions to those of us in the queer community since the time of Stonewall. It was a game-changing moment that would "hopefully" lead more progressive movements that reflect the time.

In the spring of 2015, I contacted Eddy Alvarez, then a graduate student in the Department of Chicana/o Studies at the University of California, Santa Barbara, if he would like to be a part of this project. I look at our collaboration as an important conveyance of generational interests in what lies ahead, and without his solid interest and keen knowledge, this project would not have come to life. After the circulation of the call for papers, I invited Magda García to join the project because of her theoretical knowledge and skills. Since then, so much has changed. We write from the different perspectives that shaped this book, and each one is critical to the development of *Transmovimientos*. Our perspectives are laid out throughout. This project began with hope, it changed to a deepening concern over our nation's leadership, and it arrives at a tumultuous turn in history. Each editor has a perspective on the book, and it is in our words.

Eddy Francisco Alvarez Jr.

As I write these words while transformative events unfold in the United States and globally, I am thinking about moments big and small, texts and memories that have shaped the work we share here, our pedacito of labor toward a world donde quepan muchos mundos, where many worlds fit, as the Zapatistas first called for many years ago. As we honor the writings, activism, and lives of the people, movements, and texts discussed in this book, I am thinking back to the immigrant rights marches of 2005 and 2006 across the country, when immigrant rights activists and supporters rallied together to denounce HR 4437, otherwise known as the Sensenbrenner Bill, which criminalized undocumented immigrants. These marches were an inspiration to many young people who had never participated in activism before. Some of these youth would go on to form the Undocuqueer Movement, a network of activists who came to the United States as infants or children and who were using the internet, art, and social media to educate about and navigate questions of citizenship status, queer identity, and anti-immigrant sentiment. Yosimar Reyes, known for his undocuqueer activism and creative artistry, reminded us in *For Colored Boys That Speak Softly* that deviating from traditional gender and sexual norms "can be punishable by death." As we move closer to the publication of *Transmovimientos*, I think of Alexandra Rodríguez de Ruiz, who along with Marcia Ochoa and Isa Noyola founded the organization El/La Para TransLatinas in 2006 after the closure of Proyecto Contra SIDA in San Francisco. I am transported to Rodríguez de Ruiz's performance in Eugene, Oregon, at the 2010 Jotería conference sponsored by the National Association for Chicana and Chicano Studies (NACCS), Lesbian Bi Mujeres Transgender (LBMT), and Joto Caucuses and the University of Oregon. Through her magical performance about "crossing the border con tacones," she asked us to consider the migration stories of trans Latinas in the United States and their movements across political and cultural landscapes. As we interrogate the current climate for transgender people in the United States, with Trump's decision to roll back transgender healthcare, I honor Zoraida Reyes, one of my former students at UCSB, who was a fierce activist and performer and whose life ended too soon in 2014. Zoraida's activism at UCSB and in Orange County, California, continues to inspire us to keep doing this critical work. Zoraida was a founding member of the organization Familia: Trans Queer Liberation Movement, as is Jennicet Gutierrez, another transgender activist. In 2015 Gutierrez became known as the Obama heckler for speaking out at an LGBTQ Pride event hosted by the White House. Gutierrez was kicked out, but not before asserting that she was a trans Latina and demanding no more deportations and release of all LGBTQ detainees.

As I remember the urgency of the scholarship and creative work in this volume, including Bamby Salcedo's, I must cite the 2019 Trans Gay Caravan that moved from Central America through Mexico, un transmovimiento that defied national borders and necropolitical and dehumanizing discourses. Through official and social media reports, we witnessed these reinas, or queens, as described by Ruben Zecena, move across borders to seek asylum in the United States.

"With tiaras, heels, and colorful banners, queens deliberately challenge the individuating violence of migration regimes and illuminate the glimmer, hope and allure of fierce relationalities," he writes (2019). In these pages, we too invoke that glimmer and hope as we imagine a different kind of world, as we move toward an abolitionist and just world rooted in what the *Abolition* journal calls a future that is anchored in actions toward decolonization, anticapitalism, antiracism, abolitionist feminism, and queer liberation (2020).

Magda García

As we worked to bring our critical collection into its published form, we found ourselves, like our readers and their communities, at the beginning of a pandemic. As universities began to close their campuses and as shelter-in-place orders were enacted along the East and West Coasts, the magnitude of the crisis had yet to reveal itself. State and federal governments widely informed the public that the United States should expect to be impacted by COVID-19 for an estimated two weeks. We then witnessed waves of hospital workers warn of an impending shortage of hospital equipment and began receiving images from inside New York hospitals located in predominantly working-class boroughs of color. Hospital workers found themselves reusing disposable face masks, Native communities received body bags instead of medical equipment, thousands of our elderly died due to weakened state or federal nursing home regulations, and thousands from our communities formed lines at food distribution sites as we awaited a federal response. For those of us with vestiges of privilege due to our heterosexuality, being potentially upwardly mobile, and/or possessing U.S. citizenship, we came to experience a neglect akin to the neglect experienced by our queer and trans communities of color during the 1980s HIV/AIDS epidemic under the Reagan administration and by our undocumented communities throughout the Bush, Obama, and Trump administrations. At the time of publication, we have lived through months of federal neglect in the face of a pandemic that has taken the lives of hundreds of thousands of the world's most vulnerable. In the United States, working-class and un/documented Latinx and Black communities rapidly found themselves in the position of essential and therefore expendable workers even as these very communities are located at the nexus of risk for COVID-19 due to lack of preventative healthcare, an economic depression, and, as the deaths of Ahmaud Arbery, George Floyd, and Breonna Taylor remind us yet again, police terror. Yet with economic collapse finally reaching its final stages even for the middle class, the deaths of thousands of people of color, and a fascist white supremacy that has finally abandoned all rhetoric of love for (white) family, community, and nation for unabashed hatred and violence, we are coming to witness historic uprisings for Black lives and against police terror with a sense of true hope traversing our minds, bodies, and spirits. As we approach what may be the vestiges of neoliberalism or the maturation of U.S. fascism amid a global pandemic, we find ourselves repeating the names Marsha P. Johnson and Sylvia Rivera as we come face to face with the potentialities of a riotous liberatory imaginary first forged by Black and Latinx transwomen, drag queens, and lesbians with glass bottles, rocks, and fire at the Stonewall Inn in 1969. Even so, we find ourselves yet again facing the erasure of Black trans people and cisgender women such as Tony McDade and Breonna Taylor in our protests and mobilizations against police terror.

References

Abolition. https://abolitionjournal.org/making-abolitionist-worlds/.

Zecena, Ruben. 2019. "Migrating Like a Queen: Visuality and Performance in the Trans Gay Caravan." *WSQ: Women's Studies Quarterly* 47 (3–4): 99–118. https://doi.org /10.1353/wsq.2019.0063.

Contributors

Carlos-Manuel is a playwright, director, and actor. He teaches theater at Contra Costa College, where he's also the chair of the Drama Department. His academic and artistic work focuses on U.S. Latinx immigrant and queer experiences. Published plays include *Esno White*, *La Vida Loca*, *Creation*, *Vaqueeros*, and *Lloronas*. He's the editor of *Vaqueeros, Calacas, and Hollywood: An Anthology of Contemporary Plays*. Several of his essays have been published in journals and/or anthologies. He's a 2015 NEH award recipient, and as a result, he wrote his second one-person show, titled *Joto: Confessions of a Mexican Outcast*. The play was presented at the Fourteenth Dublin Gay Theatre Festival in Ireland in 2017.

Carlos Ulises Decena is an interdisciplinary scholar whose work straddles the humanities and social sciences and whose intellectual projects blur the boundaries among critical ethnic, queer, and feminist studies, social justice, and public health. His first book, *Tacit Subjects: Belonging and Same-Sex Desire among Dominican Immigrant Men*, was published by Duke University Press in 2011. He is currently at work on *Circuits of the Sacred*.

Nicholas Duron was born in Waco, Texas, and received his education at the University of Texas at Austin and the University of Texas at San Antonio. He is a PhD candidate at New York University working on his dissertation on Chicanx literature, affect theory, and desire. He also teaches full time as a high school ELA instructor in Brooklyn, New York, where he currently resides.

Omar González, PhD (he/him), is a poz, pochx, putx, Puebloan Pisces from El Paso, Texas, nurtured and groomed by fierce Xicana and Black lesbian activists in Austin and later by fierce mujer scholars at California State University, Northridge, where he earned a BA and an MA in Chicana/o studies. He completed his PhD on the work of John Rechy in Chicana/o studies at UCLA in 2019 under the guidance of la maestra of queer Chicanx letters, Dr. Alicia Gaspar de Alba, and her fabulous spouse, the world-renowned Chicana lesbian artist Alma Lopez Gaspar de Alba.

Verónica Mandujano was born and raised in the San Francisco Bay Area in East Oakland and San Leandro, where she first encountered and was inspired by ethnic studies and spoken word as a youth. She holds a double BA in Chicana/o studies and Black studies and is pursuing her PhD in Chicana/o studies at UC Santa Bárbara. She retreats to Guanajuato, Mexico, whenever possible to spend time with her family and pursue her research. As a partera in training, she merges her work in practitioner ethics and sensibilities with a Xicana feminist epistemology by seeking to re-member and recover traditional birthing ways held by her late abuela Herlinda Hernandez Mandujano. She engages her family history as a microcosmic representation of the macrocosmic phenomenon of the disappearance of home births in Mexico. Verónica utilizes the field of epigenetics to consider the sociocultural and generational context of birth for the colonized subject in relation to the technocratic birthing industry and its Euro-Western origins.

Lorena Muñoz is an urban/cultural geographer whose research focuses on the intersections of place, space, gender, sexuality, and race. Dr. Muñoz's transdisciplinary research agenda has been focused on Latinx communities, particularly in the areas of (in)formal economy, labor, and productive/transformative agency. Dr. Muñoz is currently working on two interdisciplinary, collaborative, and comparative projects. The first project is a study of informal access to food, labor, and health in three different urban populations of migrant and immigrant laborers in the Global South (Colombia and Mexico) and the United States. The project focuses on the intersection of food, health, and labor in relation to street vending and food-ways systems. The second project is a comparative study on immigration and the impact of family separations in South Africa and the United States. Muñoz is an associate professor of ethnic studies at Mills College and a research associate at ACMS University of Witwatersrand, Johannesburg, South Africa.

Joanna Núñez is a queer Chicana feminist educator, activist scholar, and organizer. She grew up in Northern California and in Las Vegas, Nevada. She is the proud daughter of immigrant parents from Baja California, Mexico. She received her bachelor's degree in women's studies and social work in 2010 from the University of Nevada, Las Vegas. In 2019 she earned her PhD in feminist studies at the University of Minnesota, Twin Cities. Her dissertation, "¡Mi mamá me enseño! Teaching and Learning *Mexicana* and Chicana Feminisms in the Home," documents the lessons that immigrant, working-class mothers offer their children in terms of transformational resistance, feminism, and oppositional knowledge within the spaces of their homes. Her work explores the connection between home and intimate community-building practices, particularly those within queer and feminist communities of color, in facilitating large-scale movements for social transformation. She is currently a postdoctoral fellow in women's and gender studies at Santa Clara University. Joanna is committed to decolonizing research practices, collaborative intellectual production, and participatory action research processes. She cowrote a chapter for the forthcoming second edition of *The Handbook of Latinos in Education* with Anita Tijerina Revilla, José Manuel Santillana, and Sergio Gonzalez titled "Radical Jotería y Muxerista Love in the Classroom: Brown Queer Feminist Strategies for Social Transformation."

Jasmine Rubalcava-Cuara is a queer muxerista, first-generation Chicana born in Long Beach, California. She is a community organizer and social justice activist. Jasmine served as an interpreter and immigration paralegal for eleven years in Las Vegas, Nevada. Currently, she is an after-school site educator offering extracurricular programming and counseling/support services for students and their families in the Berwyn-Cicero suburbs of Chicago. Her research interests focus on jotería and muxerista pedagogy, migration testimonios, queer motherhood, and healing through ancestral knowledge. Jasmine earned a BA at the University of Nevada, Las Vegas, in women's studies. Her thesis examined how jotería and muxerista (Latina/o/x queer and/or feminist) activists who were DACA eligible narrate their experiences. Jasmine is now pursuing her master's degree in social work at Northeastern Illinois University, where she will continue with this work. Jasmine believes in a world without borders and prisons and a world where Black Lives Matter. She is a proud daughter, sister, tía, y mamá. Jasmine resides in Chicago with her three-year-old, Tonalli Luna.

Bamby Salcedo is a nationally and internationally recognized transgender Latina woman who received her master's degree in Latin@ studies from California State University, Los Angeles. Bamby is the president and CEO of the TransLatin@ Coalition, a national organization that focuses on addressing the issues of transgender Latin@s in the United States. Bamby developed the Center for Violence Prevention & Transgender Wellness, a multipurpose, multiservice space for trans people in Los Angeles. Bamby's remarkable and wide-ranging activist work has brought voice and visibility not only to the trans community but also to the multiple overlapping communities and issues that her life has touched, including migration, HIV, youth, LGBT, incarceration, and Latin@ communities. Through her instinctive leadership, she has birthed several organizations that created community where there was none, and she advocates for the rights, dignity, and humanity for those who have been without a voice. Bamby's work as a collaborator and a connector through a variety of organizations reflects her skills in crossing various borders and boundaries and working in the intersection of multiple communities and multiple issues. Bamby has served and participated in many local, national, and international organizations and planning groups. This work mediates intersections of race, gender, sexuality, age, social class, HIV+ status, immigration status, and more. Her activist public speaking has ranged from testifying to governmental bodies, human rights and social justice organizations, universities and colleges, demonstrations and rallies, and national and international conferences as featured speaker. Bamby speaks to diverse audiences on many topics and intersecting issues. Bamby has spoken about transgender-related issues, social justice, healthcare, social services, incarceration, immigration, and detention, as well as professional and economic development for transgender people. Bamby has been invited to participate in several panels at the White House, including in 2016 "The United State of Woman," where she shared the stage with Vice President Biden at the opening plenary session, and in 2015 at the Transgender Women of Color and Violence and LGBTQ People of Color Summit. Bamby has also participated as the opening plenary speaker at several conferences, including the 2015 National HIV Prevention Conference and the United States Conference on AIDS in 2009 and 2012. She has participated as facilitator with the PanAmerican Health Organization while developing the blueprint on how to provide competent healthcare services for transgender people, as well as healthcare for LGBT people and human rights in Latin America and the Caribbean. Her powerful, sobering, and inspiring speeches and her warm, down-to-earth presence have provided emotional grounding and perspective for diverse gatherings. She speaks from the heart as one who has been able to transcend many of her own issues and to truly drop ways of being and coping that no longer served her, issues that have derailed and paralyzed countless lives. Her words and experience evoke both tears and laughter, sobriety and inspiration through the documentary made about her life, *TransVisible: Bamby Salcedo's Story*. Bamby has been featured and recognized in multiple media outlets such as *People en Español*, *Latina Magazine*, *Cosmopolitan*, the *Los Angeles Times*, *Los Angeles Magazine*, and *out 100*, and she was featured in the HBO documentary *The Trans List*, among many others. Bamby has also being recognized for her outstanding work by multiple national and local organizations.

José Manuel Santillana is a doctoral candidate in the Gender, Women and Sexuality Studies Department at the University of

Minnesota. He has a disciplinary background in Chicana and Chicano studies. His research examines Mexican social life and death in rural Central California, where there is ongoing environmental degradation. His academic expertise is located at the intersections of critical environmental studies, critical race and ethnic studies, women of color feminism, and jotería studies. He is the coauthor of "Jotería Identity and Consciousness: The Formation of a Collective," published in *Aztlán: A Journal for Chicano Studies*.

Katherine Steelman (PhD candidate, UC San Diego Department of Ethnic Studies) is a cultural historian and writer. Broadly, her work examines how sexually nonnormative spaces are socially and materially constructed in Tijuana, Mexico. She takes up U.S. cultural production, as well as the Tijuanense response to the U.S. narrative of the city and its communities that might be called queer. This work juxtaposes critical analyses of cultural texts with ethnographic interviews. Currently, she is working on a project that engages cultural representations of Haiti in the United States and Mexico, as well as collaborative ethnographic work with Haitian migrants in Tijuana.

Dr. Anita Tijerina Revilla is a muxerista and jotería activist-scholar and professor in the Department of Chicana(o) and Latina(o) Studies at Cal State Los Angeles. Her research focuses on student movements and social justice education, specifically in the areas of Chicanx/Latinx, immigrant, feminist, and queer rights activism. Her expertise is in the areas of jotería (queer and Latinx) studies, Chicanx education, Chicana/Latina feminisms, and critical race/ethnic studies. After receiving her bachelor's degree from Princeton University and a master's degree from Teachers College, Columbia University, she earned her doctorate from UCLA Graduate School of Education in social sciences and comparative education with an emphasis in race and ethnic studies. She is also a visual artist who specializes in acrylic and oil portraiture of the muxerista and jotería community.

Index

home, 109, 111–12, 143–45, 162, 166; separation from, 20–22; stereotype of homophobic Chicanx, 88–89; and UCLA jotería conference committee, 48–52

Farmer, Paul, 193–94

femininity: and butch/femme dichotomy, 88, 92–93, 172; and effeminacy, 66, 103–4; traditional classification of, 100–101, 104

feminism, 50

Fernandez-Kelly, Patricia, 5–6

financial aid, 6

Flores, Juan, 67

Floyd, George, 209

Gabriel, Juan, 87

Gaither, Nell, 199–200

Galarte, Francisco J., xix

García, Deyaneira, 199

García, Peter J., 82

Garza, Alicia, xxi

Gaspar de Alba, Alicia: *Desert Blood: The Juárez Murders*, 80

gay bars, 79–80, 107–8, 109, 110–14

Gay Men's Health Crisis, 60, 69, 77n2

gay pride/rights parades, 89–91, 103

gender identity, as term, 193

gender roles: and family responsibility, 13–15; in heteronormative discourses, 164–66, 169; and male/female classification, 100–101; performed in vending landscapes, 168–70; as transnational, 92–93; violation of traditional, 81, 83–85. *See also* femininity; masculinity

gender self-determination, as term, 193

GEO Group, 190

Gevisser, Mark, 113

Gomez, Letitia, 77n1

government policies. *See* immigration policies

El Gran Paro Estadounidense, 35

Green, Kai, xvii–xviii

grief, 155–57

Guerrero, Dan, 104

Gutiérrez, Jennicet, xx, xxi, 199

Gutierrez, Jorge, 199

Guzmán, Manolo, 78n3

Halberstam, Jack, 172

Harper, Philip Brian, 72–73

hate crimes, 81, 87–88, 187–88, 199

Hebert, Patrick "Pato," 61

Hernandez-Montiel v. Immigration and Naturalization Service, 194–95

heteronormativity: and gendered vending practices, 168–70; and marginalization, 9, 39, 178–79, 193; and spatial imaginaries, 164–67; transgressing, 81, 83–85

HIV/AIDS crisis, 67, 68–70, 74, 113–14, 133, 208

home, sense of, 109, 111–12, 143–45, 162, 166

hooks, bell, 72

HR 4437, Border Protection, Antiterrorism, and Illegal Immigration Control Act (2005), 3, 35, 206

hunger strikes, 199

ICE (U.S. Immigration and Customs Enforcement), 6–7, 191, 192, 196–99

identity negotiation: of border queers, 80, 88–89, 92–95; and language knowledge, 146–48; racial, 82–83, 148–50; and reclamation of homophobic terms, 31n14, 37, 38–45; and secrecy, 102, 132–33, 173; through space-making practices, 46–47, 161–62, 163–64, 168–74; transgender, 63–65, 88, 109–11, 131–33. *See also* femininity; masculinity

Iglesias, Gabriel, 79

illegal/legal dichotomy, 4–5, 30n4, 54n1

Illueca, Jorge, 185

immigration policies: in Arizona, 13; HR 4437 (2005), 3, 35, 206; Immigration Reform and Control Act (1986), 27; and NAFTA, 5–6; in Nevada, 6–7; under Obama, 4, 189–90, 191; under Trump, 190–92, 195–96. *See also* DACA

Immigration Reform and Control Act (1986), 27

Improper Conduct (documentary), 65

incarceration. *See* prisons; privatized deportation centers

Institute of Gay Men's Health, 60, 77n2

"Invalid Litter Dept." (At the Drive-In song and video), 80

Jiménez Leal, Orlando, 65

Johnson, Marsha P., 209

José (case study participant), 13–15

jotería (jota/joto/jotx), as term, 31n14, 37, 39–45

jotería analytic, 9, 31n15

La Jotería de UCLA, 34. *See also* UCLA jotería conference committee

Juárez, Mexico: gay pride parade in, 89–90; historical context of border, 81–82, 83–85, 95; religion in, 94; violence in, 80, 81, 88, 95

Kennedy, Jonathan, 81
Ku Klux Klan (KKK), 43

LA. See Los Angeles CA
La Fountain-Stokes, Lawrence, xx
language: and identification, 146–48; intelligibility in translation, 74–77; of love, 154–56. See also derogatory language
LASA (Latin American Studies Association), 51
Las Vegas NV, 11–12
Leclerc, Perrine, 186–87
Lee, Clement, 198
lesbian community invisibilities, 170–71
Lewis, Vek, 108–9
Leyva, Yolanda, 88
Lezama, José Luis, 166–67
Lisbet, Dayanara, 187
literature, Chicanx and Latinx, 143, 144–46
Livingston, Jennie, 72–73
Loaeza, Guadalupe, 101
Lopez, Jennifer, 80
Lorde, Audre, 143
Lorente, Diego, 187
Los Angeles CA: AIDS crisis in, 113–14; immigrant neighborhoods in, 167–68; La Plaza nightclub, 107–8, 109, 110–14. See also UCLA jotería conference committee; vending landscapes
love: archiving, 156–57; and desirability, 151–53; language of, 154–56; and openness, 153–54; search for, 131–33; of self, 61–62, 63–65
Luibhéid, Eithne, 9, 163, 164, 167
Lupe (case study participant), 41, 47–48, 53

machismo mentality, 92–93, 101–2, 103–4. See also masculinity
MALCS (Mujeres Activas en Letras y Cambio Social), 51
Manalansan, Martin, 163
marginalization: through DACA, 8, 16, 25; and heteronormativity, 9, 39, 178–79, 193; of trans community, 109, 138, 139, 178–79, 193. See also derogatory language
Maria (case study participant), 15–17
Marías (ambulant vendors), 166–67

maricón, as term, 39
marriage: legal residency through, 9–10; same-sex, 9, 187, 195, 205–6
masculinity: and butch/femme dichotomy, 88, 92–93, 172; and desirability, 151–52; and effeminacy, 66, 103–4; and family responsibility, 14–15, 129; and machismo mentality, 92–93, 101–2, 103–4; misconceptions of Mexican/Latino, 101; and sexual positions, 92, 99, 102–3; traditional classification of, 100
Massey, Douglas, 5–6
McDade, Tony, 209
MEChA (Movimiento Estudiantil Chicanx de Aztlán), 35, 51
Mejia, Max, 108–9
memory: archiving, 156–57; family and cultural, 148, 155; and nostalgia, 166; versus official histories, 85
Menchú, Rigoberta: I, Rigoberta Menchú, 71–72
Méndez, Juan E., 198
Mercado, Walter, 87
Mexican Revolution, 83–85
Mexico: street vending in, 166–67; transphobic violence in, 108–9, 187–88. See also Juárez, Mexico
Mexico City, 166–67
Mignolo, Walter, 86
Migration Policy Institute, 7, 8
Milk (film), 87
Milk, Harvey, 87, 93
Mirandé, Alfredo, 100–101, 105
Monsiváis, Carlos, 105
Moore, Lisa Jean, xviii, xix
Moraga, Cherríe, 40, 41–42, 45, 53, 104, 143
Morales, Carlos, 90
Moran, Lee, 80
Movimiento Estudiantil Chicanx de Aztlán (MEChA), 35, 51
movimientos, as concept, xx–xxi
Mujeres Activas en Letras y Cambio Social (MALCS), 51
Muñoz, José Esteban, 107, 108, 111–12
Murguía, Francisco, 85
muxerista, as term, 31n14
muxerista action research, 10

In the Expanding Frontiers series

Undesirable Practices: Women, Children, and the Politics
of the Body in Northern Ghana, 1930–1972
by Jessica Cammaert

Intersectionality: Origins, Contestations, Horizons
by Anna Carastathis

Abuses of the Erotic: Militarizing Sexuality in the Post–Cold War United States
by Josh Cerretti

Queering Kansas City Jazz: Gender, Performance, and the History of a Scene
by Amber R. Clifford-Napoleone

Postcolonial Hauntologies: African Women's Discourses of the Female Body
by Ayo A. Coly

Terrorizing Gender: Transgender Visibility and the Surveillance Practices
of the U.S. Security State
by Mia Fischer

Romance with Voluptuousness: Caribbean Women and Thick Bodies in the United States
by Kamille Gentles-Peart

Salvific Manhood: James Baldwin's Novelization of Male Intimacy
by Ernest L. Gibson III

Nepantla Squared: Transgender Mestiz@ Histories in Times of Global Shift
by Linda Heidenreich

Transmovimientos: Latinx Queer Migrations, Bodies, and Spaces
edited by Ellie D. Hernández, Eddy Francisco Alvarez Jr., and Magda García

Wrapped in the Flag of Israel: Mizraḥi Single Mothers and Bureaucratic Torture
by Smadar Lavie

Queer Embodiment: Monstrosity, Medical Violence, and Intersex Experience
by Hilary Malatino

Staging Family: Domestic Deceptions of Mid-Nineteenth-Century American Actresses
by Nan Mullenneaux

Hybrid Anxieties: Queering the French-Algerian War and
Its Postcolonial Legacies
by C. L. Quinan

Place and Postcolonial Ecofeminism: Pakistani Women's Literary and Cinematic Fictions
by Shazia Rahman

Gothic Queer Culture: Marginalized Communities and the Ghosts of Insidious Trauma
by Laura Westengard

To order or obtain more information on these or other University of Nebraska Press titles,
visit nebraskapress.unl.edu.